REVOLUTION AND TRANSITION IN EAST-CENTRAL EUROPE

DILEMMAS IN WORLD POLITICS

Series Editor

George A. Lopez, University of Notre Dame

Dilemmas in World Politics offers teachers and students of international relations a series of quality books on critical issues, trends, and regions in international politics. Each text examines a "real world" dilemma and is structured to cover the historical, theoretical, practical, and projected dimensions of its subject.

EDITORIAL BOARD

FORTHCOMING TITLES

Thomas G. Weiss
Humanitarian Action, Intervention, and World Politics

□   □   □

James A. Caporaso
Challenges and Dilemmas of European Union

□   □   □

Janice Love
Southern Africa in World Politics

SECOND EDITION

REVOLUTION AND TRANSITION IN EAST-CENTRAL EUROPE

■ ■ ■

David S. Mason
BUTLER UNIVERSITY

WestviewPress

A Division of HarperCollins*Publishers*

To my parents

Dilemmas in World Politics Series

Copyright © 1992, 1996 by Westview Press, A Division of HarperCollins Publishers, Inc.

Published in 1996 in the United States of America by Westview Press, 5500 Central Avenue, Boulder, Colorado 80301-2877, and in the United Kingdom by Westview Press, 12 Hid's Copse Road, Cumnor Hill, Oxford OX2 9JJ

Library of Congress Cataloging-in-Publication Data
Mason, David S. (David Stewart), 1947–
    Revolution and transition in East-Central Europe / David S. Mason.
    —2nd ed.
        p.   cm. — (Dilemmas in world politics)
    Rev. and updated ed. of: Revolution in East-Central Europe. 1992.
    ISBN 0-8133-2834-9 (hc). — ISBN 0-8133-2835-7 (pbk.)
    1. Europe, Eastern—Politics and government—1945– 2. Communism—
Europe, Eastern.   I. Mason, David S. (David Stewart), 1947–
Revolution in East-Central Europe.   II. Title.   III. Series.
DJK50.M38   1996
947–dc20   96-24718
                                                                                          CIP

The paper used in this publication meets the requirements of the American National Standard for Permanence of Paper for Printed Library Materials Z39.48-1984.

10   9   8   7   6   5   4   3   2   1

Contents

List of Tables and Illustrations   ix
Preface and Acknowledgments   xi
List of Acronyms   xiii

    Introduction   1

**1 The Establishment and Decay of
Communism in East-Central Europe**   9

The Western Reaction and the Onset
    of the Cold War, 12
The Institutions of Communism, 14
Socioeconomic Changes in the Early Years
    of Communism, 17
Challenges to Communist Orthodoxy, 19
System Performance and Decay, 29
Conclusion, 39

**2 Reform and Revolution in the Soviet
Union and East-Central Europe**   41

Gorbachev's Reforms (1985–1989), 42
1989: Revolution in Eastern Europe, 51
Social Movements and Revolutions, 63
Conclusion, 71

**3 Redrawing the Borders in Europe:
Germany, the Soviet Union,
Yugoslavia, Czechoslovakia**   75

The Unification of Germany, 75
The Collapse of the Soviet Union, 80
The Tragedy of Yugoslavia, 87

The Velvet Divorce of Czechoslovakia, 95
Conclusion, 96

□   □   □   **4   Rebuilding the Political and
          Economic Orders**   **99**

Rebuilding the Political Order, 100
The Postrevolutionary Political Process, 112
Theories of Democratization, 115
Constructing a Market Economy, 121
The Reemergence of Nationalism in Europe, 141
Conclusion, 152

□   □   □   **5   The Postcommunist Era in
          International Politics**   **155**

Revising the Alliance Systems, 156
The Restructuring of Europe, 158
The Impact on Europe of the
        Collapse of the Soviet Union, 168
The End of the Cold War, 171
The Impact on the Third World, 179
The New Global Order, 183
Conclusion, 189

Discussion Questions   191
Notes   195
Suggested Readings   205
Video Resources   211
Glossary   213
Chronology   219
About the Book and Author   225
Books in This Series   227
Index   229

□   □   □

Tables and Illustrations

Tables

1.1   Percentage of labor force employed in agriculture   18
1.2   Economic growth in Eastern and Western Europe, 1950–1967   19
1.3   Changes in relative positions of Eastern European countries
        in bilateral comparisons with market economy countries   20

2.1   Eastern European communist party leaders, 1954–1991   50

4.1   The dissolution of the communist parties   101
4.2   The postcommunist governments of East-Central Europe   103
4.3   Hard currency debt of Eastern European countries   129
4.4   The economics of the transition   140
4.5   Nationalities in East-Central Europe   150

5.1   Membership in European organizations, 1995   162

Figures

1.1   Slowdown in economic growth   30
1.2   Gross hard currency debt of the Eastern European countries 32

4.1   The left turn in Eastern European elections   114
4.2   A visual representation of regime change from
        authoritarian rule to democracy   117
4.3   The phasing of economic reform   130
4.4   Ethnic composition of the former Soviet Republics   145

Photos

The importance of symbols   27
Solidarity's distinctive trademark   28
Berlin Wall—before   57

Berlin Wall—after 59
Destroyed buildings in the Muslim enclave of Stari Vitez,
 Bosnia and Herzegovina, May 1994 90
A Muslim prays near his young son's grave, May 1994 91
Polish local election poster, May 1990 105
A 1994 Solidarity demonstration in Warsaw 106
Campaign poster of the Hungarian Federation of
 Young Democrats, 1990 108
Campaign poster of the Hungarian Democratic Forum, 1990 109
A new private food store in downtown Warsaw 125

Cartoons

Yugoslav cartoonists view the invasion—Prague, 1968 25
The perennial shortage of machinery parts 31
"Freedom" 119
Foreign direct investment 128
Supermarket 1983, 1993 134
Freedom versus sausage 137
"My sovereign hut—my castle" 148
Communism . . . nationalism 187

Maps

Eastern Europe 8

3.1 Commonwealth of Independent States 84
3.2 The former Yugoslav republics 89
3.3 Significant areas that will change hands with the
 signing of the Dayton Agreement 93

5.1 The European Union 166

□ □ □

Preface and Acknowledgments

Soon after the first edition of this book appeared in 1992, Jennifer Knerr, my editor at Westview Press, asked me to start thinking about a second edition. This was both gratifying and dismaying. It was gratifying to know that the book was well received by professors and students but dismaying to think of wrestling once again with the difficult issues raised in a book I thought was finished! It turned out that revising and updating this book was almost as difficult and time consuming as starting from scratch with the first edition, given the enormous number of changes in the postcommunist states since 1992: the horrible escalation of the war in Bosnia; the 1993 crisis in Russia; the rapid consolidation of democratic institutions in Eastern Europe; the disturbing rise of poverty, crime, and inequality throughout the region; and the startling "left turns" in elections in Lithuania, Hungary, Poland, Russia, and elsewhere.

As with the first edition, though, I have tried to keep the book relatively simple in organization and relatively straightforward in presentation. For teachers who used the first edition, there are several changes that should be pointed out. A new chapter (3) addresses the collapse of old states and the creation of new ones in the former Yugoslavia, the former Soviet Union, Germany, and Czechoslovakia. Besides presenting much new material, particularly on the war in Bosnia, this chapter brings together material that appeared in other chapters in the previous edition. The first edition had a separate chapter (4) on theories of social, economic, and political change. Almost all of that material still appears in the book, though each of the theories is "farmed out" to the sections and chapters to which it is most relevant.

Like any academic enterprise, this book benefited from the assistance, comments, and suggestions of many people. George Lopez, the series editor, first broached the idea of this book with me and got me hooked on the idea of a readable and accessible text that integrates history, politics, and theory. As I began writing the first edition, I had just finished teaching a course entitled "Perestroika in Central Europe," and the book was in some ways an extension of that course. When I began to work on the second edition, I was teaching a freshman honors course entitled "The

Trauma of Transition in East-Central Europe." Students in both of those courses helped me to refine some of the ideas and concepts that are developed here. Lori Jancik, as my undergraduate research assistant, contributed enormously to the first edition in many ways: helping with bibliographic research; fact-checking; proofreading; and preparing the chronology. I am also indebted to Carla Randolph, a former Butler student who is now a Ph.D. candidate at Indiana University. She read and commented on an early version of the manuscript and helped me out with speedy and efficient research in Bloomington, which included digging up some of the political cartoons that appear in these pages. Because this book is intended for students, the comments of Lori, Carla, and others were particularly helpful. Marta Goertemiller and Donna Charles, our departmental secretaries, also helped out with the book in innumerable ways.

Jennifer Knerr, senior editor at Westview Press, was patient and encouraging in prodding this project along, with both editions. She found some wonderfully thorough and thoughtful readers in F. Neil Richardson and Robin Remington, who provided detailed and helpful criticism of the first draft of the book. The manuscript also benefited from suggestions from Gerhard Loewenberg of the University of Iowa, Luan Troxel of Smith College, Dan Nelson of Georgetown University, and Paul Marer at Indiana University. Of course I did not account for *all* of the suggestions of all of these friends and colleagues, so any remaining errors are entirely mine.

Finally, I want to thank the three women who are the most important part of my life. My wife and best friend, Sharon, read parts of the manuscript, talked me through some of the ideas and organization of the book, and put up with me when I was absorbed and distracted by this project. My daughters, Dana and Melanie, always full of life and (almost) always cheerful, provided perspective on all this and often asked questions about communism, world politics, and East-Central Europe that I could not easily answer. My fondest wish is that this new world that they will inherit will be more generous, charitable, and peaceful.

David S. Mason

☐ ☐ ☐

Acronyms

ANC	African National Congress
ASSR	Autonomous Soviet Socialist Republic
BBC	British Broadcasting Corporation
BSP	Bulgarian Socialist Party
CDSP	Current Digest of the Soviet Press
CDU	Christian Democratic Union (Germany)
CFE	Conventional Forces in Europe
CIS	Commonwealth of Independent States (former USSR)
CMEA	Council for Mutual Economic Assistance
Comecon	Council for Mutual Economic Assistance
Cominform	Communist Information Bureau
CPSU	Communist Party of the Soviet Union
CSCE	Conference on Security and Cooperation in Europe
DCR	Democratic Convention of Romania
DLA	Democratic Left Alliance (Poland)
EBRD	European Bank for Reconstruction and Development
EC	European Community
ECE	East-Central Europe
ECSC	European Coal and Steel Community
EEC	European Economic Community
EU	European Union
FBIS	Foreign Broadcast Information Service
GATT	General Agreement on Tariffs and Trade
GDP	Gross Domestic Product
GDR	German Democratic Republic, or East Germany
GNP	Gross National Product
HSP	Hungarian Socialist Party
HSWP	Hungarian Socialist Workers' Party
IGO	Intergovernmental Organization
IMF	International Monetary Fund
INF	Intermediate-Range Nuclear Forces (Treaty)
KGB	Committee on State Security (USSR)
KOR	Workers' Defense Committee (Poland)

KPN	Confederation of Independent Poland
KSS	Committee for Social Self-Defense (Poland)
LCY	League of Communists of Yugoslavia
LDP	Liberal Democratic Party (Russia)
MDS	Movement for Democratic Slovakia
MKS	Interfactory Strike Committee (Poland)
MPLA	Popular Movement for the Liberation of Angola
NATO	North Atlantic Treaty Organization
NEM	New Economic Mechanism (Hungary)
NPT	Non-Proliferation Treaty
NSF	National Salvation Front (Romania)
OECD	Organization for Economic Cooperation and Development
OSCE	Organization for Security and Cooperation in Europe
PFP	Partnership for Peace
PRC	People's Republic of China
PSL	People's Peasant Party (Poland)
PUWP	Polish United Workers' Party
PZPR	Polish United Workers' Party
ROPCiO	Movement for the Defense of Human and Civil Rights (Poland)
SALT I	Strategic Arms Limitation Treaty I (1972)
SALT II	Strategic Arms Limitation Treaty II (1979)
SEA	Single Europe Act
SLD	Democratic Left Alliance (Poland)
SPD	Social Democratic Party (Germany)
SSR	Soviet Socialist Republic
START I	Strategic Arms Reduction Treaty (1991)
START II	Strategic Arms Reduction Treaty (1992)
UDF	Union of Democratic Forces (Bulgaria)
UN	United Nations
UNICEF	United Nations International Children's Emergency Fund
UNITA	National Union for the Total Independence of Angola
USSR	Union of Soviet Socialist Republics
WEU	Western European Union
WTO	Warsaw Treaty Organization (Warsaw Pact)

□ □ □

Introduction

The year 1989 marked a turning point in world history. During the last six months of that year, the world witnessed the collapse of communism in Europe. Two years later, communism was abolished in the Soviet Union, and that country began to fall apart. These changes were stunning and unprecedented in terms of their breadth, depth, and speed. The popular revolutions in Eastern Europe led to fundamental transformations of all of those countries, but they also caused epochal changes in both European politics and international politics. The collapse of the Soviet Union and the reunification of Germany fundamentally altered the face of Europe, geographically, strategically, economically, and politically. The disappearance of both the Soviet Union and European communism meant an end to the Cold War, the defining element of postwar international politics. The disintegration of the multinational states of the Soviet Union and Yugoslavia unleashed pent-up nationalism and ethnic hostility that led to the worst violence in Europe since World War II. And the ripple effects of the East European revolutions spread far and wide, influencing domestic politics in the United States, Nicaragua, South Africa, Israel, Cuba, and many other countries.

The enormity of the changes in this part of the world recalled other eras of epochal changes. In some ways, the exhilaration and optimism that swept East-Central Europe in 1989 resembled the mood after World War II, when these same countries emerged from years of violence, deprivation, and oppression. In 1989, as in 1945, their populations faced the enormous task of rebuilding the political and economic order. Now, as then, they were about to begin this effort with new leaders, a new political orientation, and a new international environment.

There are other historical parallels as well. The events of 1989, in terms of their likely impact on domestic and international politics, rival the French Revolution of 1789 and the Russian Revolution of 1917. The 1789 revolution marked a sudden transformation for France, of course, with the overthrow of the monarchy and the Old Regime and the initiation of a republican political experience. The impact of the French Revolution, however, was felt

1

all over Europe and the rest of the world. The seeds of democracy and nationalism planted in Paris were carried throughout Europe by Napoleon and his armies, marking the beginning of the end of monarchy and aristocracy on the continent. Napoleon's conscript armies, fighting for a cause rather than a salary, also revolutionized the nature of warfare.

If 1789 was the first democratic revolution, based on the Enlightenment ideas of freedom and property, 1917 was the first socialist one, inspired by the nineteenth-century ideals of political and economic equality. The seizure of power by Vladimir Lenin and the Bolsheviks in November 1917 inaugurated a transformation of Russia even more fundamental and thoroughgoing than that of France in 1789. The Russian Marxists, like the French revolutionaries, believed that their revolution had international relevance. With the establishment of the Communist International (the Comintern) in Moscow in 1919, the Russian revolutionaries committed themselves to world revolution. Whether because of or in spite of their efforts, by the 1970s half of the world's population lived in communist party states.

The events of 1989 were equally far-reaching and, like the revolutions of 1789 and 1917, had both domestic and international effects. Within the countries of East-Central Europe, the social, economic, and political changes were as fundamental as were those in France and Russia after their revolutions. In every country in the region the transition to Western-style parliamentary democracy meant a fundamental restructuring of the political system, a proliferation of new interest groups and parties, and upheaval within the bureaucracy and administration. At the same time, all of these new regimes attempted an economic transition from centrally planned economies to market-oriented ones with increasing degrees of private ownership of property. Trying to accomplish *both* of these transitions simultaneously, from authoritarianism to pluralism and from plan to market, was a huge task, and the two occasionally pulled against each other. To further complicate matters, there were enormous *social* costs involved in these changes, particularly with the reemergence of unemployment, bankruptcies, inflation, and inequality. The transitions would not be easy, and they would take a long time.

The international impact of the revolutions of 1989 and 1991 was just as great—and potentially as significant—as those of 1789 and 1917. For Americans, the most obvious impact was the disappearance of the communist threat, however exaggerated that may have been. With the collapse of communism in Eastern Europe and the Soviet Union, the problem of communist expansionism simply no longer existed. Indeed, communism seemed to be on the retreat all over the world. For the whole postwar period, U.S. foreign policy had been based on the "containment" of communism. Because communism no longer needed containing, this

U.S. policy became irrelevant, and the Cold War conflict between the superpowers finally came to an end. These changes dramatically reshaped the international political environment and required a fundamental rethinking of U.S. foreign policy.

The effects of the anticommunist revolution were felt not just in the United States. Europe was being reshaped as thoroughly as it had been after World War II, and perhaps as dramatically as after World War I (in the aftermath of the dissolution of the Austrian, German, Russian, and Ottoman empires). The collapse of the Warsaw Treaty Organization (WTO), the Eastern European military alliance (otherwise known as the Warsaw Pact), called into question the role and purpose of the North Atlantic Treaty Organization (NATO), the Western Alliance. The unification of Germany created a large new European power that could dominate Europe economically, politically, and perhaps even militarily. The new democratic states in East-Central Europe aspired to membership in NATO and the European Union (EU) at the same time that the EU was moving toward closer internal integration. At the same time, the wars in the former Yugoslavia, especially the protracted conflict in Bosnia, challenged NATO, the United Nations, and the EU, which were unable to find ways to settle the conflict.

The Third World was also affected by the changes in the communist world. The Gorbachev leadership in the Soviet Union declared in 1987 and afterward that it no longer viewed the Third World as an ideological battleground and would sharply reduce its economic and military commitments to those countries. The Soviet economic deterioration and political collapse made this virtue into a necessity. The removal of the Third World from the theater of the Cold War seemed to portend well for these countries. But instead, the grievous problems of poverty, hunger, and inequality in the Third World became even more invisible as the first world's attention shifted to the economic restoration of the former second world. The already limited foreign aid resources from the Western powers were strained by the demands of both East-Central Europe and the Third World. Because the former seemed to promise quicker results (and higher returns), that is where the resources were deployed. The de-ideologization of the Third World, in combination with the end of the Cold War, was likely to shift the dominant division of the international system from East-West to North-South.[1]

If the point still needed proving, the events of 1989 demonstrated once again the growing interdependence of the countries of the world. As we have seen, the Eastern European revolutions of 1989 had a dramatic and almost immediate impact on the United States, Western Europe, and the Third World. Even more important, however, was the symbiosis of change *within* the Soviet bloc. In earlier years a political crisis in one bloc country could, in large measure, be contained to that one country. There was some spillover from Poland to Hungary in 1956, but the Prague Spring of 1968 in Czechoslovakia and the Polish Solidarity movement of 1980–1981 did not spread beyond national boundaries. In 1989, the revolution spread like wildfire from one country to the next. Furthermore, the reform program in the Soviet Union stimulated changes in Eastern Europe, which in turn stepped up the pressures for change in the Soviet Union. The collapse of communism in Eastern Europe accelerated the collapse of communism in the Soviet Union.

All this testifies to the increased interconnectedness of countries, which is manifested in many forms: communications, transportation, culture, education, tourism, trade, and so forth. These linkages were perhaps even more important in a region such as Eastern Europe, where the political, economic, and social infrastructures were so similar and where the problems that each country faced were so uniform. This standardization facilitated coordination and control by the national communist parties and by Moscow, but it also accelerated communication during 1989 and created a sense of common grievance and common purpose in the populations of the various countries.

This book addresses a number of dilemmas in world politics that have confronted the communist states, the West, and the postcommunist states of East-Central Europe. For the Soviet Union, probably the principal foreign policy dilemma in the postwar period was the issue of conformity versus diversity in Eastern Europe. This was a region of fundamental strategic, economic, and political importance for the Soviet Union. From the Kremlin's point of view, the question was how best to keep the region under Moscow's thumb. Joseph Stalin insisted on conformity, but ended up losing control over Yugoslavia. Nikita Khrushchev allowed more diversity, but the result was insurrection in Poland and Hungary. The leadership of Leonid Brezhnev applied repression in Czechoslovakia in 1968, but that country then fell into a sullen stagnation. When Mikhail Gorbachev eventually allowed unprecedented diversity, the communist system collapsed.

The tension between conformity and diversity in states and empires is an ancient one. In the fifth century B.C., Thucydides wrote (in *The Peloponnesian War*) of similar quandaries facing Athens with its far-flung Mediterranean empire. The communist leaderships of Eastern Europe also had to face this dilemma. For some of them, especially in the Stalinist era, the question was only how best to maintain power. But by the mid-1950s, it was clear that the Eastern European leaders had to respond in some way to the popular demands for national autonomy and political participation. To ignore this altogether risked rebellion and instability. Until the rise of Gorbachev, then, these leaders had to tread a narrow line between the Kremlin's demands for conformity and their populations' yearnings for change. For example, in 1981, when Poland's party leader Wojciech Jaruzelski banned the independent trade union Solidarity and declared martial law, he said that he was doing so to avert a greater tragedy—presumably a military intervention by Moscow. After 1985, when the Gorbachev leadership began encouraging change in Eastern Europe, the dilemma was reversed but equally acute. At that point the problem for the communist parties in Eastern Europe was how to manage change without being consumed by it. As we have seen, they were not able to solve that problem.

The old dilemmas previously faced by the communist regimes have recently been replaced by new and equally pressing ones for the postcommunist states. All of these countries are now trying to pursue fundamental changes in the political system and the economy *simultaneously*. This is a formidable task that few countries have even attempted in the past. Usually such multifaceted and thoroughgoing change is only possible after a violent revolution that sweeps away most remnants of the old order. Furthermore, the postcommunist economic transformations, from plan to market, entail many dislocations and much sacrifice on the part of the populations. Such intense and wrenching change can only be accomplished by a government that has *either* very firm central control *or* a large-scale popular mandate. The fledgling democratic governments of the region have neither: They rejected the centralism of communism; and within a year of their revolutions they had lost the unanimity and solidarity of the revolutionary mandate. Many of them faced the choice of retarding either democratization or economic liberalization. In the multinational states of the former Soviet Union and Yugoslavia, these problems were compounded by the divisive and explosive forces of nationalism.

Eastern Europe has always posed a dilemma to the West as well, especially to the United States. The United States voiced support for democracy and human rights, but in the delicate and dangerous Cold War environment also wanted stability. The area was never one of central concern in U.S. foreign policy. But the United States never accepted the domination of Eastern Europe by the Soviet Union and never officially recognized the 1940 absorption of the Baltic states (Estonia, Latvia, and Lithuania) into the Soviet Union. In the early postwar period, the U.S. government professed to favor the "liberation" of the "captive peoples" of Eastern Europe from Soviet-imposed communism. But when it came right down to it, such as when Hungary attempted to leave the Soviet camp in 1956, the United States was unwilling to risk a major confrontation with the Soviet Union in the Soviet sphere of influence. The United States instead began to pursue a policy of "differentiation" in which economic aid and trade was doled out to those Eastern European states (for example, Romania) that seemed most willing to challenge Moscow. A similar dilemma confronted the United States in the period after 1989, when the Bush administration agonized over whom to recognize in the collapsing multinational states (e.g., Slovenia and Croatia; the Baltic states; the other former Soviet republics). As in earlier times, the United States claimed to support national self-determination and democratic rule, but it was also worried about the collapse of political and economic stability that might follow national fragmentation. This was another classic foreign policy dilemma: whether to pursue a policy based on idealism or realism. This dilemma arose even more forcefully with the war in Bosnia. From the U.S. point of view, here was a clear-cut case of aggression by Bosnian Serbs against Bosnian Muslims. The Serbian policy of seizing territory, "ethnic cleansing" of Muslims in those areas, and artillery shelling of population centers like Sarajevo seemed to call for a firm response from the Western democracies, including the United States. But the idealism that stimulated such a response was tempered by a realism that recognized the limits of U.S. diplomacy and military power in the region. Diplomatic negotiations and economic sanctions seemed to have little effect; yet a military solution would require, it seemed, a large-scale and long-term commitment of troops that Americans (and most Europeans) were unwilling to support.

With the collapse of communism in Europe, the United States seemed to have "won" the Cold War. But with the disappearance of communism and the Cold War, the United States faced a novel and somewhat uncomfortable dilemma: What to do now? Postwar U.S. foreign policy had been based on the containment of communism, but now there was nothing to contain. Ironically, just as the United States emerged as the world's sole superpower, the country had lost its major role in world affairs. This dilemma carried over into the domestic arena, as the United States now had the opportunity to address some of the pressing social and economic concerns that had long been ignored in the face of perceived external threats.

The alert reader will have noticed the mixed references in this chapter to Eastern Europe and East-Central Europe. The use of these terms requires some explanation. The issue here is not just a geographic one, though geographers also disagree on the use of these terms. It is also a political and cultural issue that relates to the self-identity and political orientations of the people of the region. This issue of nomenclature has occasioned an intense debate by intellectuals both in Europe and elsewhere. This debate (which also revolves around yet another designation—Central Europe) will be addressed more fully in Chapter 1.

In this book, however, the following conventions will be followed: "Eastern Europe" refers to the European communist party states—primarily before 1990; "East-Central Europe" refers to the same countries, but after the collapse of communism (see map of Eastern Europe). These states will sometimes be referred to as the "ECE" countries. Thus, the Eastern European countries are Poland, East Germany, Czechoslovakia, Hungary, Romania, Bulgaria, Yugoslavia, and Albania. The Soviet Union is sometimes also included in this category (in that geographic Europe extends to the Ural Mountains in the Soviet Union). East-Central Europe encompasses those same countries, though East Germany no longer exists as a separate state and Czechoslovakia is now two separate states, the Czech Republic and Slovakia.

These designations are not always clear-cut, of course, and would become even more difficult as new states emerged out of the old. The Soviet Baltic republics of Lithuania, Latvia, and Estonia became independent states in 1991 and cast their lot with Europe. The other former western Soviet republics of Moldova, Belarus, and Ukraine, all geographically part of Europe, could also follow the same path. Slovenia, Croatia, Bosnia-Herzegovina, and Macedonia all declared their independence from Yugoslavia in 1991 or 1992, adding even more states to the East-Central European quilt.

This book focuses on the revolutions in East-Central Europe and their impact on the region, the world, and on international politics. Because of the close ties between the Eastern European countries and the Soviet Union, it also contains a discussion of the developments in the latter. Chapter 1 provides an overview of the postwar history of the region, from the establishment of communist rule in the 1940s to the fragmentation and decay of the communist system through the early 1980s. Chapter 2 looks at the roots of reform in the Soviet Union and reviews the 1989 revolutions in Eastern Europe. Chapter 3 discusses how the revolutions led to the collapse of old states in the Soviet Union, Czechoslovakia, and Yugoslavia (with special attention to the war in Bosnia) and the formation of new states out of those as well as of the formerly divided Germany. Chapter 4 considers the rebuilding of the political and economic orders in the former communist states and their often difficult transitions toward political democracy and market economies. Chapter 5 discusses the international dimensions of the East European revolutions and the realignment of the international political and economic system that is taking place. Throughout the book, but especially in Chapters 3 and 4, these events and issues are related to some important theories of comparative and international politics: theories of social movements and revolutions, democratization, nationalism, and economic transition. The volume also includes discussion questions, an annotated list of relevant readings on the region and on recent events, a list of video resources, a chronology, and a glossary. Terms highlighted by bold type may be found in the Glossary.

Eastern Europe

ONE

□ □ □

The Establishment and Decay of Communism in East-Central Europe

In February 1945, Franklin Roosevelt, Winston Churchill, and Joseph Stalin (the Big Three) met at the Soviet resort town of Yalta to plan the final stages of World War II and to negotiate the postwar order in Europe. The Anglo-Americans were not in a very strong bargaining position because they had liberated only France, whereas the Soviet army had pushed the Germans out of most of Poland, Hungary, Yugoslavia, Czechoslovakia, and Romania and were only about 100 miles from Berlin (which they would take three months later). Among the provisions of the **Yalta Agreements,** as they came to be known, were: the movement of Poland's borders some 100 miles westward (leaving parts of eastern Poland to the Soviet Union), the division of Germany into occupation zones (with the Soviets occupying the eastern part), and the agreement that the nations of Eastern Europe were to be democratic and "friendly" to the Soviet Union. In an earlier meeting between Churchill and Stalin in Moscow, the two had agreed that "Russia" would have predominant influence in Romania and Bulgaria and equal influence with the West in Yugoslavia and Hungary.[1]

In later years Yalta became a symbol of betrayal for many of the people in Eastern Europe who felt that the Allies had left Stalin with a free hand in the region. Indeed, in the three years following the Yalta Conference, the Soviets systematically established Soviet-style communist regimes throughout the area. Given the circumstances of 1945, however, it was almost inevitable that the Soviet Union would come to dominate Eastern Europe. As a result of the postwar military operations the area was by then largely under Soviet military occupation, and, by the time of the Nazi surrender in May of 1945, it was almost completely so. (Although parts of Yugoslavia and Albania were not occupied by the Russians, parts of Finland and Austria were.) During the war, Poland, Yugoslavia, and the Czech lands had been occupied by the Germans; and, in 1940 and 1941, Hungary, Slovakia, Romania, and Bulgaria had actually sided with the Germans by signing the Tripartite Pact (the wartime alliance of Germany, Italy, and Japan). So just as the American, British, and French forces swept the Germans out of the western part of Europe and initiated Western-style democratic governments in those countries, the Soviets occupied Eastern Europe and established "peoples' democracies" that were "friendly" to the Soviet Union. Of course, from the Soviet point of view, and especially from Stalin's, *friendly* meant *communist*—a capitalist state would by nature be hostile to the communism of the Soviet Union. For the Soviet Union, furthermore, the lands of Eastern Europe were much more important strategically than they were for the West: Most of these lands bordered on the Soviet Union; and the region had constituted the principal route of invasion into Russia and the Soviet Union by countless armies, including those of Napoleon in 1812 and of the Germans in both world wars. Control over the area was of critical importance for the Soviet Union but was of marginal interest to the West. The major exception to this pattern was in Yugoslavia, where Josip Broz Tito and the Yugoslav resistance managed to liberate the country from the Germans without substantial Soviet assistance.

In the West at the time, and particularly in the United States, there was little inclination to challenge the Soviets on Eastern Europe. The United States had just *finished* a war, after all, and the Soviet Union had been an ally in the defeat of Nazi Germany. The United States was rapidly demobilizing its troops and bringing them home from Europe. Additionally, the Big Three's "Declaration on Liberated Europe" (part of the Yalta Agreements) had provided that these states would have freely elected governments "responsive to the will of the people." In the United States, citizens and leaders alike felt that they had done their duty. The last wartime summit, at Potsdam in July 1945, provided that the Allies would take reparations only from their own zones of occupation. This hardened the division between East and West and facilitated the application of the Soviet economic agenda in Eastern Europe.

Politically, the Soviets were already in the process of extending their control into the region, using a procedure that the Hungarian communist party chief referred to as "salami tactics"—one slice at a time. In the earliest stage, in 1945 and 1946, Soviet occupation authorities in each of the countries sponsored the formation of coalition governments that included both communist and noncommunist parties. In most cases, the first parliamentary elections were competitive and fair. In the 1945 elections in Hungary, for example, the prewar Smallholder's party won 57 percent of the votes and their leader became prime minister. In the same election, the Communist party won only 17 percent of the votes, though they did assume some key ministerial posts, such as Interior, which controlled the police and security apparatus.

These early coalition governments pursued reformist policies that were generally welcomed by both the local populations and the Western governments: the purging of fascists and others who had collaborated with the Nazis; the implementation of social reforms, especially agricultural reforms that distributed the land more widely; the provision of political freedoms and freedom of expression (except criticism of the Soviet Union); and a foreign policy that was sympathetic to the Soviet Union and to the West.

During 1946 and 1947, however, these policies were modified and the coalition governments were restructured in favor of the communists. Newspapers and media outlets increasingly came under the control of the communists, and censorship was imposed. Noncommunist political leaders were intimidated, blackmailed, or even assaulted. Party meetings that were critical of these actions or of the communists were broken up by the police (who were controlled by the communist-dominated Interior Ministry). Ultimately, new parliamentary elections, characterized by intimidation of voters and candidates as well as outright fraud, led to new government configurations. In the Hungarian elections of 1947, the Smallholder's party this time won only 14 percent of the vote, compared to 22 percent for the Communist party. The leader of the Smallholder's party, Ferenc Nagy, fled the country. The next year, the small Communist party was merged with the Social Democratic party into the Hungarian Workers' party, which dominated the political system for the next thirty years. The pattern was similar throughout the region, with the "fusion" of left-wing parties into a renamed Communist party (e.g., the Workers' party) occurring almost everywhere in 1948.

Although intimidation and force were used to consolidate communist power in Eastern Europe, it is important to recognize that there were also indigenous sources of support for the communists in most of these countries. There were many reasons for this. In Czechoslovakia, Hungary, and Bulgaria, for example, there had been strong communist parties even before the war. In some cases, the communists had played an important role in the wartime resistance movement to the Nazis and in the liberation of the country from German control. This contributed to popular support for the communists in Bulgaria, Yugoslavia, and Albania. (The communists' role in the resistance also contributed to widespread support for the Communist party in France after the war.) Many people supported the political parties on the left because they welcomed their programs for change and social reforms that promised economic modernization and the end of the semifeudal prewar system. Memories of the economic depression in the interwar period had convinced many people that capitalism was in crisis, fostering a receptiveness (especially among intellectuals) to other approaches, including the Soviet system. Finally, there were many people who *favored* an alliance with the Soviet Union, seeing this as the only realistic protection for small countries with a history of outside domination.

THE WESTERN REACTION
AND THE ONSET OF THE COLD WAR

In the early postwar years, as we have seen, Western relations with the Soviet Union were reasonably friendly. Roosevelt, Churchill, and Stalin, despite their differences in temperament and ideology, were able to reach a broad consensus on the postwar order in Europe and worldwide with the founding of the United Nations. Within five years after the end of the war, though, U.S.-Soviet relations were poisoned, both sides were remilitarizing, and the world was in the throes of the **Cold War.** Many of the causes for this lay in Eastern Europe.

The origin of the Cold War is one of the most studied and debated issues in U.S. history, and there is an enormous literature on U.S.-Soviet relations in the early postwar years.[2] Among Western historians, there are two major schools of thought on the origins of the Cold War. The *traditional* interpretation places the blame largely on Moscow, asserting that the Soviet Union was intent on expanding its influence and its ideology and that the United States had no alternative but to resist and "contain" this expansionist tendency. The *revisionist* school does not accept the contention that the Soviet Union alone caused the Cold War. Some revisionists argue that the United States overreacted to a minimal or dubious threat from the Soviet Union. The more radical revisionists place the blame squarely on the United States, arguing that an expansionist United States was attempting to extend its influence worldwide, including into the Soviet sphere of influence. Some of the more recent literature combines elements of these two schools, producing *postrevisionist* interpretations.

To some extent, the revival of U.S.-Soviet animosity after World War II was inevitable. The two countries were ideological enemies from the time of the 1917 revolution that brought the communists to power in Russia. Mutual distrust and suspicion were reinforced by allied intervention in Russia in the early years of Bolshevik (communist) power, the U.S. refusal to extend diplomatic recognition to the new regime (until 1933), and Soviet efforts to undermine worldwide capitalism through the **Comintern** (an international organization of communist parties founded by Moscow in 1919). Even apart from these differences, one would have expected tension between these two major powers as they were sucked into the power vacuum in Europe created by World War II.

Both powers were intent on trying to avoid a repetition of the war they had just fought, but they had different conceptions about the causes of World War II and the ways to prevent another. From the Soviet point of view, this had not been a world war at all, but the Great Patriotic War: a fight for survival against German aggression in which the Soviet Union lost twenty million lives. For the Soviet Union, the main task was to avoid future aggression from the Germans or from other "Western imperialists." This meant obtaining control over the Eastern European corridor through which the Germans had passed twice in the last generation. Such control entailed the existence of friendly states in Eastern Europe (in the language of the Yalta Agreements), which to Stalin meant communist.

From the U.S. point of view, and particularly from that of President Harry S Truman (who succeeded Roosevelt upon the latter's death in April 1945), the conflict in Europe had come about because of "appeasement" of Hitler's aggression, symbolized by the 1938 Munich Agreement (in which the Western Allies acceded to Hitler's demands for the Sudentenland region of Czechoslovakia). To avoid another war meant to avoid appeasement of aggression. When the Eastern European states began one by one to fall under the sway of the communists, Truman and the United States saw this as a form of Soviet aggression, not unlike that of Hitler in the 1930s.

As the lines between the two powers began to harden, both became more doctrinaire and less flexible. Visiting Fulton, Missouri, in March 1946, former British Prime Minister Winston Churchill said that "an **iron curtain** has descended across the continent" of Europe. In 1947 an important article by George Kennan, a State Department official and Soviet specialist, argued that the Soviet Union was expansionist by both tradition and ideology, and that U.S. policy should therefore be a "firm and vigilant containment of Russian expansive tendencies."[3] President Truman adopted a similar point of view in his March 1947 appeal to Congress for money to support Greece and Turkey: "It must be the policy of the United States to support free people who are resisting attempted subjugation by armed minorities or by outside pressure." This speech became known as the **Truman Doctrine** which, along with the "**containment** of communism," became the guiding doctrine of postwar U.S. foreign policy.[4] The doctrine was implemented with a series of policies and treaties that were meant to establish a bulwark against the further expansion of communism in Europe and elsewhere: the Marshall Plan, a commitment of $17 billion to promote European economic recovery from the war; the North Atlantic Treaty Organization (**NATO**), which extended the U.S. military and nuclear umbrella over Western Europe; and the U.S. participation in the Korean War (1950–1953) to block the expansion of communism in Asia.

The U.S. view of expansionist communism, as expressed by Kennan and Truman, was matched by a similarly hostile view of the United States by Stalin and his advisers and associates. At the founding meeting of the **Cominform** (an international organization to coordinate policies among the communist states) in 1947, Soviet politburo member Andrei Zhdanov argued that U.S. leaders "mask their expansionist policy . . . by fictious [sic] considerations of defense against communism." "America's aspirations to world supremacy," however, encountered an obstacle in the USSR and "in the new democracies [i.e., Eastern Europe] which have escaped from the control of British and American imperialism." Zhdanov criticized both the Truman Doctrine and the Marshall Plan as being parts of U.S. expansionist policy.[5] These policies, therefore, were matched by Soviet-sponsored international organizations meant to protect their allies against Western expansionism: the Cominform; the Council for Mutual Economic Assistance (**Comecon,** or CMEA); and later the **Warsaw Pact,** the Soviet counterpart to NATO. The lines had hardened on both sides of the iron curtain.

THE INSTITUTIONS OF COMMUNISM

Over the next five years, from 1948 to 1953, the communist governments of the region proceeded to establish in their own countries the institutions and policies of Soviet-style communism. This was a time of very rapid change. The Eastern European states accomplished in five years what had taken perhaps twenty years to accomplish in the Soviet Union under Vladimir Lenin (1917–1923) and then Joseph Stalin (1920s through 1953). In part, this was possible because the Eastern Europeans had a ready-made model based on the Soviet experience, and they simply imitated the Soviet pattern in the economic, social, and political spheres.

The social policies of the new regimes had elements that were both benevolent and oppressive. Like most modernizing governments, and all socialist ones, the new governments (even in the coalition phase) seized most of the large landed estates and redistributed the property to ordinary peasants and farmers. In some areas, for example in the "Western Territories" of Poland, newly acquired from Germany, this involved a huge amount of land. The government's distribution of this property, often to refugees from farther east, understandably fostered considerable goodwill toward the regime. On the one hand, the new communist-dominated governments also pursued socialist social policies that were often well-received by the population: subsidized housing, health care, education, and guaranteed employment. On the other hand, these more generous policies were accompanied by the restrictive apparatus of the Soviet state as well: an increasingly powerful secret police; restrictions on independent organizations and media; and censorship.

Economically, each of the Eastern European states pursued the twin policies of rapid industrialization and collectivization of agriculture (the linchpins of Stalin's first Five-Year Plan begun in 1928). As in the Soviet Union, emphasis was placed on heavy industry (metallurgy, machine tools, engineering, petrochemicals) at the expense of light industry and consumer goods. The economy could be steered in this direction because of increasing state ownership of industry and because of state-controlled central economic planning. A state planning agency (modeled on the Soviet Gosplan) worked with the Council of Ministers and the various governmental ministries (e.g., Ministry of Heavy Industry, Ministry of Metallurgy) to set annual targets for growth of national income and gross output of industry, transportation, construction, and agriculture as well as specific output goals for important producer and consumer goods.[6] Prices and wages were also fixed by government agencies. A central state bank controlled and distributed financial and investment resources. The state also regulated foreign trade through a Ministry of Foreign Trade.

Collectivization of agriculture also followed the Soviet pattern from the late 1920s and early 1930s, though the process was not nearly as brutal as in the Soviet Union. Two types of socialized farms were established: Collective farms were those in which the farmers pooled their land, livestock, and equipment and shared in both the work and the proceeds of the farm; state farms, however, were owned and operated by the government (through the Ministry of Agriculture), and the farmers were simply employees. Employees of state farms had more job and income security but were not usually allowed the small private plots for truck farming as were the collective farmers.

During the 1950s, most farmland was brought into one of these two institutions. As in the Soviet Union a generation earlier, there was much resistance from private farmers, many of whom had only recently been given land as part of the early postwar reforms. The pressure to join the socialized farms was both physical and financial. In some countries more than in others, this pressure on farmers was more intense, and resistance often led to arrest or deportation. In other cases the pressure was more subtle. Individual farmers suffered higher taxes and had more difficulty acquiring seed and equipment. Furthermore, employees of state farms were eligible for government-sponsored health care, vacations, and pensions. At any rate, by the early 1960s, most farmland was in the socialist sector. The only exceptions were in Poland (where the socialized sector never encompassed more than a quarter of the farmland) and Yugoslavia;

in both countries the private sector in agriculture became an important economic and political force in later years.

The political systems of Eastern Europe were also modeled closely on the Stalinist political structure; the institutions even adopted the Soviet names in most cases. As in the Soviet Union, the Eastern Europeans adopted a parallel political structure of party and government. The formal structures of government were constitutionally defined and, in theory at least, democratically elected by the population. In practice, in elections to state bodies there was only one candidate per seat, and voters simply voted for or against the single candidate. Moreover, candidates had to be cleared by party authorities at the appropriate level. At the national level, there was a national parliament elected by direct popular vote every four or five years. The parliament chose from among its members a **Council of Ministers** whose members also acted as the heads of the numerous government ministries (many of them economic). The chairman of the Council of Ministers, equivalent to a prime minister, acted as head of the government. This pattern of organization was replicated at lower levels, down to the city or village, where city councils had chairpersons who had powers equivalent to a mayor.

This whole structure was paralleled by the communist party organization (though, as we have seen, it was often called a "Workers' party," as in the Polish United Workers' party). In each country, only about 10 percent of the adult population belonged to the party, which was considered the leading and guiding force in society. At the national level, a party congress was elected by party members every four or five years. Its power was largely symbolic in that it met for only a few days, but it did elect from its members a **Central Committee** (usually several hundred members), a Political Bureau (or **politburo,** ten to fifteen members), a Secretariat, and a first secretary, who was the national party leader. After the early 1950s, at least, the first secretary in most countries was not really a dictator; he was the first among equals in a politburo that was the key decision-making institution in the political system.

The relationship between the party and the state was very close, extending even to common membership. The politburo, for example, included in its members the top figures in both the party and the state, typically including several party secretaries and the most important members of the (government's) Council of Ministers (e.g., the minister of Defense and the chairman of the State Planning Commission). Furthermore, as noted above, party executive bodies at each level exercised some control over the appointment of key persons in the government. A list of those positions requiring such clearance was referred to as the **nomenklatura,** a term which came to describe the political elite itself. Theoretically, though, the functions of party and state were to be separate: The party was to provide leadership and guidance (and make general policy decisions); the government was responsible for policy implementation, administration, and day-to-day decision making.

The adoption in Eastern Europe of the institutions and policies of the Soviet Union created the Soviet bloc, as it was called in the West. Soviet **hegemony** (influence) over the region was reinforced by a common foreign policy of "socialist internationalism" and a series of international organizations that tied the region together and insured conformity. The first of these institutions was the Communist Information Bureau, or Cominform. At the founding session of the Cominform, in September 1947, the concept of separate national paths to socialism was condemned and the leaders of the people's democracies (as the Eastern European communist states were called) were told that their policies and political systems should conform to that of the Soviet Union.[7] Beginning in 1948, these principles became the basis for a series of purges of Eastern European communist leaders who were considered too nationalistic in their approach. In 1949, Moscow sponsored the creation of the Council for Mutual Economic Assistance, or Comecon, which was meant to coordinate trade among the European communist states and to tie them more closely together economically. And in 1955, as a response to the West German entrance into the North Atlantic Treaty Organization (which had been founded in 1949), the Soviet Union and the people's democracies created their own military alliance, the Warsaw Treaty Organization (or the Warsaw Pact). With the establishment of these three organizations, Cominform, Comecon, and the Warsaw Pact, the Soviet Union and the Eastern European states became closely integrated politically, economically, and militarily, and they became increasingly cut off from the rest of Europe. Winston Churchill's statement about the "iron curtain" was even more true in 1955 than it was in 1946.

SOCIOECONOMIC CHANGES
IN THE EARLY YEARS OF COMMUNISM

From the end of World War II through the 1960s, all of the Eastern European states experienced high degrees of economic growth and rapid social changes. Perhaps the biggest social change was a result of the rapid urbanization and industrialization of these countries and the consequent decline in the percentage of people living and working in the countryside (see Table 1.1). From 1950 to 1970, all except Albania were transformed from primarily rural, agricultural societies to industrial, urban ones. Urbanization continued during the 1970s and 1980s.

TABLE 1.1 Percentage of labor force employed in agriculture

Country	Ca. 1930	1950	1960	1970	1978
GDR	–	24	18	13	10
Czechoslovakia	37	38	26	19	11
Hungary	53	49	37	25	17
Poland	64	56	47	39	32
Bulgaria	80	73	57	47	36
Yugoslavia	78	70	58	50	40
Romania	–	74	66	49	40
Albania	–	85	71	66	62

Source: Paul M. Johnson, "Changing Social Structure and the Political Role of Manual Workers," in Jan F. Triska and Charles Gati, *Blue Collar Workers in Eastern Europe* (Boston: George Allen and Unwin, 1981), 31. Reprinted by permission.

This was also a period of very rapid and sustained economic growth throughout the region. The average annual rates of growth of the **gross national product** (GNP), the total value of goods and services produced in a country, was above 3 percent for most of the countries for most of the years up through the mid-1970s. Very few countries historically have experienced such rapid and long-term growth; it is even more unusual for a whole region. Even the per capita growth in the economy was remarkably high, particularly during the 1950s (see Table 1.2).

There has been much controversy in the West about the meaning of this economic growth in Eastern Europe and about the reliability of the data used to calculate GNP growth rates. Many Western economists have pointed out that the economies of Western Europe have been much more successful and reached much higher levels of development than those in Eastern Europe. They also point to the relatively low standard of living of Eastern Europeans compared to Western Europeans and to the periodic shortages of consumer goods in the East. Such observations are largely correct, but they should be balanced with other considerations. First, generally, the Eastern European countries were less developed in the first place (i.e., before World War II) than those in Western Europe; some might more accurately have been grouped with Third World countries in terms of economic development. So these countries had farther to go. Second, the lower standard of living in Eastern Europe (in terms of income and consumption) is balanced in part by higher indicators in other respects: lower (in fact negligible) rates of unemployment; broader accessibility (and lesser cost) of health care (as measured by physicians and hospital beds per capita); a more egalitarian social and economic structure.

But even apart from these considerations, the Eastern European states held their own in economic development in comparison with other states. This was particularly the case during the 1950s and 1960s. Table 1.3

TABLE 1.2   Economic growth in Eastern and Western Europe, 1950–1967 (average annual rate of growth of real per capita gross domestic product, percentage)[a]

Country	1950–1960	1960–1967
Albania	6.1	3.0
Bulgaria	7.9	7.2
GDR	11.0	3.7
Hungary	4.2	4.9
Poland	6.0	5.1
Romania	7.6	8.5
USSR	8.6	5.6
Yugoslavia	6.2	6.9
USSR and Eastern Europe	7.7	5.4
EEC (Western Europe)	4.7	3.6
Federal Republic of Germany	6.6	3.1
Italy	4.6	4.0

[a]For the Soviet Union and Eastern Europe, growth rates are measured in net material product; for Western Europe in gross domestic product. These are both similar measures to gross national product, which is the total value of goods and services produced by a country.

Source: United Nations, Yearbook of National Accounts Statistics, 1968, Vol. 2, International Tables (United Nations, 1969), 109, 112.

shows a way of comparing Eastern European countries, by pairing them with countries at similar levels of economic development. As the table indicates, in the early postwar years (up to 1960), most of the Eastern European countries actually gained on the market economies of the West. As is also evident from this table, this pattern began to change in the 1960s and the Eastern Europeans began to fall farther and farther behind. This was a key factor that led to the reforms in the 1980s and the revolutions in 1989, and will be further discussed later in this chapter.

CHALLENGES TO COMMUNIST ORTHODOXY

By 1948, as we have seen, people's democracies based on the Soviet model were established all over Eastern Europe. But even from the beginning, the communist bloc was not as monolithic as most Westerners perceived it. The first challenge to Soviet domination came from Yugoslavia. Along with Albania, Yugoslavia was exceptional in that the Soviet army had played only a minor role in liberating it from the Nazis at the end of World War II and had occupied only the northern part of the country. The main role in dislodging the Germans was played by the Partisans under

TABLE 1.3   Changes in relative positions of Eastern European countries in bilateral comparisons with market economy countries (ratios x 100)[a]

Country	1937	1960	1970	1980
East/West Germany	100	70	71	64
East Germany/U.K.	77	60	66	80
Czechoslovakia/Austria	90	91	78	70
Hungary/Italy	89	86	70	74
Poland/Spain	105	125	88	77
Romania/Greece	88	100	78	78
Yugoslavia/Greece	87	97	83	81
Bulgaria/Portugal	81	122	113	153

[a]This table compares levels of economic development over time between countries in Eastern and Western Europe. Looking at the last line, for example, Bulgaria's economic development was approximately 81 percent of that of Portugal in 1937, but by 1960 it was 122 percent, that is, 22 percent *higher* than Portugal's.

Source: Paul Marer, "The Economies of Trade of Eastern Europe," in William E. Griffith, ed., *Central and Eastern Europe* (Boulder, Colo.: Westview Press, 1989), 62.

the direction of the communist leader Josip Broz Tito. Nevertheless, in the early postwar years Tito seemed to be the most slavishly Stalinist leader in Eastern Europe and Stalin's most reliable ally. Tito, more quickly than any other Eastern European leader, ensconced his communist party, purged the country of opposition leaders and parties, and embarked on the collectivization of agriculture and on rapid industrialization. Partly in recognition of Yugoslavia's model of progress, the Cominform's headquarters was established in Belgrade in the fall of 1947.

Before 1947 there were already hints of friction between the strong-willed leaders of the two countries. Stalin had not been pleased with Yugoslav complaints about the behavior of Red Army troops in Yugoslavia at the end of the war. Tito had refused the Kremlin's offer to establish a joint Soviet-Yugoslav bank. Stalin was also unhappy with Yugoslavia's support for the communists in Greece's civil war and with its efforts to win control over the border city of Trieste from Italy. Stalin feared these efforts would complicate Soviet-Eastern European relations with the British and the Americans at a time of sensitive postwar negotiations.

The major issue at this point was Yugoslav autonomy in foreign affairs because domestically Yugoslavia was the most orthodox of Eastern European regimes in 1945–1947. Tito and the Yugoslav communists were willing to follow the Soviet lead, but on their own terms. Stalin wanted unconditional subordination. This issue came to a head over Tito's efforts in 1947 and 1948 to establish a Balkan federation that would include Hungary, Romania, Bulgaria, Albania, and Yugoslavia. Stalin rejected Tito's plan and instead proposed an alternative, which Tito then rejected. The issue was not so much over the federation itself, which both leaders favored in some form, but over Tito's right to pursue such regional initiatives without Soviet approval. This was the Kremlin's first confrontation with its dilemma of control versus diversity, and Stalin opted for the former. Stalin was determined to teach Tito a lesson and to make of him an example for the rest of the bloc. In the first half of 1948, Soviet advisers were withdrawn from Yugoslavia, Tito was accused of heresy, and, finally, in June the Cominform expelled Yugoslavia from its ranks and removed its headquarters from Belgrade. With the implementation of a Soviet economic blockade on Yugoslavia, Stalin apparently felt that Tito was doomed: "All I need to do is shake my little finger and there will be no more Tito," he is quoted as saying.[8]

Stalin was wrong. Tito had the support of a unified party and much of the population, which viewed him as a war hero. The economic blockade was blunted by aid from Western countries, which were happy to drive a wedge into the communist bloc. Even worse from the Soviet point of view, Tito and the Yugoslav communists proceeded to establish their own "separate road to socialism" in the domestic realm, based on extensive decentralization, worker self-management of enterprises, and a mixed market economy. The early success of this experiment was a standing rebuke to the more authoritarian and centralized Soviet model, and it set a pattern of diversity that was to plague the Soviet leadership for the next forty years.

Unable to humble Tito, Stalin turned his frustration on the countries that were under Soviet control with a series of anti-Titoism purges. Most of these were directed against "home" communists—communist leaders who had remained in their own countries during World War II and who were therefore considered susceptible to "nationalist" tendencies (and therefore to **Titoism**). Purge trials of prominent communist leaders took place in Czechoslovakia, Hungary, Bulgaria, and Albania. The most prominent of these trials were in Czechoslovakia; they culminated in 1952 with a spectacular trial of former party leader Rudolf Slansky and thirteen others who were charged with being "Trotskyite-Zionist-Titoist-bourgeois-nationalist traitors, spies, and saboteurs, enemies of the Czechoslovak nation, of its People's Democratic order, and of Socialism."[9] All fourteen were found guilty and eleven were hanged.

Tension between the Soviet Union and Yugoslavia eased somewhat after the death of Stalin in March 1953, and even more so after the new Soviet party leader, Nikita Khrushchev, began the process of "destalinization" of the Soviet Union. At the Twentieth Congress of the Soviet Communist party in February 1956, Khrushchev criticized Stalin and acknowledged that the paths to socialism may differ. But even earlier, in May 1955, Khrushchev had visited Yugoslavia and signed a communiqué with

Tito recognizing the right of "national roads to socialism." In April 1956, the Cominform was dissolved. Two months later, Tito visited Moscow and signed a joint declaration reemphasizing the separate roads principle and reestablishing formal state and party relations between Moscow and Belgrade. Khrushchev was experimenting with diversity in the bloc, but the consequences were unexpectedly troublesome.

1956: The Polish Challenge and the Hungarian Revolution

The death of Stalin and Khrushchev's destalinization unleashed well-springs of frustration and tension throughout Eastern Europe. In every country except Yugoslavia, the party leaders in 1956 were the same people that had come to power in the wake of the anti-Titoism campaigns. All these "little Stalins" therefore were sensitive to the criticisms that Khrushchev leveled against Stalin and Stalinism. They were also made vulnerable by the Soviet reconciliation with Tito, who also continued to criticize Stalinist methods. The apparent liberalization in the Soviet Union had resonance in the populations of Eastern Europe as well, as people saw an opportunity to voice grievances long suppressed and repressed.

The first manifestation of unrest broke out in the western Polish city of Poznan in June 1956, just one week after Tito's visit to Moscow. The Poznan demonstrations against low wages and poor economic conditions became a riot that was brutally put down by Internal Security forces. The demonstrations spread to other cities, however, and led to demands for political reforms as well. The Stalinist party leader, Boleslaw Bierut, had died while attending the Twentieth Party Congress in Moscow, and his successor, Edward Ochab, expressed sympathy for some of the demonstrations and political demands. He finally agreed to step aside in favor of Wladyslaw Gomulka, the "home" communist party leader who had been purged for his Titoist tendencies in 1948. Khrushchev and other members of the Soviet politburo flew to Warsaw in October and were assured by Gomulka that Poland would remain communist and within the Soviet alliance. Gomulka assumed the party leadership, promising Poles the creation of a more "Polish" form of communism; he eased pressure on the Roman Catholic church, abandoned the collectivization of agriculture, and dismissed the Soviet general who was Poland's defense minister.

Hungary had also undergone some liberalization since 1953, and in July 1956 the Stalinist party leader Matyas Rakosi was replaced as party leader. Until the fall, the changes and reform efforts were largely confined to the political elite in Hungary. With the October events in Poland, however, the impetus shifted to the population, and particularly to students, who saw the Polish events as the abdication of Soviet domination of the region. Demonstrations at the end of October demanded the return to power of the "Hungarian Gomulka," the moderate communist and former premier Imre Nagy. Young people also toppled the huge statue of Stalin in the center of Budapest, the Hungarian capital.

As with Poland, members of the Soviet politburo flew to the Hungarian capital to supervise the transfer of power to Nagy, as prime minister, and Janos Kadar, as party leader. Unlike Gomulka, however, Nagy was unable or unwilling to restrain the Hungarian revolution, which continued to spread. Some of the old noncommunist political parties reemerged, and their leaders were brought into Nagy's cabinet. Nagy began to negotiate for Hungary's withdrawal from the Warsaw Pact and, on November 1, proclaimed Hungary's neutrality. These events were beyond the limits of the permissible for the Kremlin, which ordered a military intervention to crush the rebellion. Janos Kadar was put in charge of restoring the communist order; Nagy, who had sought temporary shelter in the Yugoslav embassy, was finally arrested, tried, and executed in 1958.

The crushing of the Hungarian revolution demonstrated that the Kremlin would not accept the Yugoslav model elsewhere in the bloc and marked a return to the pattern of conformity and control. It also set, implicitly at least, the limits to reform in Eastern Europe: maintenance of the leading role of the communist party; continued membership in the Warsaw Pact; and the maintenance of a dichotomous image of the world through the mirror of **socialist internationalism.** For the rest of the world, the Hungarian tragedy also confirmed that Eastern Europe was a Soviet sphere of influence. This had been challenged by the United States when Secretary of State John Foster Dulles had pledged earlier to "roll back" communism from Eastern Europe.[10] In the context of the 1950s, this was an *idealistic* approach in foreign policy, but in the end *realism* dominated. There was little the United States could do to help the Hungarian freedom fighters on the Soviet doorstep in 1956, and the U.S. pledge was revealed as a hollow one. The United Nations was also powerless in this case, both because of the absorption of the UN Security Council with the Suez Crisis (Israel was attacking Egypt at the same time Soviet troops were invading Hungary) and because of the Soviet ability to veto any action by the Security Council. Nevertheless, the revolt in Hungary also demonstrated how deep was the disaffection with communism among many Eastern Europeans and illustrated the limited success of the Soviets in grafting the Soviet system onto Eastern Europe.

In the early 1960s, there were other signs of fragmentation of the Soviet bloc. Khrushchev's criticisms of Stalin and his rapprochement with Yugoslavia disturbed the more dogmatic communist leaders in the People's Republic of China (PRC) and Albania. Ideological, territorial, and political disputes between the Soviet Union and Mao Zedong's China became increasingly bitter and open until relations ruptured altogether and the

Soviets withdrew their economic and military advisers from China. At about the same time, Khrushchev severed state relations with Albania, which then became the ally and client of the PRC. Meanwhile, the Romanian party leadership broke with Moscow over a Soviet plan to more closely integrate the economies of Comecon. Although Romania remained orthodox in terms of its domestic political structure, its foreign policy during the 1960s became increasingly independent of Moscow. Romania reduced its commitment to the Warsaw Pact, refused to allow Warsaw Pact maneuvers on its territory, and adopted a neutral stance on the Sino-Soviet conflict (the conflict between communist China and the Soviet Union). Writing in 1965, a prominent academic specialist on Eastern Europe referred to all of this as "the breakup of the Soviet empire in Eastern Europe."[11]

1968: The Prague Spring

The next major challenge to communist rule and Soviet hegemony came from Czechoslovakia. This country, which had been the most economically advanced in Eastern Europe before World War II, had suffered more than any other from the wrenching economic reorientation under the communists. A steady economic decline after 1963 made the party leadership more receptive to economists' demands for reforms, and a decentralizing market-oriented economic reform program was implemented in January 1967. The changes in the economic sphere, however, only stimulated demands for political liberalization and for freedom of expression and debate.

The accelerating demands for change led the party to replace the conservative party leader, Antonin Novotny with the more liberal Slovak, Alexander Dubcek. This leadership change, much like the accession of Nagy in Hungary in 1956, sparked popular expectations for even more substantial changes. Dubcek spoke about the creation of a "socialism with a human face," and during the spring of 1968, Czechoslovakia was awash with change, inside and outside the party. The party's April Action Program attacked the concentration of party power and proposed freedom of press, assembly, and travel. In June, advanced censorship of the media was abolished. The party relaxed its control over writers and over trade unions, and other organizations.

As the Prague Spring progressed, the leadership in the Kremlin—and also in Czechoslovakia's northern neighbors, Poland and the German Democratic Republic (GDR, or East Germany)—became increasingly alarmed with the pace of change and with the possibility of transnational infection. A July meeting of the Warsaw Pact members warned that Czechoslovakia's affairs were not purely internal, and the members demanded that Czechoslovakia reimpose censorship and curb the changes. Later that month, virtually the entire Soviet politburo came to Czechoslovakia to counsel and warn. When the Czechoslovak leadership rejected the advice, the Soviet Union led an "allied socialist" invasion of Czechoslovakia, and 750,000 troops from the Warsaw Pact crossed into the country on the night of August 20–21. Dubcek and the reformers had pushed liberalism and nationalism too far. Dubcek was retired from the party and replaced by Gustav Husak, who began a process of "normalization" of Czechoslovakia. The Prague Spring was over.

A month after the Soviet intervention in Czechoslovakia, the Soviet Communist party daily *Pravda* elliptically justified the invasion by invok-

Yugoslav cartoonists view the invasion—Prague, 1968. Czechoslovakia is forced to sign away its freedom. *Source: Vjesnik* (Zagreb), August 27, 1968. Reprinted by permission.

ing a principle dubbed in the West as the **Brezhnev Doctrine,** named after Soviet party leader Leonid Brezhnev. *Pravda* reaffirmed the principle of many roads to socialism but insisted that no action in any socialist country "should do harm either to socialism" in the country involved "or to the fundamental interests of other socialist countries. . . . This means that each communist party is responsible not only to its own people but also to all the socialist countries and to the entire communist movement."[12] In effect, the Kremlin was claiming the right to intervene in any country in the bloc to prevent counterrevolution or the deterioration of communist party control. Thus, the Brezhnev Doctrine is also sometimes referred to as the "doctrine of limited sovereignty": The sovereignty of the East European states was limited by their obligations to others in the socialist camp.

1980: Poland's Solidarity

The Brezhnev Doctrine cast a pall over Eastern Europe for the next decade, but it did not deter the Poles from periodic bouts of strikes and unrest. Indeed, Poland had a tradition of revolt, often against the Russians, that dated back to the eighteenth-century era of the Partitions when the Polish state was gobbled up by its three powerful neighbors, Russia, Prussia, and Austria. This tradition continued even after the consolidation of communist power. In 1956, as we have seen above, demonstrations and riots effected the transfer of party leadership to Wladyslaw Gomulka. In 1968, students and professors staged huge demonstrations following the regime's closing of a performance of a nineteenth-century play that contained the line: "The only things Moscow sends us are jackasses, idiots and spies."[13] One of the slogans during the student demonstrations was the rhyming "Polska czeka na swego Dubczeka"—Poland is waiting for its own Dubcek.

The 1968 demonstrations were met with harsh reprisals and purges of students and professors, especially those of Jewish origin. In 1970, the initiative returned to the workers, this time in the port cities of Gdansk and Szczecin, who mounted demonstrations against a Christmastime increase in food prices. Gomulka fell from power the same way he had risen, on the basis of popular unrest, and he was replaced as party leader by Edward Gierek. Gierek rescinded the price increases, but when the regime tried to raise them again in 1976 they were met by another round of strikes and demonstrations. The 1976 strikes, and the subsequent crackdown by the authorities, brought workers and intellectuals into an alliance for the first time with the formation by the latter of KOR, the Workers' Defense Committee.

In 1978, a small group of workers in the shipyards along the coast illegally formed a Committee of Free Trade Unions for the Baltic Coast. One of the founding members was a shipyard electrician named Lech Walesa. In October of the same year, Karol Wojtyla of Krakow was elected pope of the Roman Catholic church, taking the name John Paul II. On his triumphal visit to Poland the next year, he was welcomed by millions of Poles and gave them a sense of both hope and power.

Thus the stage was set for an even more powerful challenge to the regime. The spark came in July 1980 with yet another effort by the regime to raise retail food prices (which by this time were considerably below the cost of producing the product, requiring huge government subsidies). Strikes spread throughout the country, eventually centering on the coast again. By mid-August, 16,000 workers were on strike at the huge Lenin Shipyards in Gdansk. Lech Walesa assumed the leadership of that strike committee and then of the Interfactory Strike Committee (MKS), which represented and coordinated the strike activity at over two hundred enterprises.

When a politburo delegation from Warsaw arrived to negotiate, the MKS presented them with a list of twenty-one demands, the first of which

The importance of symbols. The 1981 dedication of a memorial to victims of the Polish uprisings of 1956, 1968, 1970, 1976, and 1980. (Photo by Anna Bohdziewicz, Foto Victoria. Used by permission.)

was "acceptance of Free Trade Unions independent of both the Party and the employers." After two weeks of negotiations inside the Lenin Shipyards, the government finally agreed to virtually all of the demands. Thus the government sanctioned the creation of the first independent trade union in the communist world, which the workers named **Solidarity.**

Over the next sixteen months, some eleven million people (out of a total work force of sixteen million) joined Solidarity or its rural affiliate. With this practically universal support, the organization became more and more powerful and increasingly challenged the political prerogatives of the party. At the same time, the communist party (the Polish United Workers' party) grew weaker and more indecisive as hundreds of thousands of members resigned, and another million joined Solidarity as well.[14] The weakening of the Polish party raised hackles in the Kremlin. Several times in 1980 and 1981, the Soviets staged threatening military maneuvers along the Polish borders. After the September 1981 Congress of Solidarity, the Kremlin described the session as an "anti-socialist and anti-Soviet orgy." In an ominous hint of things to come, in October the Polish party leader, Stanislaw Kania, was replaced by General Wojciech Jaruzelski, who was already prime minister and defense minister. Finally, under pressure from the Kremlin, on December 13 Jaruzelski declared martial law, arrested the Solidarity leadership, and banned the union.

Though the Brezhnev Doctrine was not explicitly invoked in the Polish case, the crushing of Solidarity was a reaffirmation of the unwillingness of the Soviet leadership to tolerate the erosion of communist authority in Eastern Europe. (Indeed, the Brezhnev leadership had in effect extended this principle outside of the region, when Soviet troops were sent to Afghanistan in 1979 to prop up a Marxist regime under siege there.) But in Poland the results were different from those in Hungary or Czechoslovakia. In the first place, the Soviet army had *not* intervened directly, ap-

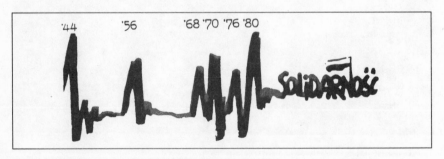

Poster of a cardiogram tracing the birth of Solidarity. The distinctive trademark resembles a surging crowd carrying the flag of Poland. (Author photo.)

parently fearing massive national resistance to the use of Soviet troops. Second, the martial law abolition of Solidarity was not entirely effective. The union was reconstituted as an underground organization and continued its activities in organizing strikes and demonstrations, publishing newsletters, and promoting independent initiatives in all spheres of society. What was most important, however, was the simple legacy of Solidarity. Adam Michnik, a founding member of KOR and a Solidarity adviser, characterized it as follows:

> In 1980 the totalitarian state gave in and signed an agreement which allowed for the existence of the first legal and independent institutions of postwar Polish political life. They lasted but a short time; long enough, however, to convince everyone that after December 1981 it was not possible to speak again about "socialism with a human face." What remains is communism with its teeth knocked out.[15]

SYSTEM PERFORMANCE AND DECAY

Western economists have found it difficult to estimate economic growth in the communist countries, complaining of unreliable data and varying degrees of exaggeration by the state agencies that collect such data. Nevertheless, by most measures, the centrally planned economies of Eastern Europe and the Soviet Union delivered hefty overall growth rates through the 1950s and most of the 1960s. However, by the late 1960s and early 1970s, Eastern European growth rates began to decline (Figure 1.1), and their economies fell further and further behind the market economies of the West (see Table 1.3). The change became particularly evident in the 1970s.

There are numerous reasons for these reversals. The international environment and economic policies pursued in the 1950s were no longer viable or possible by the 1970s. The economist Paul Marer describes the 1950s in the following way: "The authorities mobilized unemployed and underemployed labor and other resources, increased investment in human and physical capital at a rapid pace, and got the resources needed to finance these activities by imposing a high rate of forced saving on the population and by neglecting infrastructure [i.e., transportation and communications, like roads and telephone systems]."[16] Resources were directed toward areas like heavy industry (steel, coal, machine building, and so on) that were not highly developed before the war, so the *percentage* growth rates were very large. The regimes also spent much more on investment in such industries than in the production or import of consumer goods.

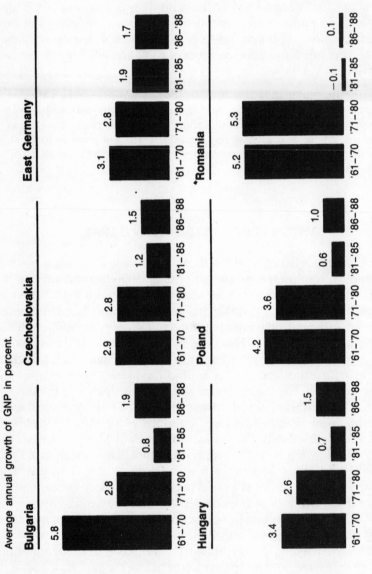

FIGURE 1.1   Slowdown in economic growth. (*Sources:* Adapted from National Foreign Assessment Center, *Handbook of Economic Statistics 1981* [Washington, D.C.: U.S. Government Printing Office, 1981], p. 30; and *New York Times*, December 11, 1989.)

The perennial shortage of machinery parts. *Source: Kooperativno Selo* (Sofia), November 20, 1960. Reprinted by permission.

During the 1960s and 1970s, these problems were held at bay by several different circumstances. First, most of the Eastern European countries did attempt some kind of decentralizing economic reforms, following the lead of the Kremlin's experimentation with its own "Liberman" reforms (named after the Soviet economist who first proposed them). Most of these reforms had some success in the short run. Second, the domestic economic problems of the Eastern European states were partially offset by increasing trade with the Soviet Union, which allowed them to import relatively cheap energy and raw materials from the Soviet Union and to sell to that country their own relatively low-quality manufactured goods, which were often not competitive in Western markets. Finally, during the 1970s Eastern Europe experienced a new source of growth through increased trade with the West, often financed by generous Western credit.[17]

By the late 1970s and early 1980s, all of these safety valves began to close up. The economic reform programs encountered resistance from bureaucrats and managers and were often ineffectual without a more thorough overhaul of the political and economic systems—which, as evidenced in Hungary in 1956, Czechoslovakia in 1968, and Poland in 1980, was not possible. The favorable terms of trade with the Soviet Union began to reverse in the late 1970s. As the Soviet Union experienced its own economic problems, the Kremlin became increasingly reluctant to subsidize the Eastern European economies; Soviet energy prices rose toward world market levels, and Moscow increasingly insisted on payment in convertible (Western) currencies.[18] Furthermore, *world* market prices for oil jumped dramatically after the 1973 Middle East conflict, impeding economic growth in West and East alike. Finally, during the 1980s, Western credit began to dry up as it became clear that the Eastern European governments were not able to repay the large amounts they had borrowed in the 1970s (see Figure 1.2).

Thus by the 1980s, the economies of all of the Eastern European states (and the Soviet Union) were in serious trouble. GNP growth rates had declined to near zero. External debts were so large that the governments often

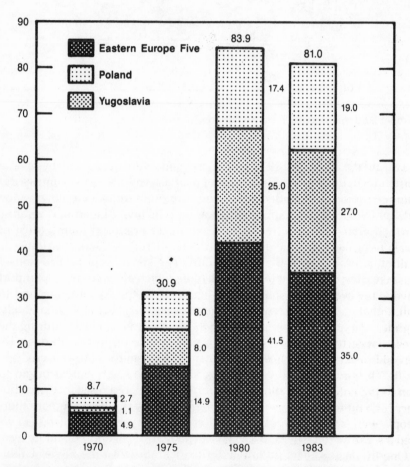

FIGURE 1.2 Gross hard currency debt of the Eastern European countries, year end, 1970, 1975, 1980, and 1983 (billions of current $). (*Source:* Paul Marer, "The Economies and Trade of Eastern Europe," in William E. Griffith, ed., *Central and Eastern Europe* [Boulder, Colo.: Westview Press, 1989], p. 62.)

had to spend all of their export earnings just to finance the debts. With the collapse of foreign credits, highly valued Western consumer goods could no longer be imported. The centrally planned economies, which were well equipped to generate rapid growth in heavy industry, were not able to generate growth in more sophisticated sectors of the economy: services, consumer goods, and high technology. To complicate matters, consumers had come to *expect* high levels of growth and were ill prepared to endure the sacrifices associated with meaningful economic reforms.

The Erosion of Political Legitimacy

All governments, democratic or authoritarian, employ some means to establish their legitimacy in the eyes of the population, and they reinforce this legitimacy through the political socialization process (civic education in schools, and so on). No regime can be based entirely on the threat or application of force. In the communist party states of Eastern Europe, political legitimacy was built on three main pillars: the communist ideology, widespread (if largely formal) participation, and socioeconomic performance. In the early postwar years, all three of these were at work, though they did not all work with all sectors of the population. As indicated above, there was considerable support for the ideas of communism (or at least, of socialism) throughout the region, and particularly in certain countries (like Bulgaria). The new communist governments were also able to gain some credibility by involving people in the political process through voting (usually with a 98+ percent turnout), through service in local elected bodies, and through participation in socioeconomic organizations, such as youth groups and trade unions. All of this participation was controlled and regulated by the communist parties but, nevertheless, gave many people a feeling that they had a stake and a voice in the system. Finally, the early socioeconomic successes of the Eastern European regimes also contributed to their political legitimacy. As we have seen, these countries experienced rapid economic growth in the 1950s and some improvement in the standard of living, especially in the 1960s and 1970s. The governments were able to deliver jobs, health care, and education to the entire populations of their countries. Furthermore, there were very high rates of social mobility within each country, meaning that many people were able to move up the social or economic scale. All of this created a sense of progress and development.

One by one, however, these sources of political legitimacy began to wither away. Most people became inured to the omnipresent political slogans and increasingly disgusted with communist political systems and societies that did not live up to the ideals of Karl Marx, or even of Lenin. Critics, such as Yugoslavia's Milovan Djilas, saw in the communist party apparatus a kind of "new class" that simply replaced the dominant classes from the precommunist period.[19] The widespread participation that had been encouraged by the new regimes now came to be seen as both hollow and coerced. More and more people began to turn away from politics altogether. (In the Russian city of Rostov-on-Don in 1978, I once asked a Russian friend, a young mother, what she thought of Leonid Brezhnev, the party leader at the time, whose image was displayed on a huge billboard where we were walking. "I don't think anything about him," she replied.)

Increasingly the political legitimacy of the regimes in Eastern Europe and the Soviet Union came to rest on their socioeconomic accomplishments. Some scholars, both in the West and in Eastern Europe, argued that there existed a kind of "social contract" or "social compact" between the governments and the populace, in which the former delivered economic goods and growth and, in return, the population tacitly agreed to leave politics to the politicians.[20] But as the economies began to deteriorate and the opportunities for social advancement began to narrow, even this source of legitimacy disappeared. In capitalist democracies of the West, the government is not always held responsible for economic slowdowns, which are often seen as an inevitable consequence of the market. In state socialist societies, however, because the government controls the economy, the government gets the blame when the economy falters. Public opinion polls from the region in the 1980s show increased popular disaffection with the economies, the governments, and the ideologies. An analysis of such surveys in Poland, for example, concluded that only about a quarter of the population could be counted as "pro" regime.[21]

After Soviet intervention to terminate the Prague Spring in 1968 and the crushing of Poland's Solidarity in 1981, the fragile political legitimacy of the communist regimes crumbled even further. As their governments' relationships to Moscow was increasingly seen by the populations as a liability, some of the party leaders in Eastern Europe replaced the emphasis on "socialist internationalism" with an appeal to "socialist patriotism." It was hoped this would win some popular support by stressing national interests and national autonomy. The Polish party leader Jaruzelski, for example, used this tactic after the crushing of Solidarity. A 1976 Berlin conference of communist parties implicitly sanctioned this approach by allowing for "indigenous, creative interpretations" of Marxism-Leninism.

In the past, when the Eastern European communist parties experienced a serious loss of legitimacy, they could count on the Soviet Union for outside support—providing another, external source of legitimacy. But with the accession of Mikhail Gorbachev to the Soviet leadership in 1985, even this external legitimation began to dry up. As the Gorbachev leadership began to reform the Soviet system, it called on the Eastern European party leaders to do the same in their countries. Additionally, Gorbachev made it increasingly clear that the Soviet Union would no longer use the military to intervene in Eastern Europe (or elsewhere). With the Eastern European communist leaderships no longer able to play the Kremlin card, the communist party states were doomed.

The Spread of Dissent

In the 1980s, mass protests shook the regimes of Eastern Europe. The roots of protest and dissent, however, went back a decade or more in most of the region. As the economies and the regimes began to weaken in the 1970s, dissident groups became more active, more visible, and more popular. In the Soviet Union, dissidence had been crushed under Lenin and Stalin and had reappeared only briefly and weakly under Khrushchev. The revival of political dissent in the 1970s was due in large part to the Soviet signature of the **Helsinki Agreements** in 1975. These documents (sometimes referred to as the Helsinki Accords), a result of a long process of negotiations among thirty-five states in Europe, plus the United States and Canada, contained a whole section on "respect for human rights and fundamental freedoms, including the freedom of thought, conscience, religion or belief."[22] The Soviet signature of these agreements stimulated a group of dissident intellectuals in the Soviet Union to form a Helsinki Monitoring Committee to publicize (in underground publications called **samizdat**) Soviet violations to the human rights they had guaranteed in Helsinki. Most of these activists (including the physicist Andrei Sakharov) were arrested or exiled, but they laid the groundwork for more substantial dissent in the 1980s.

In Eastern Europe, dissent was always stronger and more sustained than in the Soviet Union, for a number of reasons: the shorter time period under Stalinism; the greater experience with democracy (before World War II); and the less draconian political regimes.[23] Nevertheless, political dissent was largely confined to a relatively small group of intellectuals in each country, only rarely taking the form of workers' protests or strikes. As in the Soviet Union, the dissident movement was given a boost by the 1975 Helsinki Accords, which led to the formation of various kinds of human rights monitoring groups in Eastern Europe as well.

The largest dissident movement developed in Poland, especially after the formation of KOR, the Workers' Defense Committee, established by intellectuals to provide legal and material assistance to the families of workers imprisoned after the 1976 strikes. The success of KOR led the organization to expand its mission and to change its name the next year to KOR-KSS (the Committee for Social Self-Defense). The next several years saw the formation of the Movement for the Defense of Human and Civil

Rights (ROPCiO in the Polish acronym), a Polish chapter of Amnesty International, the nationalist Confederation of Independent Poland (KPN), and an incipient Free Trade Union movement. All of these organizations produced their own samizdat publications, which frequently reported cases of political arrests and the regime's violations of the country's constitution or international covenants on human rights. In the mid-1980s, there were over 2,000 regular samizdat publications in Poland, some printed in tens of thousands of copies.

In Czechoslovakia, a group of intellectuals circulated a document entitled **Charter 77,** which called on people to speak out on behalf of human rights guaranteed by Czechoslovak laws and the Helsinki Accords. The playwright Vaclav Havel became the spokesman for the signatories of the charter, who later became the core of the Civic Forum that brought down the communist government in 1989. Elsewhere in Eastern Europe, dissident organizations were not as well organized, but there were often alternative channels for expression of dissent, either through samizdat (as in Hungary) or through the churches. In East Germany, for example, the Evangelical church served as an umbrella for the unofficial peace movement, which also harbored dissidents in the democratic and ecological movements.

According to political scientist Robert Sharlet, who has written frequently about the dissident movements in Eastern Europe, political dissent served three key functions. First, dissidents who spoke out, especially through samizdat, helped break "the bonds of fear that immobilize the individual" and therefore served as role models for others. Second, the samizdat network broke the regime's monopoly on information, establishing an "alternative, unofficial communication system." Finally, political dissent in the controlled political environments of Eastern Europe led to the "gradual reprivatization of social life," carving out a growing sphere of activity independent of state control. This is part of the notion of a "civil society," which became an important concept in challenging the state.[24]

The Ideas of Civil Society and Central Europe

One cannot overemphasize the power of ideas, particularly in Central Europe. Marx argued that ideas are simply part of the "superstructure" of society and therefore have no independent determining force; they are simply functions of the underlying economic "substructure." It is perhaps ironic, then, that in the Marxist societies of Eastern Europe, powerful ideas helped to undermine and subvert the system. Often these ideas were developed and discussed by a relatively small number of intellectuals; nevertheless, these concepts subsequently became part of the culture of change. The most important concepts concerned civil society and Central Europe, and the two are related.[25]

The notion of a **civil society** was used in different ways by different groups and intellectuals, but the basic notion is that people can and should try to live as much as possible *outside* of the official structures and patterns sponsored by the communist authorities. This could take the form, for example, of producing and reading samizdat, buying or trading goods in the **second economy** (the black market or the private market), participating in informal self-educational groups (such as the Flying University set up in Poland in the 1970s), and supporting those few organizations, like some churches, that were not controlled by the political authorities. In pursuing these kinds of independent activities, the population would help to create an "alternative society" or a "second society" that was beyond the reach of the authorities. As this civil society grew, the power of the state would weaken. Eventually, the official structures would simply disappear and be replaced by the civil society.

The advocates of civil society generally called for people not to participate in the official political system and even to ignore it. This idea was developed by Czechoslovakia's Vaclav Havel in his important 1979 essay, "The Power of the Powerless," which was later published as a book.[26] Havel contends that the totalitarian political system is built on lies and that people allow the system to exist by accepting the lies and living within them. So the only appropriate response is for the individual to reject the lies: "He rejects the ritual and breaks the rules of the game. He discovers once more his suppressed identity and dignity. He gives his freedom a concrete significance. His revolt is an attempt to *live within the truth*."[27] This entails not just speaking the truth and rejecting the official lies (including the ideology), but living independently of official structures and norms and participating in parallel structures constituted independently of the official ones. The more people who do this, the greater the erosion of state power.

Along the same lines, the Polish dissident Adam Michnik called for a strategy of "social self-organization" or "social self-defense."[28] Michnik was one of the founders of KOR that pursued precisely this goal. The Czechoslovak Vaclav Benda used similar arguments in his 1978 essay entitled "The Parallel Polis." The Hungarian philosopher Gyorgy Konrad goes even further in his book *Antipolitics*, arguing that all power is antihuman, and therefore so is all politics.[29]

Not all of these writers explicitly used the term *civil society*, but all of them had the same concept in mind. Discussion of these ideas were circulated widely through samizdat, both within and among countries. There was considerable cross-fertilization of ideas among the writers in the different countries. And the appeals struck a chord with the people, who were already feeling resentful, frustrated, and apathetic.

Many of the intellectuals who developed the concept of civil society linked it to the notion of "Central Europe," contending, as Gyorgy Konrad did, that "the demand for self-government is the organizing force of the new Central European ideology."[30] Konrad, Havel, and others began to employ the term *Central Europe* following the publication in 1983 of an important essay by the Czechoslovak writer Milan Kundera entitled "The Tragedy of Central Europe."[31] In this essay, Kundera argued that culturally and spiritually, the peoples in East-Central Europe more properly belonged to the West than to the East and that it was only because the region was "kidnapped, displaced and brainwashed" after World War II that it was consigned to "East Europe." Historically, he argued, Europe was always divided into two halves, one tied to Rome and the Catholic church and the other to Byzantium and the Orthodox church. "After 1945," he wrote, "the border between the two Europes shifted several hundred kilometers to the west, and several nations that had always considered themselves to be Western woke up to discover that they were now in the East."

Kundera's argument, like those for civil society, had widespread appeal in the region. It relegated politics to the sidelines and elevated the importance of culture in Central Europe's identity. As such, it suggested that the peoples of the region could find identity, affirmation, and autonomy in culture and could do so without bowing to politics. It was another means of "living the truth." Furthermore, in Kundera's argument at least, the peoples of Central Europe were not to blame for their fate; it was the fault both of Russia, a non-European state that "kidnapped" the region, and of the West for forsaking Central Europe (echoes of Yalta) and ignoring its own cultural identity.

The concept of Central Europe provided both hope and dignity to many people in the region and constituted yet another node in the network of challenges to the communist system. There was, however, a darker underside to the ideas and the history of Central Europe. The cultural legacy that Kundera referred to, the writers and artists of prewar Central Europe, did help to shape the national and cultural identity of those states. But nationalism is two-edged: It can be a positive force for unity and common purpose; but it can also be intolerant and exclusivist. There are hints of this in Kundera's essay, which is anti-Soviet but also anti-Russian. Similarly, the cultural and political history of Central Europe may be rich and cosmopolitan, but it is also full of radical nationalism (i.e., Nazism), **anti-Semitism** (hostility toward Jews), and racism. So a revival of a Central European culture has the potential both to unite

Eastern Europe with Western Europe and to divide Eastern Europeans from each other.

CONCLUSION

This chapter showed how quickly communism was established in Eastern Europe and how quickly it began to erode. Joseph Stalin once admitted that "communism fits Poland like a saddle fits a cow," and this was true in varying degrees all over Eastern Europe. It is fruitless, however, to assign blame for this state of affairs, as is done both by Western historians of the Cold War and by Eastern European intellectuals. The fact was that the Soviet Union was in control of Eastern Europe as a result of World War II military operations and was bound to establish Soviet-style governments in that area. After the war, Western Europe was prostrate and unable to help Eastern Europe. The United States was absorbed enough with the rebuilding of Western Europe and was unwilling to confront the Soviet Union in its own sphere of influence, particularly if there was a risk of a major war over the issue. The only Eastern European countries that were able to distance themselves from the Soviet Union, Yugoslavia and Albania, had not been "liberated" by Soviet forces during the war, did not share borders with the USSR, and were outside of that country's area of central strategic concern.

In the end, at any rate, Eastern Europe solved the problem on its own and with almost no violence. The Cold War began in Eastern Europe, and it ended there. One could argue that the West "won" the Cold War without resorting to a hot war, simply by waiting for the inevitable. It was clear by the late 1940s, with the Tito-Stalin rupture, that the imposition of Soviet-style communism in Eastern Europe was not going to be easy. Despite strict political controls, censorship of the media, intense political socialization, and restrictions on contacts with the West, Eastern Europe never looked like the Soviet Union, as any visitor to the two could attest.[32] The periodic unrest in the region, often requiring Soviet intervention, demonstrated how thin was the veneer of the legitimacy of the communist party regimes.

By the early 1970s, many Eastern Europeans had simply tuned out from politics, but they could take some comfort in their own economic security. By the end of that decade even that had disappeared, as the national economies lost the dynamism characteristic of earlier decades and standards of living in some countries actually declined. What had been relatively small political dissident movements grew to encompass new constituencies, including workers. Poland's Solidarity movement of

1980–1981 demonstrated the power of an alliance between intellectuals and workers. In the 1980s, the ideas of civil society and of Central Europe came to provide a common ideology for the opposition movements throughout the region. By then, the only real glue holding the communist bloc together was the Soviet Union and the threat of Soviet military intervention. With the accession of Mikhail Gorbachev to the Soviet party leadership in 1985, however, even this began to change. The next chapter will examine the changes introduced into the Soviet Union by Gorbachev and the revolutionary impact of these changes on Eastern Europe.

TWO

□ □ □

Reform and Revolution
in the Soviet Union
and East-Central Europe

By the late 1970s, economic decline had chipped away at the already fragile political legitimacy of the Eastern European governments. With the formation of Solidarity in 1980–1981, an Eastern European population had once again challenged the dominance of the communist party and the hegemony of the Soviet Union, and once again they had been crushed by the application of force. By June 1981, six months before the martial law crackdown, the Soviet leadership had raised the specter of the Brezhnev Doctrine with a letter addressed to the Polish party's Central Committee: "Continued concessions to anti-socialist forces and their demands have led to a situation in which the PZPR [the Polish communist party] has been falling back step by step under pressure of internal counter-revolution, supported by imperialist foreign centers of subversion."[1] Martial law in Poland opened the 1980s with yet another demonstration of the limits to change in Eastern Europe.

Within a year, however, Leonid Brezhnev died at the age of seventy-six, after eighteen years as leader of the Communist Party of the Soviet Union (CPSU). The politburo selected the former head of the Committee on State Security (KGB), Yuri Andropov, as his successor. Andropov quickly initiated a number of reform programs meant to revive the Soviet economy, but he too died, in 1984. His successor, Konstantin Chernenko, was aged and infirm, and it was only when he died in March 1985 that the reformers in the politburo were able to prevail with the election of Mikhail Gorbachev as general secretary of the party. At the age of fifty-four, Gorbachev was by far the youngest member of the politburo, the first party leader to be born after the Russian Revolution, and the first to begin his party career after the death of Stalin. With a degree in law from Moscow State Univer-

sity, his background and training were different from the more technological orientation of his predecessors. Even so, neither Western nor Soviet observers expected him to be a radical reformer. As the foreign minister, Andrei Gromyko, observed of Gorbachev when he nominated him to the
leadership: "This man has a nice smile, but he has iron teeth."[2]

GORBACHEV'S REFORMS (1985–1989)

Gorbachev was able to use both the smile and the teeth to push through a
whole series of increasingly radical reforms, both economic and political.
All of the reforms were interrelated, but they can be classified into four
main categories: **perestroika,** the Russian word for *restructuring* of the
economy; **glasnost,** meaning *openness* or *publicity;* **democratization;** and
new thinking in foreign policy. The impetus for these reforms came from
a number of directions, but the factor of fundamental importance was the
economic one. Gorbachev's economic reforms were meant to revitalize a
stagnant Soviet economy that had been growing at only about 2 percent
annually for a decade. The reasons for the slowdown were partly internal
and structural and partly external. The early years of rapid economic and
industrial growth in the USSR had been possible because of abundant
and accessible natural resources (particularly of energy); a growing and
relatively moveable work force; the capacity of the regime to mobilize resources, including human ones, by force if necessary; and a concentration
on quantitative rather than qualitative goals. All of these factors began to
wither away in the 1970s as cheap resources disappeared, population
growth and mobility tapered off, and the post-Stalinist regimes became
increasingly disinclined or unable to use Stalinist means of mobilization.

These internal economic problems were compounded in the 1980s by a
sharp decline in world petroleum prices and a consequent drop in Soviet
export earnings, 80 percent of which were derived from the sale of petroleum, natural gas, and other energy raw materials.[3] In addition, the military burden on the Soviet economy, which had always been high, posed
an even greater strain in the 1980s as the administration of Ronald Reagan fired up military research, procurement, and spending in the United
States. Western estimates held that Soviet defense spending was about
the same as U.S. spending, about $300 billion annually, but since the So-
viet economy was only about half the size of the U.S. economy, the same
level of absolute spending consumed twice as much of the economy on a
percentage basis: about 12.5 percent of the Soviet GNP compared to 6.6
percent in the United States.[4] Thus, the Kremlin had compelling economic
reasons for easing East-West relations and for slowing the arms race.

These economic problems had a deleterious effect on living standards
in the USSR. Even the official press admitted in 1988 that the Soviet Union

ranked between fiftieth and sixtieth of the world's countries in per capita consumption of goods and services and that the share of government expenditures going to human needs was higher in the United States than in the Soviet Union![5] These assertions were even more pessimistic than most Western estimates of the state of the Soviet economy.

The dismal state of the economy provided the underlying need for the reforms, but the spark of initiative came from the advent of a new and younger leadership under Gorbachev and a Soviet elite that had become increasingly educated, critical, and assertive.[6] Gorbachev admitted to what both Western observers and domestic critics had been saying for years: that the legitimacy of the Soviet regime (and other communist regimes) was increasingly dependent on economic success and consumer satisfaction; that economic success could no longer be based on *extensive* growth and the policies of forced industrialization; that an *intensive* pattern of growth required commitment, hard work, and support from the population; and that such commitment would only come from a public that had some voice and input into the process. As Gorbachev himself put it, "A house can be put in order only by a person who feels he is the owner."[7]

Perestroika

Because of the economic problems, the Soviet leadership issued a series of increasingly radical reform proposals. In the first year of his leadership, Gorbachev talked mostly of the need for "acceleration" (*uskorienie*) of the economy. Beginning with the summer of 1986, however, his speeches became increasingly radical, changing the focus to "restructuring" (perestroika) rather than acceleration and eventually equating restructuring with "radical reform" and even with "revolution."[8] "Openness and public airing of issues" (glasnost) and "democratization" were increasingly seen as necessary concomitants of economic restructuring and were the centerpiece of the reform proposals at the January 1987 Plenum of the CPSU Central Committee.

Under these early economic reforms, the scope of central planning was reduced by consolidating central ministries and restricting them to long-term and strategic planning.[9] Under the new Law on State Enterprises, industrial and agricultural enterprises were to be phased into a system of economic accountability, self-financing, and autonomy that would eventually allow them to establish their own prices and production schedules and conclude their own contracts with suppliers and distributors. It also allowed unprofitable companies to go bankrupt, a prospect made real and visible for the first time in 1987 when the government announced the bankruptcy of a state farm.[10] The reform also called for the introduction of "socialist self-management" into state enterprises, by which workers would elect their managers and foremen. The 1988 Law on Cooperatives allowed for the creation of small-scale private and cooperative firms, free from government planning directives. By mid-1989, over three million people were employed in the cooperative movement. The arena for the private market was further expanded in March 1989 when the Party approved the establishment of private agricultural cooperatives and leasehold farming.

Glasnost

In his efforts to revitalize the Soviet system, Gorbachev linked perestroika with "glasnost," which is usually translated as *openness* but is closer in meaning to *publicity*. It was meant to open Soviet society to a critical evaluation of its past and present problems. This policy served a number of purposes for the Soviet leadership: It helped identify problems that needed correction; it served to build popular support for the regime, particularly among intellectuals; it reduced the population's dependence on foreign and unofficial sources of information (e.g., samizdat and the U.S.-sponsored Radio Liberty); and it helped to dislodge vested interests and shake up the bureaucracy, which was often identified as the main obstacle to perestroika and democratization.[11] The justification for glasnost was enunciated by Tatyana Zaslavskaya, the reform-minded sociologist from Novosibirsk who in 1983 had authored a secret report calling for a dramatic overhaul of the Soviet economy:[12] "If we continue to keep from the people information about the conditions under which they live," she wrote in *Pravda*, "we cannot expect them to assume a more active role in economic or in political life. People will trust and support you only if you trust them."[13]

The result of the new glasnost was a broadening and deepening of Soviet news coverage and an accessibility of information, unlike anything since the 1920s. Previously taboo subjects began to receive coverage: joblessness, drug abuse, prostitution, urban blight, catastrophes (such as earthquakes, plane crashes, and the Chernobyl nuclear reactor meltdown), hijackings, homelessness, youth gangs, homosexuality, and traffic deaths. Censorship was relaxed in 1986 and then virtually abolished with the Law on Press Freedoms of June 1990. By that time, almost any subject or personality (including Gorbachev and Lenin) was open for discussion. As independent newspapers flourished and then became legal, the range of debate broadened even further. Political tracts and sex manuals became hot sellers in the numerous sidewalk newsstands in the cities. Apparently feeling more confident about the regime's legitimacy and the credibility of the Soviet media, the Soviets in 1987 and 1988 ceased jamming the Russian-language broadcasts of Voice of America, the British Broadcasting Corporation (BBC), and Radio Liberty.

This new media openness also had a dramatic impact on the treatment of Soviet history and, in particular, of the role of Joseph Stalin. Stalin's rule had been criticized by Khrushchev in the late 1950s and early 1960s, but such criticism was off-limits during the long Brezhnev era. The new wave of destalinization in the 1980s unleashed by glasnost appeared first in the cultural realm, in the less-direct voice of literature and film. Tengiz Abuladze's film *Repentance,* released in 1987, showed in allegorical fashion the oppression and compromises of the Stalin era and mused on the continuing legacy of Stalinism. Novels that had earlier been denied publication for their anti-Stalinism were now released, as was the case with Anatoly Rybakov's *Children of the Arbat.* Historians began to publish articles and books exposing the real dimensions of the purges and the famines of the 1930s and the labor camps during the whole Stalin era. The historian Roy Medvedev publicly estimated that Stalinism claimed the lives of twelve million people.[14] Gorbachev himself issued some tentative criticisms of the Stalin era in his 1987 speech celebrating the seventieth anniversary of the Revolution. With the emergence of a more activist legislature in 1989, the Supreme Soviet condemned Stalin's deportations of people and promised that "the violation of human rights and norms of humanity at a state level will never reoccur in this country."[15]

Democratization

The campaign for glasnost was accompanied by an appeal for "democratization" of the Soviet Union. In the first years of Gorbachev's tenure, Soviet leaders and writers began to admit now that there was "not enough democracy" in the country, and Gorbachev called for a series of political reforms to reinforce the economic ones. At first, the changes were modest. The regime instituted competitive elections and secret ballots in both the party and the state, but only below the national level. But by 1988 Gorbachev was calling for "radical reform" of the political system. Constitutional reforms adopted at the end of that year provided for multicandidate competition in elections at all levels and for the creation of a full-time parliament. In the March 1989 elections for the newly created Congress of People's Deputies, Soviet citizens exercised choice with a vengeance, rejecting thirty-four regional party secretaries, a politburo member, and a host of other party luminaries, some of whom ran unopposed. The new Supreme Soviet (the permanent legislature) elected by the Congress quickly became a lively and feisty institution.

The Gorbachev leadership also sanctioned, and even encouraged, the emergence of independent groups and associations in an effort to stimulate "socialist pluralism." By early 1989, over 60,000 informal groups had emerged, with a broad range of agendas. Some of these were grass roots voluntary associations to promote various types of civic improvement, but others had definite political agendas and came to resemble political parties.[16] The "national fronts," which first appeared in the Baltic republics, were ostensibly established to promote perestroika, but they eventually spread to every republic and became platforms for campaigns for national autonomy and independence.

As Gorbachev strengthened the pluralist elements of Soviet society, he also attempted to reduce the dominating influence of the communist party. There was a reduction in the role of nomenklatura, the practice of restricting certain leadership positions to party members or party-approved people. Gorbachev said that the promotion of nonparty people to leading positions was "an important aspect of the democratization of public life."[17] The executive authority of the party was diminished by creating a U.S.-style president who was elected by the Supreme Soviet. And in March 1990, Article 6 of the Soviet Constitution was amended to eliminate the party's "leading role" in the political system. This change opened the political arena to a competitive party system.

The Gorbachev leadership also made overtures to the regime's past enemies and rivals. In April 1988, Gorbachev met with the top hierarchy of the Russian Orthodox church and called for a more tolerant attitude toward religion. Hundreds of churches were returned to their congregations, and thousands of new Orthodox congregations were registered and churches opened. Between 1987 and 1989, almost all political prisoners were released. The most important of these was the dissident physicist Andrei Sakharov, who was released and rehabilitated, ran for and won a seat in the supreme Soviet, and became a leader of the democratic forces there until his death in December 1989.

Perestroika, glasnost, and democratization were all efforts by the Soviet leadership to introduce reforms *from above* and, as such, were to be directed, controlled, and limited by the authorities. As these changes deepened and accelerated, however, they became impossible to control. Decentralization meant pluralization, so more and more groups and individuals became active participants in the society, the economy, and the political system. Almost imperceptibly, the Soviet system evolved to a point at which the clock could not be turned back.

New Thinking in Foreign Policy

The domestic economic and political changes were accompanied by a dramatic shift in Soviet foreign policy as well. Here too the basis of the change was economic: If Moscow wanted to develop an economy that was more efficient and more oriented toward consumer goods, it needed to expand trade, attract technology, reduce military spending, and cut back on aid to other countries. All of this required a more relaxed international atmosphere and, in particular, an improved relationship with the United States. Thus, there was a sweeping reorientation of Soviet foreign policy, both ideological and pragmatic.

The ideological basis for the changes was provided by Yevgeniy Primakov, a prominent academic adviser to Gorbachev, in a major article in *Pravda*.[18] Primakov emphasized the "organic link between our country's domestic policy and its foreign policy" and pointed out that the "radical qualitative change" in the country affected domestic and foreign policy alike. The Soviet Union, he asserted, now emphasized political rather than military means of insuring its security. Military doctrine should be reoriented to be primarily defensive and be based on "reasonable sufficiency" rather than on superiority. Bilateral relationships were less important than global ones because the world was increasingly characterized by "global interdependence." The foreign minister at the time, Eduard Shevardnadze, made the same point, saying that "the struggle between the two opposing systems is no longer the defining tendency of the present era." What was decisive, he said, was international cooperation "to restore and protect the resources necessary for the survival of humanity."[19] In their discussions of foreign policy and international affairs, Soviet analysts and politicians placed a reduced stress on ideology and downplayed the notions of socialist internationalism (a key element in the Brezhnev Doctrine and a principle used to justify Soviet support for Third World national liberation movements).

In terms of policies toward the Third World, Soviet leaders and writers conceded that socialism might not be the best path for all poor countries, and some argued that capitalism may even be beneficial for them, at least in the short run. As one academician put it: In the 1970s, "we attempted to expand socialism's sphere of influence to various developing countries that . . . proved totally unprepared to adopt socialism."[20] Soviet leaders admitted that they could not afford to support progressive movements all over the world and that they would do so only when resources allowed it and when it was "mutually beneficial."

These rhetorical and ideological reversals were matched by a host of Soviet actions to reduce armaments and military spending, negotiate arms-control agreements, and cut back on Soviet military commitments in Eastern Europe and the Third World. The official Soviet press often linked the military reorientation to the economic imperative, pointing out that defense spending and the arms race with the West was "one of the basic reasons for the grave condition of the Soviet economy and the slow growth in the people's standard of living."[21] In December 1988, Gorbachev told the United Nations General Assembly that Moscow would unilaterally demobilize a half million troops and scrap 10,000 tanks, including some 50,000 troops and 5,000 tanks from Eastern Europe. In June 1989, Prime Minister Nikolai Ryzhkov announced plans to cut defense spending in *half* by 1995. This lowered strategic and military profile was accompanied by a reduced level of activity in the Third World: the withdrawal of Soviet troops from Afghanistan; pressure on Vietnam to withdraw its troops from Cambodia; support for the pullout of Cuban troops from Angola; and dramatic cutbacks in economic and military assistance to Nicaragua, Ethiopia, North Korea, and other socialist Third World governments.

The End of the Brezhnev Doctrine

As Soviet policies toward the rest of the world changed, so too did the Kremlin's orientation toward Eastern Europe, the region of primary economic, strategic, and ideological importance to Moscow. These changes were the most important element of "New Thinking" and had the most far-reaching consequences. They also fit in with the broader elements of new thinking: the notion of interdependence and the increased reliance on political rather than military solutions to international problems.

The Soviet Union conducted over half of its trade with the Comecon countries, and to support the economic reforms in the Soviet Union Moscow hoped to accelerate the import of high-quality machinery and consumer goods from Eastern Europe. So to a large extent the success of the Soviet economic reform depended on increased productivity and on increases in the quality of output in Eastern Europe. This required that the Eastern Europeans pursue the same kinds of decentralizing and market-oriented reforms that the Soviets were implementing. Exposing the Eastern European economics more directly to international markets, especially Western ones, would also make them more competitive and contribute to qualitative improvements.

Thus, as the reform process accelerated within the Soviet Union, so did soviet encouragement for reform in Eastern Europe. In 1987, Gorbachev began a series of visits to the Eastern European capitals to press home the message of reform. In a speech in Prague, Gorbachev explained and outlined the process of reform in the Soviet Union and gently prodded the Czechoslovaks to study the Soviet experience: "Today a reliable yardstick of the seriousness of a ruling communist party is not only its attitude toward its own experience but its attitude toward the experience of friends." He also spoke of "the sharply growing importance of exchanges of experience in socialist construction and its *generalization*."[22] Similar messages were passed to all of the Eastern European leaders, and, in 1987 and 1988, economic reform programs were initiated in Poland, Hungary, Bulgaria, and Czechoslovakia. Only in East Germany, whose economy was relatively healthy, and in Romania, where Nicolae Ceausescu ruled with an iron hand, were there no movements in this direction.[23] Hoping to expose Eastern Europe to market pressures from the West, the Kremlin encouraged Romania and Bulgaria to enter the **International Monetary Fund (IMF)** and Hungary, Poland, Romania, and Czechoslovakia to join the **General Agreement on Tariffs and Trade (GATT).**

Moscow's encouragement of Eastern European reform was accompanied by a steady march away from the principles of the Brezhnev Doctrine, the policy used to justify Soviet intervention in Czechoslovakia in 1968 (and elsewhere). Consistent with the ideological elements of new thinking, the Gorbachev leadership downplayed the notion of socialist internationalism (a key element of the Brezhnev Doctrine) and repeatedly stressed "the right of every people to choose the paths and forms of its own development."[24] Gorbachev drove home these principles when he visited Prague in 1987:

> The entire system of political relations between the socialist countries can and should be built unswervingly on a foundation of equality and mutual responsibility. No one has the right to claim a special position in the socialist world. The independence of each party, its responsibility to its people, the right to resolve questions of the country's development in a sovereign way— for us these are indisputable principles.[25]

This language was strikingly different from that enunciated nineteen years earlier in the Brezhnev Doctrine, with its notion of limited sovereignty. Both the content and the location of Gorbachev's speech suggested an effort to move Soviet–Eastern European relations out of the shadow of 1968.

Setting the Stage for 1989

By 1988, the Soviet leadership had cleared the ground for major changes in Eastern Europe. Soviet perestroika and glasnost provided a model for reform in Eastern Europe, and legitimized the kind of economic and political reforms advocated by intellectuals and workers alike. The Kremlin's withdrawal of the threat of military intervention broadened the possibilities for change and strengthened the hands of the reformers in the region. At the same time, the opponents of change, the hard-liners, could no longer count on the support of the Kremlin. Eastern Europe was opened for change; it was up to the Eastern Europeans to take advantage of the opening.

A major obstacle to such change was the age and tenure of the Eastern European leaders (see Table 2.1). In mid-1987, for example, Gorbachev was far younger than any of his Eastern European colleagues (only Poland's Wojciech Jaruzelski and Albania's Ramiz Alia were under sixty-

TABLE 2.1   Eastern European communist party leaders, 1954–1991

	Party leader (in 6/1987)	Age	In office since	Replaced by	Date	Age
Czechoslovakia	Gustav Husak	74	1969	Milos Jakes	12/1987	64
				Karel Urbanek	11/1989	48
Poland	Wojciech Jaruzelski	64	1981	M. Rakowski	7/1989	62
Hungary	Janos Kadar	75	1956	Karoly Grosz	5/1988	58
				Imre Pozsgay	6/1989a	52
				Reszo Nyers	6/1989	66
				Miklos Nemeth	6/1989	41
East Germany	Erich Honecker	75	1973	Egon Krenz	10/1989	52
				Gregor Gysi	12/1989	41
Bulgaria	Todor Zhivkov	76	1954	Petar Mladenov	11/1989	53
				Alexander Lilov	2/1990	57
Romania	Nicolae Ceausescu	69	1965		12/1989	
Albania	Ramiz Alia	62	1985	Fatos Nano	5/1991	

aIn June 1989, the Hungarian Socialist Workers' Party created a four-man presidium of leaders, consisting of Grosz, Pozsgay, Nyers, and Nemeth.

five) and had far less experience as first secretary (three years compared to an average of twenty years among the allied Eastern European leaders). Not only did this give Gorbachev a different (post-Stalinist) perspective but it made it far easier for Gorbachev to criticize past leaders and past failings (e.g., the Brezhnev and Stalin eras) because he assumed no responsibility for those mistakes. For most of the Eastern European leaders, to criticize the past was to criticize the present; it was, in fact, self-criticism. Hungary's Janos Kadar and Czechoslovakia's Gustav Husak, for example, had assumed their party leadership positions in the wake of the crackdowns of 1956 and 1968. For them to reassess the events of those years would have undercut their own "accomplishments" and even their own legitimacy.

This obstacle eased away as most of the older party leaders stepped down, sometimes under pressure from the Kremlin. Husak and Kadar were the first to go. In 1987, there were signs of tension between Husak and the Soviet leadership. For example, Husak and the rest of the Czechoslovak delegation left Moscow in the middle of the seventieth anniversary celebration for their own Independence Day ceremonies in Prague but did not return for the important November 7 parade through Red Square. Six weeks later, Husak stepped down as party leader "because of his age" (he was seventy-five) and was replaced by Milos Jakes.

Kadar's situation in Hungary was different from that of Husak in Czechoslovakia. Although the latter, since 1968, had supervised the most repressive regime in Eastern Europe, Kadar had created a more relaxed environment. Beginning in the early 1960s, he eased up politically with the slogan "those who are not against us are with us." And in 1968, his regime initiated the **New Economic Mechanism (NEM),** the most liberal economic reform program in the bloc. Hungary's more liberal path was dubbed "goulash communism." Nevertheless, by the 1980s Hungary's economy was also experiencing difficulties (slow growth, high debt), and Gorbachev's Soviet reforms stimulated demands for further economic and political liberalization within Hungary. In May 1988, the aged Kadar was replaced as party leader by Karoly Grosz, who was the same age as Gorbachev. The retirements of Husak and Kadar cleared the way for further and faster change in Czechoslovakia and Hungary. Poland had already laid the groundwork in 1980–1981. It was these three countries that started the ball rolling into 1989.

1989: REVOLUTION IN EASTERN EUROPE

Since the martial law crackdown on Solidarity in December 1981, Poland had muddled along in political stalemate and economic stagnation. After

1981, most Poles turned apolitical and apathetic, reluctant to support either the martial law regime of General Jaruzelski or the underground opposition of Solidarity. Even after the lifting of martial law in 1983, neither the government nor the opposition could muster enough popular support to break the stalemate. As one Solidarity leader put it: "People prefer to wait. The prevailing feelings are those of passivity, reservation and perhaps even tiredness. There is no will to come up with action."[26]

Poland: Electing a Noncommunist Government

People were disillusioned with the government and its policies—even with socialism. Public opinion polls in the early 1980s showed most people supporting the ideal, at least, of socialism. By 1987, however, a study of university students found a majority opposed to "the further construction of socialism."[27] And few saw any hope that the reforms of the system would work.

The Jaruzelski government had initiated a decentralizing economic reform in 1982 but had little success in implementing it due to bureaucratic inertia, conservative opposition, and popular antipathy. The economy experienced almost no growth from 1981 to 1985, and only very small growth in the years after that (see Figure 1.1). The country's huge hard currency debt continued to grow, reaching $40 billion in 1988. The government's efforts to rationalize the pricing structure simply led to skyrocketing inflation (60 percent in 1988), workers' demands for compensating wage increases, and a wage-price spiral that further lowered the standard of living.

In 1988, a combination of circumstances led to yet another round of Poland's periodic protests. Eight years since the founding of Solidarity, there was a new generation of young people in the work force, and some of them felt neither committed to the old organization nor intimidated by the legacy of 1981. By now, there was a reforming leadership in the Soviet Union that would not necessarily support the conservatives in Warsaw. The protests were sparked by a new round of price hikes that, as in 1956, 1970, 1976, and 1980, angered the workers and led them into two rounds of protests and strikes, first in the spring and then in August.

In the spring, the strikers' demands were largely economic, but in August they included calls for political changes, including the legalization of Solidarity. On August 31 (the anniversary of the signing of the Gdansk agreements in 1980), Interior Minister Czeslaw Kiszczak met with Solidarity leader Lech Walesa and offered to discuss the legalization of Solidarity if Walesa could persuade the striking workers to return to work. After some difficulty with strike leaders who feared a sellout, Walesa was able to prevail, and the strikes came to an end.

For the rest of the year, though, Solidarity and the government were unable to settle on ground rules for negotiations. Finally, after a stormy session of the party's Central Committee in January 1989, in which Jaruzelski threatened to resign if they didn't approve his recommendation, the party approved a resolution allowing political pluralism, a political opposition, and the legalization of Solidarity. This cleared the way for a series of roundtable negotiations among representatives of the government, the Catholic church, and Solidarity.

The negotiations were concluded on April 5, 1989, with a path-breaking set of agreements that went even further than the party's Central Committee had promised in January. Solidarity would be reinstated and would receive air time on radio and television as well as its own national and regional newspapers. New parliamentary elections would be called, and the Solidarity-led opposition would be allowed to compete for 35 percent of the seats in the restructured lower house of the Polish parliament, the Sejm. Even more far-reaching was the reconstitution of a second legislative chamber, the Senate, for which elections would be completely free and open. At the signing ceremony of this historic pact, Lech Walesa proclaimed, "This is the beginning of democracy and a free Poland."

The elections were scheduled for early June, just two months after the roundtable agreements. Under the agreements, the opposition was allowed to contest 35 percent of the seats in the Sejm (161 of 460) and all 100 seats in the new Senate. In the Sejm, the Polish United Workers' party (PUWP, the communist party) reserved 38 percent of the seats for itself, the balance (27 percent) going to its allied parties in the government. The Solidarity-led opposition was at an incredible disadvantage, trying in that short time to transform itself from illegal underground to legal electoral contestant. Despite the lack of time, resources, and organization, the opposition staged a stunning victory, winning *all* of the contested seats in the Sejm and 99 of the 100 seats in the Senate.

Solidarity's startling electoral success transformed the political climate in Poland. As agreed in advance, Jaruzelski was elected president by the new parliament but with the absolute minimum number of votes necessary. In the election for prime minister, the PUWP's allied parties refused to support the communist's candidate and instead swung their support to Solidarity. With this unexpected turn of events, the Party no longer commanded a majority in the parliament (and therefore the ability to form a government). Finally in August, a coalition cabinet was formed under Tadeusz Mazowiecki, an attorney, editor, and Solidarity supporter. Communists remained in control of the military and internal security, with ministerial appointments to those two portfolios and two others, but the rest of the government was noncommunist. For the first time in the history of the communist bloc, a noncommunist government was in power.

The roundtable negotiations, the election results, and the formation of the Solidarity-led government were increasingly blunt challenges to the principles of the Brezhnev Doctrine. In the past, maintaining the leading role of the communist party was the sine qua non for the people's democracies of Eastern Europe. With the formation of the Mazowiecki government in August, the Polish communist party had lost this leading position and was now in the unaccustomed role of an opposition party. But all through this process, the Kremlin looked on with equanimity—and even approval. Though the April roundtable agreements insisted neither on the preservation of party dominance nor on the preservation of socialism, the Soviet government newspaper *Izvestia* treated the potential loss of communist dominance in an almost offhand way: the opposition "will take their place in the parliament," it reported, "where, incidentally, the PUWP will no longer have a majority."[28] That summer, a Gorbachev spokesman jokingly referred to Moscow's new "Sinatra Doctrine." This was a reference to Frank Sinatra's song "My Way" and implied that the Soviet satellites would be allowed to go their own way. Soon after Mazowiecki's election as prime minister, he traveled to Moscow, where he was warmly received. The message for both Poland and the rest of the bloc was clear: the Brezhnev Doctrine was dead.

Hungary: Burying the Past and Breaching the Iron Curtain

On June 16, just twelve days after the important and symbolic elections in Poland, Hungary celebrated an equally symbolic occasion: the ceremonial reburial of Imre Nagy, the liberal party leader hanged for treason after the 1956 Revolution. Nagy had been buried in an unmarked grave in a cemetery outside Budapest. In 1988, a citizens' group was formed to press for the rehabilitation and reburial of Nagy. But it was not until Kadar retired (May 1988) that the government would sanction such a reappraisal. In early 1989, the government announced that it would allow the exhumation and reburial of Nagy. A few days later, liberal party member Imre Pozsgay revealed that a party panel investigating Hungary's postwar history judged the 1956 events to have been "a popular uprising against an oligarchy which was humiliating the nation." The June reburial was preceded by a funeral ceremony in Budapest's Heroes' Square, with some 200,000 people in attendance. Three weeks later, on the same day that the Supreme Court announced Nagy's full legal rehabilitation, Janos Kadar died.[29]

The rehabilitation of Nagy and the official reassessment of 1956 opened the floodgates of change. The popular revolution of 1956 was now legitimized (even, apparently, by the Kremlin), so both the party and the opposition began to consider and campaign for the same kinds of political changes that had been crushed thirty-three years earlier. In February 1989, in response to increasing pressure from below, the party's Central Committee approved the creation of fully independent noncommunist political parties. In June, a few days before Nagy's funeral, the government and the opposition entered into a Polish-style series of negotiations on the future of Hungary. After three months, an agreement was signed that called for constitutional reform, the creation of a multiparty system, and the holding of free parliamentary elections in 1990. In October, the thirty-third anniversary of the 1956 Revolution, the parliament approved the constitutional changes, including altering the name of the state by dropping "People's" from the Hungarian People's Republic. The preamble to the constitution now declared that "the Hungarian Republic is an independent, democratic state based on the rule of law, in which the values of bourgeois democracy and democratic socialism are equally recognized."[30] The same month, the Hungarian Socialist Workers' party (the communist party) dissolved itself and was reconstituted as the Hungarian Socialist party.

By the fall of 1989, Hungary had leapfrogged over Poland on the path to democratization. Before Poland, Hungary changed the name of its country, dissolved the communist party, and resolved the most sensitive historical issue in its relationship with the Soviet Union. (The new Polish government, at that time, was still negotiating with the Soviet Union over when and how the latter would admit that the Soviet Union, not Nazi Germany, had massacred some ten thousand Polish army officers in Katyn during World War II.) Hungary would also be the first country in the bloc to conduct completely free parliamentary elections in the spring of 1990. The pace of change in Hungary had picked up, however, precisely because of the roundtable talks and the elections in Poland. Poland pushed the limits of the possible, and the Hungarians charged forward.

Although these startling changes in Poland and Hungary provided a useful model for other countries in the region, no others at that point were quite prepared to follow suit. And perhaps the internal changes in Poland and Hungary would have been confined to two countries were it not for another important development in Hungary: the opening of the country's borders to the West. This began in May 1989 with a ceremonial cutting of the barbed wire barrier on the Austrian border, attended by some of the country's leaders and filmed by the Western media. The unexpected consequence of this breach in the iron curtain was that thousands of East German tourists began to flee Hungary (and thus the bloc) through Austria and then, for most of them, to West Germany. The East German government complained that this was a violation of bilateral treaty obligations. When Budapest responded by enforcing exit permission requirements, East Germans who had come to Hungary to leave the bloc were now stranded. By September, some 3,000 were camped at the West German embassy in Budapest, with perhaps 100,000 elsewhere in the country. On September 10, the Hungarian government finally gave the order to dismantle all barriers on its Austrian border and to allow the East Germans to leave. The East German government vehemently objected and closed down travel to Hungary. The result was a new flood of tourists hoping to reach the West through Poland and Czechoslovakia and similar encampments of young East Germans at the West German embassies in those two countries. By November, nearly 200,000 East Germans had escaped to the West.

The GDR: The Fall of the Berlin Wall

East Germany was somewhat of an anomaly in East-Central Europe: it was one of the most politically repressive regimes in the region, but it had remained aloof from the Soviet-led reforms. In part, the Gorbachev leadership had not pressed reform on Erich Honecker, the East German party leader, because the GDR had the most successful economy and the highest standard of living in the bloc. The East German media paid scant attention to the reforms in the Soviet Union, and the country's leaders evinced little enthusiasm for replicating the Soviet changes. As the GDR's party ideologist put it: "If your neighbor chooses to repaper the walls of his house, would you feel obliged to do the same?"[31]

The official silence on perestroika, however, did not prevent the population from knowing what was going on elsewhere in the bloc. An estimated 85 percent of East German households could receive West German television broadcasts, so were able to follow world news better than most people in Eastern Europe. Gorbachev had won supporters among intellectuals, bureaucrats, and the population at large. In 1987, during three nights of clashes between East German rock fans and police near the Berlin Wall, there were chants of "Gorbachev! Gorbachev!" and "The wall must go!"[32]

Tensions in East Germany came to a head in October 1989 as a result of two circumstances: the popular exodus through Hungary, Poland, and Czechoslovakia; and Gorbachev's visit on October 7. The flood of refugees out of East Germany opened some old wounds in the country and focused the spotlight once again on the Berlin Wall. Berlin, like Germany, had been divided by the Allied powers after World War II. But because the city was located in East Germany, it became easy for East Germans to flee to the West simply by walking from East Berlin into West Berlin and then transiting to West Germany. An earlier flood of Germans from East to West had drained the East of talent and caused the country's population to actually shrink in size in 1961. The Berlin Wall, constructed in August 1961, was meant to stop the hemorrhage. It became a stark symbol of communist repression and a physical manifestation of the iron curtain.

The Hungarian opening to Austria allowed a way around the Wall, because East Germans were generally free to travel to other Eastern European states. As news of the exodus spread, more and more people made plans to leave. The opportunity to resettle in West Germany, where East Germans were welcomed by the West German government, made such moves more attractive and more feasible for East Germans than for people elsewhere in the bloc. The exodus posed a sharp dilemma for the East German government. To allow such large-scale emigration would bleed the country of its population, especially its young people and intellectuals. To prohibit travel altogether risked bottling up the pressure within the country. The Honecker government waffled back and forth. On October 1, the government agreed to allow East German refugees in Prague and Warsaw to leave for West Germany by convoys of trains across East Germany (where more refugees boarded). Then the government tried to stem the flow with a ban on visas for travel to Czechoslovakia. The new restrictions led to protests and demonstrations in East Berlin, Dresden, Leipzig, and other cities.

It was at this time that Gorbachev came to East Berlin to participate in the country's fortieth anniversary celebration. Wherever he went, he was greeted by chants of "Gorby! Gorby!" and police broke up several demonstrations and protests. Gorbachev's statement that "Life itself pun-

Berlin Wall—before. (Photo courtesy of the German Information Center.)

ishes those who delay" was seen as a rebuke of Honecker and as tacit support for the advocates of change.[33] After Gorbachev's departure on October 8, the demonstrations grew larger and more political and spread to other cities. There were demands for free emigration, the resignation of Honecker, and the legalization of **New Forum,** the coalition of opposition forces that had emerged out of the protests.

The largest demonstrations were in Leipzig where, since the summer, regular Monday evening prayers for peace at the Church of St. Nicholas had been followed by small demonstrations nearby. On October 9, some 70,000 people joined the demonstration; on October 16, 100,000 did. That week, there was high tension in Leipzig as the Honecker leadership debated whether to use force to break up the demonstrations. Apparently, the local police decided against this course and were backed up by Egon Krenz, the politburo member in charge of internal security.[34] On October 18, Honecker was replaced as party leader by Krenz, the politburo's youngest member.

Over the next three weeks, the East German regime eased up on travel restrictions and granted amnesty to political prisoners. But the demonstrations continued to grow, reaching 300,000 in Leipzig and a half-million in East Berlin. In the first few days of November, first the entire government resigned, then the party's politburo did the same, and it was replaced by a smaller body. With the relaxed travel restrictions, people were once again pouring out of the country, and Krenz pleaded with East Germans to stay home, promising further changes. In a desperate attempt to stem the tide, the government ended all travel restrictions, and the Berlin Wall was opened.

That day, November 9, 1989, was the beginning of the end of East Germany. Over the next months, the communist party made an effort to reform and democratize itself, as was happening in Hungary and Poland. Egon Krenz resigned as party chairman and was replaced by forty-one-year-old Gregor Gysi, who presided over the transformation of the party from communist to socialist. The country's parliament voted to end the communists' leading role and promised free elections in the spring of 1990. But by then, there was a flood tide, from both East and West, for unification of the two Germanys. East Germany disappeared on October 3, 1990, within a year of the collapse of the Berlin Wall.

Bulgaria: Evolutionary Revolution

In the midst of these dramatic and photogenic events in East Germany, important developments in Bulgaria were almost lost in the excitement. Bulgaria, a Slavic state with a language and alphabet similar to Russian, had always had close relations with Moscow. Party leader Todor Zhivkov, in

Berlin Wall—After. (Photo courtesy of the German Information Center.)

that position since 1954, had managed to ride the bumpy political succes-
sions in the Soviet Union and remain a loyal client of each of the Soviet
leaders since Stalin. After some initial reluctance and some sharp criticism
from Moscow, Bulgaria began to fall in behind the Soviet line of reform.

But after Gustav Husak and Janos Kadar had stepped down from the
party leadership in Czechoslovakia and Hungary in 1987 and 1988,
Zhivkov was by far the oldest (seventy-eight) and most senior party
leader in the bloc. In the Gorbachev era, this increasingly seemed to be a
disadvantage. Zhivkov's tenure was challenged more and more by several major issues, including the government's effort to assimilate or
expel the large Turkish population in Bulgaria and a growing dissident
movement led by an environmental group calling itself Eco-Glasnost. In
Bulgaria, there had never been a very substantial political opposition,
and Eco-Glasnost had been formed to promote change in an arena, the
environment, that seemed relatively safe from the political standpoint.
The revolutionary movements sweeping through the rest of the region,
however, gave courage to dissident groups in Bulgaria, and their demands became increasingly political. On November 3, 1989, Eco-Glasnost held a prodemocracy demonstration in Sofia that attracted some
9,000 supporters.

On November 10, the day after the fall of the Berlin Wall, Zhivkov suddenly resigned as president and party leader. The reformist foreign minister, Petar Mladenov (fifty-three years old), replaced him in both positions. Over the next several months, a combination of Hungarian-style reform from above and East German–style "people power" led Bulgaria toward democratization. Nine independent opposition groups, including Eco-Glasnost, merged in early December to form the Union of Democratic Forces (similar to East Germany's New Forum). The Bulgarian Communist party reshuffled its leadership, but after a prodemocracy demonstration by some 50,000 on December 10, Mladenov called for ending the party's leading role and for free elections. Demonstrations in Sofia continued, however, demanding a faster pace of change, and by the end of the year, the Bulgarian government and the Union of Democratic Forces agreed to open negotiations on the political future of the country—setting the stage for Bulgaria's own roundtable talks.

Czechoslovakia: The Velvet Revolution

By the fall of 1989, the revolutionary spirit had spread all over Central Europe. The startling changes in Poland, Hungary, and East Germany had shown how much could be accomplished by grass roots activism and internal party reform. With the increasingly radical changes in each country, people began to realize that the Soviet Union had no intention of blockading change in Eastern Europe. If East German communism could collapse, anything was possible.

In Czechoslovakia, the old party hard-liner Gustav Husak had reluctantly initiated some Soviet-style reforms under pressure from the Kremlin, and the reforms had been continued under his successor Milos Jakes. By early 1988, an experiment in economic decentralization had been extended to state enterprises accounting for about 30 percent of industrial production. A small-scale Czechoslovak glasnost had opened up the press somewhat and allowed the publication of works by previously banned authors, such as Franz Kafka. In December 1988, the government ceased jamming Radio Free Europe broadcasts, just as Moscow had done some months earlier. The regime no longer tried to isolate Alexander Dubcek, the liberal party leader during the 1968 Prague Spring, and they allowed him to conduct several interviews with the Western media.

As in other countries, the Soviet example and the internal relaxation of controls had the unintended consequence of stimulating *unofficial* political activism as well. In Czechoslovakia, as in the Soviet Union, there was a boom both in underground publishing and in the formation of independent associations. In August 1988, 10,000 people marched through the streets of Prague to mark the twentieth anniversary of the Warsaw Pact intervention in Czechoslovakia. Religion and the church also became a locus of political activism; a half million people, Catholics and non-Catholics, signed a petition for religious rights and freedoms after Cardinal Frantisek Tomasek urged them to do so in a letter from the pulpit. As a leader of the Charter 77 human rights organization observed, "Gorbachev has opened up a new climate here. He is destroying the old atmosphere of fear."[35]

In January 1989, several thousand people marked the anniversary of the death of a student who twenty years earlier had set himself on fire to protest the Soviet intervention.[36] Despite forceful action by the police, the demonstrations continued for five straight days. Vaclav Havel, the playwright, Charter 77 activist, and author of "The Power of the Powerless," was arrested at this demonstration and sentenced to nine months in jail. The sentencing of Havel, the major spokesman for Charter 77, became a rallying point of protest around the country and focused international attention on Prague. This commotion and attention may have contributed to the government's decision to parole him early, in May.

The underlying tension in Czechoslovakia was exacerbated by the turmoil in East Germany in October and November. Czechoslovak young people, in particular, were impressed by the flood of East German refugees, many of whom passed through Czechoslovakia, and by the increasingly large and peaceful demonstrations of Leipzig, Berlin, and other cities. On November 12, party leader Jakes warned that protests in Czechoslovakia would not be tolerated. At a demonstration five days later, however, nearly 100,000 gathered to march on Wenceslas Square in central Prague. The forceful police reaction was in marked contrast to the restraint exercised by East German authorities, and it provoked further rounds of protest and larger and larger demonstrations. Vaclav Havel and other opposition groups put together the **Civic Forum** to coordinate the protests and to demand the resignation of Jakes and of Gustav Husak, who was still president of the country.

Every day, the demonstrations in Prague grew larger and more insistent. Meanwhile, the regime itself began to wither and fragment. While Jakes still stonewalled, Prime Minister Ladislav Adamec met with Havel and other members of the newly created Civic Forum. On November 24, after 350,000 people had gathered in Wenceslas Square to cheer Alexander Dubcek and Vaclav Havel, the entire party leadership resigned. Jakes was replaced by Karel Urbanek and the politburo was reshuffled. At that point, this was not a large enough concession. A general strike paralyzed the country and within a week forced the government to agree to the formation of a coalition government, to free elections, and to freer travel to the West. The communists had bowed out without a fight, and Czechoslovaks exalted over their "velvet revolution." As Havel claimed with only slight exaggeration, the revolution had taken ten years in Poland, ten months in Hungary, ten weeks in East Germany, but only ten days in Czechoslovakia.[37]

The collapse of the communist regime, accomplished in fact by the end of November, was insured the following month with a remarkable series of leadership changes. On December 12, the young and liberal communist Marian Calfa became prime minister of a government made up mostly of noncommunists. On December 28, Alexander Dubcek was elected speaker of the Parliament. And on December 29, 1989, in one of the most rapid, stunning, and symbolic political reversals in history, Vaclav Havel replaced Gustav Husak as president of Czechoslovakia.

Romania: Blood and Vengeance

The satisfying and peaceful conclusion of the year in Czechoslovakia was darkened by a much more violent turn of events in Romania. The regime of Nicolae Ceausescu was different from the others in Eastern Europe: The government was more repressive; the leadership more personalist; and the policies more iconoclast. Since Ceausescu had come to power in 1965, he had pursued an independent line, especially in foreign policy. He had resisted Soviet efforts to integrate the economies of Comecon in the 1960s, had refused to participate in the Warsaw Pact invasion of Czechoslovakia in 1968, had prohibited Warsaw Pact maneuvers within Romania, and had refused to take sides in the Sino-Soviet dispute from the 1960s on. The frosty relations between the Soviet Union and Romania became even more frigid after 1985 as Ceausescu staunchly resisted Gorbachev-style reforms in spite of Romania's dismal economy.

Ceausescu's snubbing of Moscow had attracted favorable attention from the United States and other Western governments, but internally Ceausescu's rule was as harsh and dogmatic as any in the region. Ceausescu was a Stalinist dictator long after Stalinism had disappeared from the rest of Eastern Europe (except Albania). In theory, the Romanian Communist party was the leading political force in society, but in practice even the party had been emasculated and subordinated to the secret police (the Securitate) and to Ceausescu and his inner circle. The latter included several members of his own family, including his wife Elena who was his second-in-command, a first deputy premier, and a member of the politburo.[38]

The rigid atmosphere in Romania had stifled any form of dissent, so there were virtually no dissident groups or intellectuals to plant the seeds of democratization or revolution. The absence of any reform program in the 1980s had also discouraged those who might have worked for evolutionary change. So when the revolution came, it did so suddenly and spasmodically. There were no leaders to speak of and no moderating influences.

The spark that lit this tinderbox was the government's decision on December 15 to arrest a Protestant minister, Laszlo Tokes, who had bravely spoken out against the repression of the two million ethnic Hungarians who live in Romania. Hundreds of supporters of Reverend Tokes battled with Securitate forces when they tried to apprehend the minister at his home parish in the Transylvanian city of Timisoara. This led to a larger protest demonstration on December 17, when some 10,000 people protested the rule of Ceausescu. Securitate forces opened fire, killing several hundred. This led to an open rebellion in Timisoara, and protests, riots, and demonstrations spread to Bucharest and other cities.

Ceausescu denounced the Timisoara demonstrators as "fascist reactionary groups," but when he made a public televised speech on December 21, 1989, he was shouted down by protestors. As the violence escalated, Ceausescu declared martial law, but key military officers (including the defense minister) refused to enforce it, and many army units joined the uprising, fighting against the Securitate forces. Ceausescu and his wife fled the capital by helicopter but were captured and returned to Bucharest. On Christmas Day, they were put on trial by an "extraordinary military court," accused of genocide, condemned to death, and executed by firing squad. The next day, their trial and their bodies were displayed on national television.

Meanwhile, a provisional government was put together by a group of liberal communists and anti-Ceausescu officials and named the National Salvation Front (NSF). Ion Iliescu, a former member of the party's Central Committee, was named interim president. The NSF promised democratization and scheduled new elections for the spring of 1990. Moscow hailed the overthrow of the Ceausescu regime as "the will of the Romanian people."[39] But the results of the Romanian revolution were both ambiguous and anomalous. The population was rid of one of the most oppressive dictators in European history, and the Romanian Communist party had virtually vanished. The new leaders, however, did not have the same democratic credentials as those in Poland and Czechoslovakia. Additionally, there was some speculation that the National Salvation Front had been secretly formed even before December and had perhaps provoked and masterminded the protests and violence in order to seize power for themselves.

SOCIAL MOVEMENTS AND REVOLUTIONS

Most western social scientists, especially those who specialized in the study of communist societies, were surprised by the suddenness and thoroughness of the revolutions in East-Central Europe. At least part of the reason for this was the tendency by most Western scholars to treat the communist states as *sui generis*—political systems that were one of a kind. Because these systems were different from all others and had no historical antecedents, one could not apply to these countries the lessons of history or experiences from other parts of the world.

This tendency was particularly strong among those who viewed the communist systems as totalitarian. **Totalitarianism** was a term that was first developed in the 1930s to describe Nazi Germany, fascist Italy, and Stalinist Russia. It imputed to these governments total control over their societies, perpetuated by a dictator, a one-party political system, a rigid ideology, censorship, and an omnipresent secret police. But even after the collapse of Hitler's Germany and Mussolini's Italy in World War II and the death of Stalin in 1953, some people continued to use the term to describe the communist systems in Europe and Asia. Dissidents in communist countries, in particular, used the term to criticize and condemn the party-dominated political systems in their countries. Some U.S. politicians, including Ronald Reagan, even brandished the term to excoriate noncommunist but leftist governments in the Third World, such as Nicaragua under the Sandinistas.

The problems with the totalitarian model were twofold: It left very little room for discussion of *differences* among states so categorized because they were all assumed to be similar; and it essentially excluded consideration of politics *within* these states because all power was assumed to be in the hands of the dictator and the single elite party. Thus, for those who adhered to the totalitarian model of communist politics, the theories of social movements, political parties, interest groups, modernization, and so on, derived as they were from the study of more open societies in the West, were not relevant for the study of communist regimes. One of the most visible and controversial advocates of this position was Jeane Kirkpatrick, a professor of political science and U.S. ambassador to the United Nations, who contended that although conservative authoritarian states could "transform themselves" democratically, "radical totalitarian regimes" could not.[40]

In the 1960s and 1970s, Western students of the Soviet Union and Eastern Europe began to take a more nuanced approach to the study of politics in those countries. "Kremlinological" works, for example, recognized that there *was* political conflict in those societies, even if it was confined to the political elite.[41] Indeed, communist regimes were more susceptible than most governments to elite conflict because of the former's lack of any formal process of political succession from one leader to the next. Later, political scientists began to identify interest groups representing different professional groups and bureaucracies, even if they were not the same kind of independent associations characteristic of pluralist societies.[42]

Even so, Western scholars rarely applied Western social science models to communist politics. Indeed, in the discipline of political science there was often a sharp and bitter division between "comparativists" who studied Eastern Europe and all of their other colleagues. At the annual meetings of the American Political Science Association, specialists on the communist countries rarely participated in regular panels on mass-elite relations, social movements, political behavior, or public policy, but rather had their own panels on topics that focused only on Eastern Europe or the Soviet Union. Because of this, much of the discipline's accumulated knowledge about these phenomena simply were not applied to the communist countries, therefore weakening our ability to explain or predict what was happening there.

A glaring example of this lack of application of knowledge was the failure of many Westerners to apply theories of social movements and revolutions to Eastern Europe. As with many other such theories, these were ignored because they did not seem relevant to societies that (1) had already *experienced* revolutions, of a sort, with the establishment of communist rule in the 1940s and that (2) appeared unable to develop social movements because of the dominant and repressive political structure. However, it was clear by the early 1980s that such movements *were* developing in Eastern Europe, first with the emergence of Solidarity in Poland and then with the development of civil society in both theory and practice. Perhaps, therefore, theories of social movements and revolutions can tell us something about the events of 1989.

A social movement may be defined as "a group venture extending beyond a local community or a single event and involving a systematic effort to inaugurate changes in thought, behavior, and social relationships."[43] A social movement is more than simply collective action in that it is organized and systematic in its efforts to achieve significant social change. In fact, if collective behavior is to achieve social change, it must transform itself into a social movement.

Traditional theories of social movements have explained their existence as a result of the dysfunctions of rapid social and economic change in society and the sense of **relative deprivation** in the population.[44] Such a consciousness develops after a period of some change and improvements in society, during which people come to expect further improvements. The sense of deprivation develops when people desire some goal, believe that they have a right to achieve that goal, but perceive that the opportunity for such a gain is being blocked by the system. On the one hand, "power oriented movements" emerge when the blockage is perceived as being structural, and the only hope for resolution of the problem is through structural changes. In "participation oriented movements," on the other hand, group action in and of itself is seen as important and beneficial to the participants, regardless of the goals or their realization.[45]

Much of the literature on social movements is based on Western experiences, particularly in the industrialized democratic states. Many of these theories, however, could be applied to modern authoritarian states and even to communist party ones. Over twenty years ago, for example, Harvard political scientist Samuel Huntington contended that theories of modernization and development had relevance even for communist societies. Modernization of a society, even a socialist one, tends to produce changes that are ultimately disruptive. Increases in literacy, urbanization, and education increase political consciousness, and economic and social change leads to diversification of the social and political elite. These changes eventually produce "new, more complex lines of cleavage cutting across the previously dominant bifurcation" between the political elite and the population.[46] In one-party political systems, as in the communist states, the party elite at first dominated all aspects of society: The scope of politics was extremely broad. But in order to accommodate these new social and economic changes, the party would have to restrict the scope of politics; consequently, other elements in society would begin to play a political role and in doing so would challenge the authority and role of the party. If a single party maintained its pervasive societal role in the face of such changes, the various nonparty interests and groups might coalesce into a social movement to effect more radical changes in the political and social system.

More recently, **resource mobilization** theories have challenged the theory of relative deprivation as the major stimulus to collective action. A number of studies have shown little or no relationship between objective or subjective deprivation and the willingness to engage in collective action.[47] Rather, movements form "because of long-term changes in group resources, organization, and opportunities for collective action."[48] Grievances are a secondary factor. Organizations must deliberately mobilize for collective action to capitalize on such grievances. Indeed, social movement organizations may themselves try to promote a sense of grievance and frustration among their members.

Resources are necessary not only for the creation of a social movement but are also determinants of its success or failure. Important resources include tangible assets (such as money, facilities, and means of communication) and intangible ones (such as organizing and legal skills and unspecialized labor of supporters). The primary task facing social movements is to attract and retain supporters; as sociologists John McCarthy and Mayer Zald put it, to convert adherents into contributors and nonadherents into adherents. In an important book entitled *The Logic of Collective Action*, Mancur Olson has argued that rational individuals will not join collectives unless specific material benefits are available to members only; rather, they will "ride free" and enjoy the benefits achieved by the collective without membership.[49] Others, however, have contended that organizations may attract members by offering collective incentives of group solidarity, commitment to a moral purpose, identity, sociability, and so forth.

These theories help us to understand the rise of social movements in Eastern Europe and to place them in a broader context. They can be applied to the emergence of the first major social movement in the region, Poland's Solidarity, and to the movements that overthrew the communist regimes in 1989. Solidarity nicely fits the definition of a social movement (above); it even defined itself as a social movement. It emerged after a period of sustained improvements in living standards in the 1970s, followed by a sharp economic downturn, thus creating feelings of "relative deprivation" in the population. Meanwhile, the modernization of Poland had created a more complex social and economic environment that required the regime to liberalize the political system somewhat. This created more space for the emergence of dissent, samizdat, and small-scale independent associations of various kinds (such as KOR)—the beginnings of civil society. The Polish United Workers' party, however, was unwilling to forsake its monopoly of politics and the official media, making it increasingly difficult for alternative strategies and points of view to be heard. The coastal strikes of the summer of 1980 fostered a coalition of workers and intellectuals that coalesced into Solidarity. The organization's main resources were human, with some nine million members. But Solidarity's leadership recognized the importance of material resources too, both to confront the regime and to attract and retain members. The original "21 Demands" of the Gdansk strikes, for example, included access to the media and publication of a Solidarity newspaper. Once Solidarity was organized as a trade union, it began collecting dues and providing material benefits to its members.

In 1980, Solidarity emerged very quickly out of the strikes and then grew at a phenomenal rate, bringing together most people of working age. Despite its size and potential power, however, Solidarity's demands were limited to a *reform* of the system; it did not demand or attempt an overthrow of the communist regime. A Polish sociologist described this as a "self-limiting revolution."[50] The main reason for this restraint was the continued presence in the Kremlin of the author of the Brezhnev Doctrine.

In 1989, however, this restraint was no longer present. At the same time, many of the conditions extant in Poland in 1980 were still present in Poland and the other Eastern European states in 1989. Most had experienced economic decline after a long period of economic improvement. The countries of East-Central Europe were largely modern industrial states but were operating under an ideology and organizational structure that was inflexible and increasingly outdated. Gorbachev's perestroika was stimulating further changes in Eastern Europe, and Eastern European–style glasnost was opening up the societies to new groups and new demands. In most cases, however, the communist parties clung to their dominating positions and to nomenklatura, preempting large-scale change.

The formation of a noncommunist government in Poland in August 1989, however, showed what was possible: It was not necessary to maintain communist party dominance in Eastern Europe. Furthermore, the more open media coverage throughout the region let people know what was happening in other countries and within their own countries. The media themselves became important resources for the emerging social movements. First in East Germany, then in Czechoslovakia, and on through Romania, Bulgaria, and Albania, people began to coalesce in Solidarity-like organizations: the New Forum in East Germany, the Civic Forum in Czechoslovakia, the Union of Democratic Forces in Bulgaria. As the communist parties weakened, these social movements became more powerful, acquired more human and material resources, and eventually swept into power.

The experience of Eastern Europe lends support to both the theory of relative deprivation and the theory of resource mobilization and illustrates how each was important in explaining different *phases* of development. In the early, formative period of these social movements, relative deprivation helps to explain what factors led to their emergence. It took *resources*, however, for them to acquire the force and power that brought them success.

The seizure of power turned these social movements into revolutions. Students of past revolutions, such as the French Revolution of 1789 and the Russian Revolution of 1917, have observed certain patterns in these processes. Crane Brinton, in *Anatomy of Revolution,* describes a "natural history" of revolutionary movements and the stages they pass through before success or defeat.[51] Other research challenges this somewhat deterministic approach. For resource mobilization theorists, the outcomes of revolutionary movements depend on the political elites, on other groups in society, and on the ability of the social movement to attract resources and support (or at least neutrality) from these other groups. A critical factor, for example, is whether the activists in the movement are able to form coalitions with the political elites in the regime or compel the authorities to allow a societal role for the movement.[52] Sociologist Theda Skocpol, for example, has argued that both the origins and the success of social revolutions are to be found not so much in societal conditions or the movement's resources but in the weakening and breakdown of the state organizations of the old regime. The latter is often a result of international structures and world events, especially wars.[53]

The Eastern European revolutions of 1989 fit many of these past revolutionary patterns. The natural history of these revolutions accord closely with those described by Brinton and others. The major difference was the accelerated time frame of the Eastern European events. Except in Poland, where the origins of the revolutionary movement date to 1980, the revolutions of 1989 proceeded much more quickly than did past revolutions. As noted earlier, this was due both to the symbiotic nature of change in Eastern Europe, with each country building on the achievements of the other, and to the accelerating impact of the mass media, which allowed people all over the region to know almost immediately what was occurring elsewhere.

In Eastern Europe, perhaps even more so than in previous revolutions, the revolutionary movements were able to win over key personnel within the political elite. In every country, there were reformist elements within the communist parties who supported substantial change, if not the total abandonment of one-party rule. As early as 1988 in Hungary, for example, the reformist wing of the communist party allied itself with the emerging forces for change. In 1989, as the revolutions progressed in East Germany, Czechoslovakia, and elsewhere, hard-line party figures were replaced by increasingly more accommodating party leaders, who eventually were willing to negotiate with the opposition and concede free elections. As we have seen, this was partly a result of the loss of confidence and morale within the communist parties and the increasing inability of the old party elites to handle the challenge of change. In Skocpol's terms, this was a breakdown of the governing apparatus, due in large measure to changes in the international situation, that is, a more progressive and tolerant leadership in Moscow.

The benevolent neutrality of the party elites in Eastern Europe and the Soviet Union was a key factor in the Eastern European revolutions, and it deserves further discussion. Not only was this an important reason for the *success* of these revolutions, it was also a major reason for their *nonviolence*. This peaceful acceptance of the inevitable by the party elites began in Hungary and Poland and lasted until the bloodbath in Romania. The Polish party's Central Committee, under pressure from both Jaruzelski and Gorbachev, agreed in 1989 to recognize Solidarity and to allow it a role in the elections. With Solidarity's overwhelming and stunning victory in the June 1989 elections, the party grimly accepted the results—the beginning of the end of one-party dominance. In East Germany, politburo member Egon Krenz refused to allow a forceful suppression of the huge demonstrations in Leipzig and elsewhere, which allowed them to grow and become more powerful. Similarly, during the mushrooming demonstrations in Prague in November, Prime Minister Adamec agreed to talk with opposition leaders rather than try to arrest them. Thus, the Czechoslovak revolution was also a "velvet" one. Only in Romania, where Ceausescu refused conciliation or dialogue, did the revolution turn violent.

It might be asked *why* these authoritarian regimes acted with such restraint in the face of their imminent demise. There were probably several factors, both domestic and international. First, the enormous public demonstrations hammered home the collapse of political legitimacy of these governments and no doubt convinced the leadership that there was little point in resisting the inevitable. Second, the substantial and peaceful changes in the Soviet Union had provided a kind of model for political evolution in Eastern Europe. In some cases the Gorbachev leadership even put pressure on the Eastern European leaders to accommodate such changes. Finally, the Tiananmen massacre in Beijing in June 1989 and international revulsion for those events may have given pause to those in Eastern Europe who favored a forceful solution.

Restraint on the part of the authorities was facilitated by the restraint and nonviolence of the social movements themselves. Here, too, the Solidarity movement had provided a model and an example. During the 1980 strikes, by staying in the shipyards and factories the workers effectively eliminated the option of violence by the authorities and made the option of dialogue relatively more attractive. The success of this strategy in the formation of Solidarity reinforced the notion that gains could be won by nonviolent tactics, which became a major element of subsequent Solidarity activities, before, during, and after martial law. Solidarity underground leader Zbigniew Bujak made explicit the case for nonviolence in 1982 after the regime's martial law crackdown: "The basic principles adopted by Solidarity, and still valid, is the use of exclusively peaceful means. . . . We are against any acts of violence, street battles, hit squads, acts of terror, [and] armed organization."[54]

In 1988 and 1989, the Solidarity-led opposition continued the tradition of nonviolent protest, leading to the formation of a noncommunist government. This then became a precedent for the protests, demonstrations, and social movements in the other bloc countries. Each successive nonviolent victory added to the store of experience. The Eastern European populations quickly learned the strength of "people power," a term coined to describe the large-scale nonviolent resistance that had overthrown the dictatorship of Ferdinand Marcos in the Philippines in 1986.

There is another less-hopeful lesson from the history of social movements and revolutions: that the revolutionary coalitions tend to fragment and divide. Indeed, this normally begins to happen even before a revolutionary movement has seized power. As the social movement grows and begins to develop an organizational structure and concrete goals, all of which is necessary if it is to win power, it also becomes more heterogeneous and, to some extent, less exciting. Lukewarm supporters begin to drift away, and conservative, moderate, and radical factions begin to develop.[55] With victory, these problems are accelerated. In opposition, the social movement attracted many supporters by offering solidarity, identity, moral purpose, and the vision of a common enemy. With the displacement of the enemy, much of this becomes lost in the messy business of democratic politics. Social movements like Solidarity, the New Forum, and the Civic Forum, which were able to prevail because they represented so many interests in society, later were too large and heterogeneous to accomplish the more focused tasks of governing. In East-Central Europe, as we have seen, these problems were compounded by the enormity, complexity, and difficulty of the economic and political tasks before the new governments. It was easier and more exciting to overthrow communism than to design a constitution or re-create private property.

CONCLUSION

The overthrow of Ceausescu in Romania was a violent and disturbing coda to an otherwise peaceful and exhilarating year in East-Central Europe. The year 1989 would go down in history as one of the most important ones ever. Never before had so many countries undergone revolutionary changes in such a short span of time. Even more remarkable, with the lone exception of Romania, all of these changes occurred peacefully. Some were managed by a reformist party leadership, as in Hungary; some by "people power," as in East Germany and Czechoslovakia; and some by a combination of the two, as in Poland and Bulgaria.

In every case, though, the ease and rapidity of change was breathtaking. Regimes that were considered well entrenched and well protected simply tumbled, one after another, into the dustbin of history (a phrase Marx had used to describe the fate of capitalist states). Virtually everyone was surprised by how quickly the populations in Eastern Europe managed to displace the communist regimes and how meekly, in the end, the ruling elites relinquished power. It is safe to say that revolution of this scope and magnitude was not expected by the Kremlin, by the Eastern European leaders, by the populations of the region, or by governments or academic specialists in the West.

The explanation for the revolutions of 1989 seems to lie in a combination of circumstances, all of which became increasingly interrelated as the year went on. In the first place, there were indicators of systemic deterioration in Eastern Europe, as discussed in Chapter 1. The economic problems led to increased popular frustration and dissatisfaction and the growth, in many countries, of political dissent and dissident publications. It is possible that this state of affairs would have continued for a long time, however, were it not for the stimulus provided by the economic and political reforms of the Gorbachev leadership in Moscow.

These affected Eastern Europe in a number of ways. There was, first of all, a kind of demonstration effect: The Soviet reforms showed what was possible and allowable elsewhere in the bloc, so most of Eastern Europe followed the Soviet lead. Second, the Soviet leadership actively encouraged the Eastern Europeans to adopt reforms and put pressure on those that did not (e.g., Gorbachev's visit to East Germany in October). Most important, though, was the impact of glasnost and the opening of the media in the Soviet Union and Eastern Europe. In the Soviet Union itself, the results of economic perestroika were quite meager and democratization had not, by 1989, been carried very far. But glasnost had taken hold and had spread to Eastern Europe as well.

As a result, when changes began to happen in each country, first in Poland, then in Hungary, then in East Germany, people throughout the bloc *knew* what was happening. What news they could not get from their own media they could get from Western radio broadcasts because most of the Eastern European governments had ceased jamming stations such as Radio Free Europe and BBC. Thus, people and governments in one country could imitate and build on the successes of those in another. When Poland created a noncommunist government, other countries could do the same, without apparent risk of Soviet objection. And when the Czechoslovak government eliminated the leading role of the communist party, other countries could follow suit. The entire political process was accelerated and telescoped. Because the political systems were so similar to each other, an apparently risky political innovation in one country, once adopted, could more easily be adopted in another. Just as communism was imposed in a more or less standard fashion in each country in the 1940s, it was whittled away with a similar process in each country in 1989. In the 1940s, though, the top-down process was coordinated by the Soviet Union. In 1989, bottom-up revolutions could only be "coordinated" with a relatively free flow of information. Before the opening of the media through glasnost, this would not have been possible.

The revolutions of 1989 transformed the political systems of every country in Eastern Europe except Albania and Yugoslavia. It was no accident that the two countries farthest away from the Soviet borders, and least subject to Soviet influence, would themselves be the least affected by Gorbachev's reforms. The magnitude of the changes in the rest of Eastern Europe, however, was too great not to affect Yugoslavia and Albania. Within two years, communism would be under siege there and in the Soviet Union itself. In Yugoslavia and the Soviet Union, as in East Germany and Czechoslovakia, the collapse of communism led to the collapse of the states themselves, which is addressed in Chapter 3. And in the whole region, the task of transformation had just begun. The revolutions of 1989 accomplished the goal of sweeping the communists out of power. But all of them confronted a task even more formidable and complicated than revolution: the rebuilding of political and economic order. This will be the theme of Chapter 4.

THREE

□ · □ □

Redrawing the Borders in Europe: Germany, the Soviet Union, Yugoslavia, Czechoslovakia

The revolutions of 1989 precipitated not only the collapse of *governments* all over Eastern Europe but also the collapse and merger of *states*, in particular of Germany, the Soviet Union, Yugoslavia, and Czechoslovakia. Three of these countries were to some extent artifacts of either the Cold War or of communism itself. Germany, because of its role in World War II and the tensions of the Cold War, had been artificially divided into two states. The USSR was a multinational empire that had counteracted the separatist forces of nationalism with the centralizing influence of the Communist Party of the Soviet Union. And Yugoslavia, something of an artificial creation anyway from its origins after World War I, had been held together in the post–World War II period first by the charismatic leadership of Marshall Tito, and after his death by the country's own communist party, the League of Communists. With the collapse of communism and the end of the Cold War, the forces that kept Germany divided, and Yugoslavia and the USSR together, were gone. While the unification of Germany proved to be relatively peaceful, the breakup of the USSR and Yugoslavia generated the most violence and conflict that Europe had experienced since World War II and posed threats of long-term instability throughout the region.

THE UNIFICATION OF GERMANY

The fall of the Berlin Wall and the communist government in East Germany accelerated the pace of change in the rest of Eastern Europe, but it also set East Germany on a different course from its allies. As soon as the wall was opened on November 9, the voices for gradual reform were drowned out by the chorus for unification. Reunification was also broadly supported by citizens and politicians in West Germany. The enthusiasm for unification could not be defused even by Mikhail Gorbachev's declaration that unification was "not a matter of topical politics" and that even discussing it constituted interference in the internal affairs of the Germans.

One should not underestimate the deep and genuine concern of the Soviets over the "German question." As discussed in Chapter 1, after two major wars between the Russians and the Germans (the two world wars), the Soviets were determined to prevent the revival of Germany as a military power. Conflicting Soviet and U.S. views on Germany contributed mightily to the development of the Cold War, and Germany remained a major irritant in U.S.-Soviet relations until the 1970s. West German entry into NATO in 1955 was a major blow to Moscow and led to Soviet sponsorship of the German Democratic Republic (East Germany) and the Warsaw Treaty Organization. There were dangerous superpower confrontations over the status of Berlin in the late 1950s and early 1960s and over the establishment of the Berlin Wall in 1961. In the early 1970s, this tension was reduced through a series of East-West agreements that came out of U.S.-Soviet détente and West Germany's "Ostpolitik"—the opening to the East initiated by the government of Chancellor Willy Brandt. But the German question was never completely resolved, and the four wartime allies (the United States, Britain, France, and the Soviet Union) continued to maintain occupation rights over Berlin and other parts of Germany. East Germany remained a crucial strategic outpost for the Soviet Union; almost 400,000 Soviet troops were stationed there. Thus, for the Soviet Union, the "loss" of East Germany would be an even bigger problem than the loss of the rest of Eastern Europe.

Nevertheless, on this issue as on so many others, the Gorbachev leadership gradually gave way. In February 1990, at a meeting of foreign ministers in Ottawa, Canada, the four occupation powers, plus East and West Germany, agreed on a framework for reunification. The formula, referred to as the "two-plus-four negotiations," called for the two Germanys to discuss the domestic aspects of unification, then to meet with the four Allies on the security and international issues. Soon after the Ottawa meeting, after West German Chancellor Kohl declined to explicitly accept Germany's border with Poland (the Oder-Neisse line defined by those two rivers), the two-plus-four participants agreed to include Poland in the remaining negotiations. But the Ottawa results showed that the Soviet Union had already virtually conceded the issue of unification. From this point on, the major issue was whether the united Germany would be a part of NATO, as West Germany and its allies wished, or neutral, as preferred by East Germany and the Soviet Union. On this issue too, the Soviet leadership seemed obdurate. In early March, Gorbachev said that NATO membership was "absolutely out of the question" for a united Germany.[1]

Gorbachev's opposition to German membership in NATO was due in part to his hope of maintaining a partial German commitment to the Warsaw Pact. But with the electoral victories of pro-Western parties in East Germany, Hungary, and Czechoslovakia in the spring and summer of 1990, the continued existence of the pact was in doubt. In the two Germanys, meanwhile, the march toward unification seemed almost inevitable, regardless of Moscow's preferences. In March 1990, East Germany held the first truly free elections in Eastern Europe, as arranged by discussions between the government and the opposition late in 1989. The electoral campaign was basically taken over by the two main West German political parties, the Social Democrats (SPD) and the Christian Democratic Union (CDU), both of which were pledged to the reunification of the two Germanys. Chancellor Kohl campaigned on behalf of the East German Christian Democratic party; and West German SPD chairman Willy Brandt worked for the East German Social Democrats. In the elections, with a voter turnout of 93 percent, the Christian Democratic alliance won 48 percent of the vote, compared to 22 percent for the Social Democrats. Kohl and the Christian Democrats, in both East and West, had pledged rapid unification under Article 23 of the West German constitution, which allowed East German states to simply accede to West Germany. The election also accelerated the move toward economic and monetary union on July 1, when Bonn offered the healthy West German deutsche mark to East Germans in a one-to-one trade for the weak and previously nonconvertible ostmark.

By this time, Germany was already unified in every sense except the strictly political and legal one. In mid-July, in yet another stunning concession, the Soviet Union dropped its objections to united German membership in NATO. This cleared the way for the final stages of the two-plus-four negotiations. On September 12, 1990, the four wartime allies met in Moscow to sign the Treaty on the Final Settlement with Respect to Germany, relinquishing all of their occupation rights. After a champagne toast to the end of Europe's postwar division, U.S. Secretary of State James Baker proclaimed, "Two plus four adds up to one Germany in a Europe whole and free."[2] On October 3, Germany was formally unified. This whole remarkable process, from the Leipzig demonstrations of October 1989, took less than one year. With almost eighty million people, united Germany was by far the largest state in Europe. It also had the continent's most powerful military, and its combined exports would exceed those of the United States or Japan. It would be one of the most formidable economic and military powers in the world.

The four-power treaty did take account of Soviet concerns about a reunified and powerful Germany and made provisions for the transition of East Germany to the West. The treaty contained a number of German guarantees, meant primarily to reassure the Soviet Union: that Germany would limit the size of its army; that it would not acquire nuclear, chemical, or biological weapons; and that it would make no territorial claims on its neighbors, including Poland. Germany also agreed to allow Soviet troops stationed in eastern Germany to remain until 1994 and pledged to pay Moscow $7.5 billion to house and resettle the soldiers in the Soviet Union.

The final stage in political unification was all-German elections to the Bundestag, the lower house of the (West) German parliament. Held on December 2, 1990, these were the first all-German elections in fifty-eight years. The results were a mixed bag: The Christian Democratic Union, or the CDU, Chancellor Kohl's party, won 36.7 percent of the vote and, together with its coalition partners, garnered 392 of the 656 seats in the Bundestag. The more leftist Social Democratic Party, or the SPD, actually won more votes than the CDU in western Germany but fared very poorly in the former German Democratic Republic and overall lost ground compared to the 1987 West German elections. The Kohl government had purposefully set the elections early (just two months after unification), hoping to capitalize on the euphoria of the previous year and on the gratitude of Germans in the east. It worked.

The political integration of the two Germanys was relatively seamless compared to the difficulties of economic merger. The economic problems were much larger than expected and did not bode well for the economic transitions in the other postcommunist states, which did not have the advantage of huge investments and assistance from western Germany. The privatization process in eastern Germany was managed by a government-created trustee agency, the Treuhandanstalt. Beginning with the economic and social merger of the two Germanys in July 1990, Treuhand was virtually put in charge of the East German economy and was charged with selling the region's state-owned enterprises. Most of these sales were to West German firms that were already successful in European and international markets. The availability of ready buyers plus the common language and cultural heritage contributed to the pace of privatization, which was much faster than anywhere else in Eastern Europe.[3] By mid-1994 Treuhand had disposed of all but 140 of the 12,000 eastern companies it had held at the beginning of the privatization process.

Despite these successes, the costs of German economic integration were enormous, both in financial and in human terms. In the aftermath of unification, East German industrial production plummeted as employees left their jobs (many going to West Germany), East Germans stopped buying products made in East Germany (now that they had West German currency), and hundreds of firms went bankrupt. It was estimated that only about a fourth of East Germany's 8,000 companies would survive in the free market environs of a united Germany. By early 1995 over 1 million eastern Germans were unemployed, for a jobless rate of almost 14 percent. Estimates of the time it would take for eastern Germany to reach Western living standards lengthened to ten to fifteen years, from three to five years estimated earlier. The expected cost of unification to West Germany was estimated at 1 to 2 *trillion* marks, at least ten times what the West German government had estimated in 1989.[4] Public transfers from western to eastern Germany absorbed 5 percent of the country's GNP.

These grim economic problems created frustrations and disenchantment in both parts of Germany. The declining production of the eastern German economy, which was reversed only in 1993, began to drag down the previously robust West German economy, which suffered a 2 percent decline in gross domestic product in 1993. With the increased eastern burdens on the German budget and economy, many western Germans came to feel that eastern Germany was a bottomless pit into which they were throwing their money. Such feelings were exacerbated when the government of Chancellor Kohl raised taxes, shortly after his electoral campaign promised not to do so. Tax increases were followed in 1993 by spending cuts, as the government had to trim some of its generous social programs in order to sustain the $60 billion annual subsidy of "the new federal states" of the east.

Germans in the east, for their part, became increasingly skeptical of the government's economic policies, which were causing so much unemployment and so many dislocations. Furthermore, polls showed that over 80 percent felt that eastern Germans were treated as second-class citizens, subject to political or managerial decisions over which they had no control. In both eastern and western Germany, the popularity of the governing CDU began to decline while radical parties on both the right and the left of the political spectrum grew in strength. The Party of Democratic Socialism, the successor to the East German communist party, mounted a revival in the eastern states and made a strong showing in 1994 both in local elections and in the fall parliamentary elections. Despite an improved showing for most of the parties on the left in those elections, Chancellor Kohl's right-of-center coalition of Christian Democrats and Free Democrats managed to hold on with a slim parliamentary majority.

In Germany, as in the rest of East-Central Europe, there was a close connection between political stability and economic recovery. The new governments in the postcommunist states could draw on a substantial reservoir of goodwill in trying to implement the difficult measures necessary to transform their economies. In Germany, the tremendous wealth and huge popularity of western Germany in 1990 suggested that the transition of East Germany would be relatively easy. The difficulties, however, were larger than expected, and the political honeymoon shorter. By 1991, Kohl's mandate seemed to have disappeared, and there was a disturbing revival of neo-Nazism throughout the country. The problems in Germany, with all its advantages, suggested that the transitions would be even more difficult in the other postcommunist states. Furthermore, Germany's own economic difficulties dashed the hopes of many of the other postcommunist states that Germany would be a major source of aid for *their* economic recoveries.

THE COLLAPSE OF THE SOVIET UNION

The rebirth of East-Central Europe coincided with the gradual decay and disintegration of the Soviet Union. The reorientation of East-Central Europe toward the West was made both desirable and possible because of the dramatically weakened international position of the USSR. This situation was an irony for the Gorbachev leadership, which had unleashed the changes in Eastern Europe with its own glasnost and perestroika in the Soviet Union (as discussed in Chapter 2). In what Berkeley historian Martin Malia has called "the boomerang effect from Central Europe," the Eastern European revolutions doubled back on the Soviet Union and accelerated the disintegration of that system too.[5]

The Eastern European Impact on the Soviet Union

The symbiosis of change that had toppled one government after another in Eastern Europe began in 1990 to affect the Soviet Union as well. In both politics and economics, precedents from East-Central Europe were adopted in the Soviet Union. During the five years of perestroika, for example, Gorbachev had always insisted on maintaining the leading role of the Communist party. But the collapse of communism in Eastern Europe weakened Gorbachev's resolve and his ability to maintain this commitment to party dominance. In February 1990, he told the party's Central Committee that the party had to earn its leading role through the ballot box and in competition with other parties. The next month, the Congress of Peoples' Deputies amended Article 6 of the Constitution to eliminate the party's political monopoly, as most of the ECE states had already done.

The decentralization and fragmentation of the Soviet Union were also hastened by the Eastern European revolutions. A 1988 election law in the Soviet Union had allowed semicompetitive elections for the new national legislature (the Congress of Peoples' Deputies) in March of 1989. But the real electoral revolutions occurred in republican and local elections between December 1989 and March 1990, after the collapse of communist governments in Eastern Europe. In the Russian republic, radical forces under the banner of the Democratic Russia Movement won over one-third of the seats in the legislature and were then able to elect Boris Yeltsin to the republican presidency in May. Soon thereafter, Yeltstin resigned from the Communist party.

In the other republics, the forces of change were more nationalistic than democratic, although the two often went together. Nationalistic forces in the Baltic republics, in particular, seemed to take courage from the democratic revolutions to their west. Independence-minded popular fronts swept the republican parliamentary elections in Lithuania, Estonia, and Latvia in early 1990 and coincided with the increasingly radical demands for sovereignty in those states. In March 1990, the Lithuanian parliament formed a noncommunist coalition government, following a precedent set by neighboring Poland the previous summer and establishing a precedent that was later followed by other Soviet republics.

In the economic sphere, too, the rapid moves toward the market in East-Central Europe prodded the Soviets to accelerate perestroika. The Gorbachev leadership all along had favored a gradual reform of the Soviet economic system. But with the application of shock therapy to the Polish economy in January 1990, this strategy quickly became a subject of discussion in Moscow. By the summer of 1990, Stanislav Shatalin and Grigory Yavlinsky had introduced their own 500-day plan for rapid transition to the market. The Shatalin plan was rejected by Gorbachev at the time, but elements of it were revived in Yeltsin's Russia after the collapse of the Soviet Union.

By 1990, the Soviet economy was near collapse. The limited decentralization of perestroika had basically destroyed the vertical chain of command of the plan without yet replacing it with the horizontal exchanges among producers and consumers characteristic of the market. Furthermore, the political liberalization had fatally undermined popular trust in government, paralyzing its efforts to make more radical economic changes. Increasingly, the national economy ground to a halt; most economic activity was taking place only at the republican or local level. These problems were reflected in increasingly gloomy economic statistics and precipitous declines in GNP and production. The dismal economic scene within the Soviet Union raised concern outside the country as well. Increasingly, Western governments insisted on substantial economic reform as a precondition for further aid.

The mounting economic problems, however, made it increasingly unlikely that "the country" would continue to exist as an integrated unit as centrifugal nationalistic forces accelerated. Gorbachev had hoped to delay the USSR's fragmentation with a new "union treaty" among the country's fifteen republics, intended to legitimize the de facto decentralization of the Union while assuring its continuation in some form. However, the Baltic republics as well as Georgia, Armenia, and Moldova refused to sign the joint declaration and shortly thereafter met in Moldova to form an Assembly of National Fronts to coordinate their efforts toward secession from the USSR.

It was as Gorbachev and the eight other republican leaders were assembling to sign this new treaty in August 1991 that a hard-line group representing the party, the army, and the KGB attempted to oust Gorbachev from power. Russian President Boris Yeltsin managed to rally opposition to the coup and face down the plotters. In the aftermath of this failed attempt the country's fragmentation accelerated. The earlier declarations of independence or sovereignty by the republics had been mostly symbolic. But within a month of the restoration of Gorbachev, the Baltic republics of Latvia, Lithuania, and Estonia became *formally* independent and were admitted to the United Nations. In early December, Ukrainians overwhelmingly approved a referendum declaring independence. With the Ukrainian population at 52 million—18 percent of the former Soviet Union—this was a fatal blow to any efforts to keep the old union together. A week later, Yeltsin and the presidents of Ukraine and Belarus signed a treaty formally dissolving the USSR. They now constituted a loosely knit **Commonwealth of Independent States (CIS),** which was subsequently joined by all the former Soviet republics except the three Baltic states and Georgia (though Georgia later signed on). At the end of the year Gorbachev resigned and retired. After seventy-two years, the Soviet Union no longer existed. (See Map 3.1.)

This was hardly the end of Russia's problems, however, as Russia and most of the remnants of the Soviet Union suffered continuing problems of political instability, economic decline, and national conflicts. In Russia, President Yeltsin had suspended the activities of the Communist Party following the abortive coup, but the Parliament he dealt with was still the one that had been elected in 1989, consisting mostly of party members. As Yeltsin attempted to implement a Russian version of economic shock therapy, he was constantly stymied by the Parliament, which in early 1993 almost succeeded in impeaching him. In September 1993, as the Russian state approached gridlock, Yeltsin issued a decree disbanding the Congress of People's Deputies and the Supreme Soviet and simultaneously called for a referendum on a new constitution and elections for a new bicameral legislature. A group of deputies led by Congress Speaker Ruslan Khasbulatov and Russian Vice President Aleksandr Rutskoi defied the President's decree and occupied the "White House" that housed the Congress. The standoff ended violently, with troops loyal to Yeltsin shelling and attacking the White House itself. The stark image of the blackened and smoking building was a sobering reminder of how easily radical political and economic change can turn violent.

Yeltsin then proceeded with this referendum and with elections, both held in December 1993. The voters approved Yeltsin's proposed constitution, which provided for a much strengthened presidency. But the electoral results for the new Duma (the lower house of the Federal Assembly) were of small comfort to Yeltsin and the reformers. Garnering the largest percentage of the popular vote of any party (23 percent) and the second largest number of seats in the Duma was the ultranationalist Liberal Democratic party (LDP), which, as some pundits pointed out, was neither liberal, nor democratic, nor even a real party. The LDP's leader was Vladimir Zhirinovski, who argued both for the restoration of the old Soviet Union, in its old borders, and for a more authoritarian government within Russia: "I'm a dictator," he said. "What I am going to do is bad, but it is good for Russia. . . . if you do vote for me, I'll make you obey my orders. And you'll be happy, all of you."[6] Overall in the elections, the antireformist parties (including the LDP and the Communist Party) received 43 percent of the vote, compared to 34 percent for the reformers. Thus the elections did not produce the outcome that Yeltsin had hoped for, and there were continuing tensions and conflicts between the presidency and the legislature.

Over the next two years, in the face of a continuing decline in the economy and the standard of living, Russians grew increasingly skeptical of the benefits of the postcommunist system, and many began to think fondly of the old communist era. Public opinion surveys in 1994 and 1995 showed overwhelming majorities of Russians rating the communist era positively in both economic and political terms, and about twice as many rating that era more highly than the "present" one.[7] Other polls showed Russians skeptical of the advantages of democracy and overwhelmingly in favor of the kinds of statist and egalitarian policies pursued by the communists.

In this atmosphere, it was not terribly surprising that in the next set of parliamentary elections, in December 1995, the reborn Communist Party of the Russian Federation, in competition with forty-two other parties, won 22 percent of the vote, twice that of any other party, and 157 seats in the legislature (the Duma), almost three times that of the next largest party. Zhirinovski's LDP also won a sizable block of seats in the new Duma but did not do nearly as well as in 1993. By this time, many people had tired of Zhirinovski's antics, which included an incident on live television when the party leader threw a glass of orange juice in the face of the governor of Nizhni Novgorod. (The LDP apparently considered this a selling point, however, and used clips of the scene in television ads during the election campaign.) It was the success of the Communist Party

MAP 3.1   Comonwealth of Independent States.

ARCTIC
OCEAN

Wrangel
Island

East
Siberian
Sea

Bering
Sea

Severnaia
Zemlia

New Siberian
Islands

Kolyma

Laptev
Sea

Indigirka

Gulf of Shelikhov

Kamchatka Peninsula

Lena

Yakutsk

Sea of
Okhotsk

INDEPENDENT STATES

Sakhalin
Island

Kuril Islands

Lena

Angara

Krasnoyarsk

Lake
Baykal

Irkutsk

Vladivostok

Sea of
Japan

MONGOLIA

JAPAN

N. KOREA

Beijing ★

S. KOREA

CHINA

| 0 | 200 | 400 mi |
| 0 | 200 | 400 | 600 km |

PACIFIC
OCEAN

and its leader, Gennadi Zyuganov, however, that was the real news, and their success spelled trouble for Yeltsin's prospects (and those of other reformers) in the presidential elections scheduled for June 1996.

The breakup of the Soviet Union also unleashed national conflicts of many kinds all over the former empire: within some of the newly independent states; within the Russian Federation itself; and between Russia and its neighbors. In the "near abroad," the term Russians used to characterize the former Soviet republics, there were conflicts, sometimes violent, between the Russian minorities and the newly dominant nationalities in Moldova, Estonia, and Ukraine (especially in the Crimea, where the Russians constitute a majority of the population). Georgia was torn by warfare over separatist movements in both Abkhazia and South Ossetia. Also in the Caucasus region, Armenia and Azerbaijan have been fighting since 1988 over Nagorno-Karabakh, an Armenian-dominated enclave within Azerbaijan. In Tajikistan, the poorest of the former Soviet republics, a protracted civil war between the postcommunist government and Islamic insurgents caused tens of thousands of casualties and hundreds of thousands of refugees, many into neighboring Afghanistan.

The Russian government was often involved in these conflicts, sometimes to maintain stability on its own borders and sometimes in an effort to protect Russians in the non-Russian republics. After the breakup of the Soviet Union, some 25 million Russians were now located in the near abroad, and the Russian government often expressed its intention to protect them—often under prodding from nationalist politicians like Zhirinovski. The Russian empire had been different from most empires in that territory was actually *incorporated* into the Russian state; the British, in contrast, did not actually incorporate their colonies. As such, the collapse of the empire was especially traumatic for Russia, which found it hard to let go, particularly of those areas where many Russians had lived. In April 1995, for example, Russian Foreign Minister Andrei Kozyrev asserted Russia's right to "protect" Russians living in the near abroad.

Apart from problems in the near abroad, Russia had its own nationalities problems within the Federation. The Federation has eighty-eight political subdivisions, including twenty-one republics, each of which represents a different (non-Russian) nationality. In March 1992 most of these subunits signed a Federal Treaty that regulated the relationships among them, but two of the republics, Tatarstan and Chechnya, refused to sign. Tatarstan, though it is deep within the Russian heartland, claimed to be sovereign and independent but still a part of the Federation—a confusing state of affairs for everyone (including American investors in Tatarstan who do not know which laws—Tatar or Russian—apply to their operations). The Chechen case became more serious and more violent when the Muslim republic declared independence from Russia, which eventually sent troops "to restore constitutional order" in the region, leading to a bloody conflict. The end of communism and of the Soviet Union solved many problems in that part of the world, but it also created a host of new ones.

THE TRAGEDY OF YUGOSLAVIA

Yugoslavia, like the USSR, was a multinational federal state held together by a single party. With a total population of only 24 million, it was an extraordinarily heterogeneous country with no majority population. The Serbs were the largest group, but they constituted only 36 percent of the total. The country had three official languages (Serbo-Croatian, Slovenian, and Macedonian) and two alphabets, one Cyrillic and one Latin. The country was also divided by culture and religion. The northern republics (Slovenia and Croatia) were predominantly Catholic and most of the remainder of the country either Eastern Orthodox or Muslim.

The area that is now Yugoslavia had a history of nationalist violence and bloody conflict. World War I was sparked by the assassination in Sarajevo (in Bosnia) of the Austrian archduke by a Serbian nationalist. In 1934, Yugoslavia's King Alexander was assassinated in Paris by terrorist Croats and Macedonians. During World War II, Croatian secessionists set up a Nazi puppet state that murdered hundreds of thousands of Serbs and Jews.

After the war, the major source of unity and stability was the legendary head of state, Josip Broz Tito. After Tito's death in 1980, the government was managed by a collective presidency made up of representatives from each of the country's six republics and two provinces, but growing national tensions increasingly paralyzed this institution. With the dissolution of the Yugoslav League of Communists (the communist party) in January 1990, the last unifying bonds disappeared. Elections in each of the republics during 1990 brought nonsocialist and independence-minded governments to power in Slovenia, Croatia, Bosnia-Herzegovina, and Macedonia. The Serbian government, under President Slobodan Milosevic, a former communist, remained committed to maintaining the integrity of the state under predominant Serbian influence.

National tensions came to a head in June 1991, when the parliaments of Slovenia and Croatia passed declarations of independence from Yugoslavia. When Slovenia tried to take control over its border posts with Italy and Austria, federal troops went on the offensive and the Yugoslav air force bombed airfields and strafed highways. Several hundred people were killed in this conflict before a cease-fire took effect.

In Croatia, the situation was much more violent. There were clashes between Croatians and the large Serbian minority (600,000 among the 4.5

million residents of Croatia), many of whom remembered the atrocities of World War II and were fearful of being marooned in an independent Croatian state. These fears heightened when the Croatian government insisted that Serbs sign loyalty oaths and when it redefined Serbs in Croatia as an ethnic minority. Serbian irregulars began fighting for independence for the Serbian portion of Croatia called Krajina (see Map 3.2) and were soon joined by the Serb-dominated Yugoslav army, navy, and air force. Serb forces battled a Croatian militia and by the end of 1991 were in control of one-third of Croatian territory. With casualties in the thousands, this became the most destructive conflict in Europe since World War II. Conflict spread even to the medieval walled city of Dubrovnik, a major seaside tourist resort and one of the most beautiful and picturesque cities in the world. Much of the town was destroyed by land and naval artillery fire by the Yugoslav army.

The **European Community (EC)** and the United Nations attempted to negotiate a number of ceasefires, but none held more than a few days until early 1992. In December 1991, the German government announced that it intended to recognize the independence of Slovenia and Croatia, and in January 1992 convinced all twelve members of the EC to do the same. The decision was criticized by Serbia and ran counter to appeals to both the United States and the United Nations. Germany claimed, however, to have received guarantees of respect for minority rights from both Slovenia and Croatia, and asserted that diplomatic recognition was the only way to force Serbia to accept a settlement. These initiatives by Germany raised concerns all over Europe about the country's new assertiveness in foreign affairs.

But the problems of Yugoslavia did not stop with Slovenia and Croatia. Just ten days after the EC recognition decision, the legislature in Bosnia-Herzegovina dismissed objections by Serb members and decided to hold a referendum on Bosnian independence. Bosnia was even more divided ethnically than Croatia: About 43 percent of the population of 4.3 million were Slavic Muslims, but Serbs made up a third of the population, and there was a large Croatian minority as well. Serbs in Bosnia had already voted in a referendum to create an independent Serb state within Bosnia, so most Serbs boycotted the March 1 referendum, which approved Bosnian independence and sovereignty. The United States and the European Community officially recognized the independence of Bosnia-Herzegovina, but Serbia did not. Serbian guerrillas backed by Serbia and the Yugoslav army began seizing Bosnian territory for the creation of a Serbian state, which they called the Serb Republic of Bosnia.

This led to a brutal and horrifying civil war that persisted until 1995. Although there was brutality and aggression on all sides of the conflict, most of the violence was perpetrated by the Serbian militias in Bosnia in

MAP 3.2   The former Yugoslav republics.

the course of their land-grabbing campaign. In their efforts to establish Serbian domination in contested areas, the Serbs often resorted to what became known as **ethnic cleansing**: ridding communities of Muslims through forcible evacuation, imprisonment, torture, rape, and murder. Human rights organizations reported that as many as 20,000 Muslim women were raped, suggesting a deliberate effort on the part of Serbs to debase and humiliate Muslim Slavs and drive them out of Bosnia. Ethnic cleansing and the traumas of the war created a huge refugee problem, the worst in Europe since the end of World War II. By mid-1993, over 2 million people had fled their homes and villages in Bosnia; of these, about a half million each had fled to other parts of the former Yugoslavia (especially Croatia and Serbia) and to neighboring countries; the other half—a million or more—were moving from place to place within Bosnia as battle lines shifted[8]. By mid-1993, over 200,000 had died in this war—most of them civilians—making this the most destructive conflict in Europe since World War II.

The Serb offensive succeeded in bringing about 70 percent of Bosnian territory under Serb control, including most of the north and west of Bosnia, bordering Croatia, and the east of Bosnia, bordering Yugoslavia (by now consisting of only Serbia and Montenegro). By early 1994 the Bosnian government, under President Alija Izetbegovic, controlled only a central strip in the country, plus some cities that were otherwise surrounded, isolated, and bombarded by Serb forces, among them Gorazde, Srebrenica, and Sarajevo, Bosnia's capital.

Americans and Europeans were appalled and dismayed by the Bosnian war, but populations and governments alike were reluctant to intervene

Destroyed buildings in the Muslim enclave of Stari Vitez, Bosnia and Herzegovina, May 1994. (UN photo by J. Isaac/186705.)

in a conflict where there were no particular strategic or economic interests and where a military response seemed unlikely to solve the underlying ethnic and political problems. Most countries preferred to work through the United Nations, which took only limited action: providing aid to refugees; establishing an international embargo on weapons shipments to either side in the fighting; declaring "safe havens" for refugees in Sarajevo, Srebrenica, Gorazde, and other cities; imposing trade sanctions on Yugoslavia; and finally authorizing NATO air strikes against Bosnian Serb artillery positions, first of all around Sarajevo. But these actions had little effect on the conflict or the outcome, as the Bosnian Serb forces continued to acquire territory, often in flagrant violation of United Nations resolutions.

The United Nations also sponsored several ambitious peace plans meant to end the bloodshed and redraw the borders of Bosnia in various ways. All of these were rejected by either the Bosnian government and President Izetbegovic, or by the Bosnian Serbs, led by Radovan Karadzic, or by both. The Bosnian government complained that these plans, in granting the Serbs much of the territory they had seized, basically legitimized Serb aggression, expansion, and ethnic cleansing. Karadzic and the Serbs, for their part, held to two basic demands: that their territory in

A Muslim prays near his young son's grave, with many other fresh graves in evidence, in Stari Vitez, Bosnia and Herzegovina, May 1994. (UN photo by J. Isaac/186742.)

Bosnia be contiguous, rather than fragmented; and that the Bosnian Serbs be allowed separate statehood or eventual integration into Serbia itself. The frustrated attempts at mapmaking were complicated by the extreme ethnic diversity and complexity of Bosnia, where almost every village contained populations of Muslims, Serbs, and Croats (or at least they had before the war began).

At the beginning of the Bosnian war, and especially in Sarajevo, Bosnian Croats had sided with the Muslims against the common Serb enemy. During 1993, however, many Bosnian Croats changed sides, and they were encouraged in this by the president of Croatia, Franjo Tudjman, who had designs for annexing parts of Bosnia to Croatia. By the spring of 1993, some of the worst fighting of the war took place between Bosnian Croat and Muslim forces, especially around the city of Mostar. Mostar had been named after the ancient and graceful stone bridge ("most" in Serbo-Croatian) that arched over the Neretva River. In November 1993, the bridge was destroyed by Croatian gunners. The destruction of the bridge, like the bombing of Dubrovnik two years earlier, showed once again how thin can be the veneer of civilization.

International revulsion at the destruction of Mostar and its inhabitants led to stepped-up Western pressure on the Tudjman government, and by the beginning of 1994 Croatia began to back away from its support of Bosnian Croat forces. Diplomats from the United States helped to broker a truce between Bosnian Croats and Muslims and a preliminary agreement to create a Muslim-Croat federation within Bosnia. With this apparent resolution of two sides of the triangular conflict, international attention turned once again to Serbia and the Bosnian Serbs.

In the summer of 1994, agreement seemed within reach on a new plan devised by the so-called "contact group" of diplomats from the United States, Russia, France, Germany, and Britain. The map proposed by this group offered the Bosnian government a more extensive and viable territory than any of the previous plans.The Muslim-led government would get 51 percent of Bosnian territory, and the Serbs would get 49 percent, with the Sarajevo area placed under United Nations control. This plan required the Serbs to relinquish a considerable amount of the 70 percent of Bosnia that they controlled at that point, and Radovan Karadzic raised a number of objections to the proposal without actually rejecting it. The Russian government (of President Boris Yeltsin) pressured the Serbian government (of President Slobodan Milosevic) to push the Bosnian Serbs to accept the plan. In August 1994, in a stunning change of policy, the government of Serbia announced that it was imposing a trade embargo on the Bosnian Serbs and sealed off its border with Bosnia.

With the loss of their only source of diplomatic, economic, and military support, the Bosnian Serbs were now totally isolated and seemed to have few alternatives to accepting the international peace plan. But Karadzic and the Bosnian Serbs claimed to be undaunted by the loss of Serbia's support and asserted that they would continue the struggle until they achieved a satisfactory resolution, including international recognition of a separate Bosnian Serb state.

The Bosnian Serb intransigence was due in large measure to their success on the battlefield, which had placed them in control of some 70 percent of Bosnian territory. But in the summer of 1995 the Serbs overextended themselves and tested the limits of Western patience in attacking several of the cities protected as "safe areas" by the United Nations. In July Serb forces overran the cities of Srebrenica and Zepa, expelled the Muslims, and massacred thousands of Muslim men, causing world outrage. The next month they launched a deadly mortar attack on a Sarajevo market, prompting NATO to begin a two-week bombing campaign designed to break the siege of the city and force the Serbs to negotiate. At the same time, a major offensive by Croatian forces drove more than 120,000 Serbian troops and civilians from the Krajina region of Croatia; and a Bosnian government offensive, following the NATO air attacks around Sarajevo, led to the recapture of about a third of the Serb-controlled portions of Bosnia. This gave the Bosnian government the 50 percent control envisioned in international peace plans and led all three parties to agree to a cease-fire and negotiations under U.S. auspices.

The Clinton administration arranged for the three Balkan presidents, Milosevic (the Serbian president who also represented the Bosnian Serbs), Tudjman, and Izetbegovic, to meet at the Wright-Patterson Air Force Base near Dayton, Ohio, hoping to keep the negotiators out of the media spotlight and away from big-city distractions. It was a daunting task, given the national and personal animosities that had developed over four years of war and a quarter of a million casualties. Even among erstwhile allies there was no great affection: Bosnian President Izetbegovic once remarked that choosing between Milosevic of Serbia and Tudjman of Croatia was like choosing between "leukemia and a brain tumor."

Nevertheless, after three weeks quartered at the spartan air base, an agreement was reached. It involved concessions by both sides, though some issues were left for later resolution. Bosnia would maintain its current borders as a single state, but it would also be divided into two roughly equal entities: a Muslim-Croat federation and a Serb republic. A central government would be retained in Sarajevo, with a rotating collective presidency, a bicameral legislature, a court, and a central bank. Refugees would have the right to reclaim their homes or receive compen-

MAP 3.3 Significant areas that will change hands with the signing of the Dayton Agreement. (*Source:* U.S. Defense Intelligence Agency.)

sation. A peacekeeping force of some 60,000 troops (including about 20,000 Americans) under NATO command would monitor the cease-fire and supervise implementation of the accord.

The Dayton accord was a major accomplishment, but there were still many questions and doubts about its ultimate effectiveness. The agreement left unresolved, for example, a dispute over the width of a corridor around the town of Brcko (see Map 3.3) linking the eastern and western areas of the proposed Serb republic. It also did not resolve the fate of Radovan Karadzic and General Ratko Mladic, the two Bosnian Serb leaders who had been indicted by an international war crimes tribunal. Furthermore, many Bosnian Serbs, including members of the Serbian delegation at Dayton, were unhappy with the proposed new territorial boundaries, particularly since they gave many Muslims the right to reclaim territory (presumably including houses and apartments) that was now occupied by Serbs.

It was also unclear just how the new federal government would work, given the legacy of hatred and warfare among its component parts. Some predicted that the whole agreement would fall apart as soon as the NATO troops were withdrawn. Given the tepid congressional and popular support for the U.S. participation in the Bosnian peacekeeping mission, the NATO mission would probably not last more than a year or two.

THE VELVET DIVORCE OF CZECHOSLOVAKIA

Czechoslovakia was a federal state, like Yugoslavia and the USSR, that was first formed from the remnants of the Austro-Hungarian Empire at the end of World War I. While Czechs and Slovaks considered themselves distinct nationalities, the Czech and Slovak languages are very similar and both written (like Polish, but unlike Russian) in the Latin alphabet, so the Czech-Slovak ethnic and cultural differences were not nearly as great as those dividing Yugoslavia or the USSR. Furthermore, the velvet revolution of November 1989 and the victory and popularity of President Vaclav Havel seemed to give the country a sense of unity and pride almost unprecedented in its history. But almost immediately after the velvet revolution, tensions and fissures began to appear in the political and national landscape of the country.

In the country's first free parliamentary elections, in June 1990, the big winners were the Civic Forum and the **Public Against Violence**, the two umbrella groups that had led the velvet revolution of 1989 in the Czech and Slovak lands, respectively. These groups were more like social movements than political parties and, like Poland's Solidarity, included a wide array of political forces and orientations.

But almost as soon as the election was over, Czechoslovakia's many problems and divisions began to erode the earlier solidarity and euphoria. Like Poland's Solidarity, the Civic Forum was a broad and amorphous coalition with greater consensus on what they did *not* want—communism—than what they *did* want. Its weak international organizational structure also made it difficult for its members to make decisions. By the beginning of 1991 the Civic Forum had declared itself a political party, but this did not solve the problem of heterogeneity, and both the Forum and the Public Against Violence soon split into various factions. As in the rest of Central Europe, the new government was also plagued by economic problems, including growing inflation and unemployment and declining production and growth.

The often bitter debate about the relationship between the Czech and Slovak lands and between the republics and the federal government complicated the political and economic problems at the national level. Slovak demands for greater autonomy within the federation were acknowledged in April 1990 with a change in the country's name to the Czech and Slovak Federal Republic and with a constitutional amendment at the end of the year that ceded many of the central government's powers to the republics. But some Slovaks wanted more radical change, including complete independence for Slovakia. This caused further tensions and divisions within the Slovakia-based Public Against Violence. When President Havel attended a Slovak rally in Bratislava (the Slovak capital) in March 1991, he was booed and greeted with cries of "Judas." This tension was evident during a fall 1991 visit to Butler University of two young Czechoslovak legislators, one Czech and one Slovak. When asked to comment about the main problems facing the country, they spent most of their time arguing about nationalities issues, sometimes bitterly. This did not seem to bode well for a smooth political and economic transition.

The biggest issue was economics. Czechoslovakia, like all of the post-communist states, suffered a serious economic recession as the country struggled with the transition from communism to capitalism. But largely because of the prevalence of so many large and antiquated heavy industrial centers in Slovakia, that part of the country suffered much more than did the Czech areas. By the end of 1992, for example, the unemployment level had reached 12 percent in Slovakia, compared to only 4 percent in the Czech Republic.

The country's finance minister, Vaclav Klaus (a Czech), was pushing for rapid privatization of state-owned enterprises and a quick transition toward the market. Slovakia's prime minister, Vladimir Meciar, argued that this would only compound Slovakia's problems and urged a more evolutionary transition. The growing strength of these two leaders and their political parties led to increasing conflict and stalemate in the federal government. In mid-1992 Meciar and Klaus met and agreed on a quick separation of the two regions. Though public opinion in both parts of the federation favored a continuation of the federal arrangement, the political leaders moved in the opposite direction, and Czechoslovakia was formally dissolved on January 1, 1993, succeeded by two new states: the Czech Republic and Slovakia.

CONCLUSION

The collapse of communism and the end of the Cold War brought the biggest changes to the geography and politics of Europe since the end of

World War I. After that earlier war, the empires that had dominated Central and Eastern Europe collapsed and were succeeded in Central Europe by new, smaller independent states and in Eastern Europe by the Soviet Union. At that time, it was a combination of war and nationalism that led to the redrawing of the borders of Europe: War had destroyed the old empires and nationalism had forged new nation-states in their aftermath. In the 1990s, the anticommunist revolutions served the function that war had played earlier in the century, forcing the collapse of the Soviet Union, Yugoslavia, Czechoslovakia, and East Germany. Nationalism, as always two-edged, fostered the reunification of Germany and the disintegration of the three multinational states.

When national borders are redrawn, the effects are wrenching and disruptive. After World War I, the new states of Central Europe were meant to be both national and democratic. Inevitably, though, there were territorial fault lines that led to tension and conflict among some of the neighboring states; and in only a few of them did democratic institutions survive very long. Consequently, the Eastern European states were easy prey for demagogues, national chauvinists, and, eventually, Nazi Germany.

Some of the same problems have appeared in East-Central Europe as new states and new leaders have emerged and have attempted to forge, simultaneously, both national and democratic identities. Of the four areas addressed in this chapter, in two of them the process has flowed fairly smoothly, with the peaceful unification of Germany and the peaceful separation of Czechoslovakia. But even in those countries, the transformations have been surprisingly difficult, costly, and disruptive, especially for Germany's attempt to merge two states with radically different political, economic, and social systems. Most people assumed that the common national identity of Germans would allow a bridging of these different institutional arrangements, but even in terms of political culture, eastern and western Germans turned out to be surprisingly distinct. East Germans welcomed the enterprise and wealth of the West but were often intimidated and frightened by capitalism's rough edges.

In Yugoslavia and the Soviet Union the process was much more violent. In some respects, the breakup of multinational states into national ones was a culmination of the post–World War I process of creating nation-states. At that time, the new countries of Yugoslavia and the Soviet Union were exceptions to the rule enunciated so forcefully by U.S. President Woodrow Wilson in his "Fourteen Points" that states should be based on nationalities. Both Yugoslavia and the USSR were multinational states, though both created at least a formal structure of federalism to maintain national identities and autonomy. Despite fissiparous tendencies in both countries, they both held together for a remarkably long time, due largely to the centralizing and homogenizing power of the communist party and, in Yugoslavia's case after World War II, the strong leadership of Tito. The collapse of communism (and Tito's death in 1980) stripped away those last unifying elements.

The breakups of these states were traumatic, both for the populations involved and for the international community. With the collapse of the central governments and the communist parties, the leaders of the smaller successor states to Yugoslavia and the Soviet Union had to find alternative sources of political legitimacy and support. In the competition for political power, figures like Milosevic in Serbia and Zhirinovski in Russia relied on primitive ethnocentrism to garner support. Such appeals undermined, or threatened to undermine, peace, stability, and democracy in both areas, complicating the already difficult transition from communism. For the rest of the world, these problems and conflicts posed dangers to peace in Europe in a much more immediate way than had ever been the case during the Cold War. These problems of domestic transition and of international politics after the Cold War will be addressed in Chapters 4 and 5, respectively.

FOUR

□ □ □

Rebuilding the Political and Economic Orders

The collapse of communism in Eastern Europe in 1989 created a broad and daunting agenda for the new coalition governments in the region: the recreation of democratic politics; the construction of market economies; and a reorientation of foreign policy toward the West. These changes required a fundamental transformation of the social and economic systems of the countries and even a psychological reorientation for much of the population. In some ways, these changes would be much more wrenching and traumatic than the relatively quick and painless political revolutions. For any country, at any time in history, any *one* set of these transformations (political, economic, international, social) would have been difficult. For the countries of East-Central Europe, the transitions were made even more challenging by a number of complicating factors: the necessity of pursing change in all spheres *simultaneously;* the uncharted territory of moving *from* communism to capitalism; the poor state of the economies, compounded by huge foreign debts; and the problem of trying to build a new society *on top of,* rather than in place of, the old.

The great revolutions of the past, for example France in 1789 and Russia in 1917, forcefully and violently displaced the personalities and institutions of the old order, clearing the ground for the construction of their new societies. In 1989, the peaceful revolutions could not be as ruthless or as thorough. The most important changes were in the political realm, and even these were limited primarily to the displacement of the communist party. The institutions of the government, the bureaucracy, and the economy largely remained in place. (A Slovak legislator visiting Butler University in September 1991 wondered whether the velvet revolution in 1989 hadn't actually been a "putsch"—implying that one group of communists had simply replaced another. I heard similar remarks from Polish workers protesting against the leftist government in 1994. It would take years, perhaps generations, for the revolutions to be consummated.

REBUILDING THE POLITICAL ORDER

The single most important task for the new postcommunist governments was the design and implementation of new constitutions. In each country, however, it was agreed that a new constitution should be formulated (or at least approved) by a democratically elected parliament. So new elections were set for 1990 (in most countries), and in order to have competitive parliamentary elections, multiparty political systems had to emerge. As a first step, the dominance of the communist parties had to be ended.

The communist parties of the region had dominated almost all aspects of life in those societies, so the elimination of the leading role of the party allowed the emergence of autonomous forces and independent initiatives in all spheres of society. By early 1990, every country in the bloc had eliminated the party's leading role, either by law or by declaration. This then allowed the emergence of new political parties, which, in turn, created the seeds of multiparty politics and laid the groundwork for competitive elections.

With the removal of the constitutional guarantees for the communist party in each country, that party began to wither and die. Membership and morale plunged, and those who wished to perpetuate communist or socialist ideals scrambled to reconstitute the parties in ways that would make them competitive in forthcoming elections. In early 1990, almost all of the old communist parties either dissolved or were renamed (see Table 4.1), though in some countries reformist and hard-line factions separated to create two new parties. In Hungary, for example, liberal communists such as Rezso Nyers and Imre Pozsgay prevailed in renaming the Hungarian Socialist Workers' party (the communist party) the Hungarian Socialist party and committing the new party to Western European–style democratic socialism. A smaller group of conservatives who opposed this change resigned from the renamed party and formed a new party with the old communist name, the Hungarian Socialist Workers' party. That group drafted the former party leader, Karoly Grosz, as their new party leader.

All over the region, the members of the renamed communist parties pledged themselves to multiparty parliamentary democracy, a mixed-market economy, and Western democratic principles. Also, they all renounced, to one degree or another, the dogmatism and authoritarianism of the past. In many cases, the new political orientations of the postcommunist parties were indistinguishable from those of the Western Euro-

TABLE 4.1 The dissolution of the communist parties

Country	Old party	New party or parties	Date
Hungary	Hungarian Socialist Workers' party	Hungarian Socialist party Hungarian Socialist Workers' party	10/1989
Romania	Romanian Communist party	National Salvation Front[a] Socialist Labor party	12/1989 12/1990
Poland	Polish United Workers' party	Social Democracy of the Republic of Poland Social Democratic Union	1/1990
GDR	Socialist Unity party	Party of Democratic Socialism	3/1990
Bulgaria	Bulgarian Communist party	Bulgarian Socialist party	4/1990
Czechoslovakia	Communist party of Czechoslovakia	Party of the Democratic Left (Slovakia) Communist Party of Bohemia and Moravia (Czech)	1/1991
Albania	Albanian Workers' party	Albanian Socialist party	6/1991

[a]Later renamed Party of Social Democracy

pean socialist or social democratic parties. But in the eyes of many Eastern Europeans, the new parties were severely compromised by their pasts.

With the ending of one-party rule and the legalization of multiparty systems, there was a virtual explosion of new political parties and movements throughout Eastern Europe. In Czechoslovakia, for example, the Federal Assembly approved a party registration law in January 1990, and by the end of July, more than one hundred parties had registered. In Poland, the proliferation of political parties after the June 1989 elections led the Polish Press Agency to publish a handbook of seventy-eight parties and political groupings to help people sort it all out.[1]

Free Elections and New Governments

Between June 1989 and June 1990, multiparty parliamentary elections were held in Poland, East Germany, Hungary, Romania, Czechoslovakia, and Bulgaria.[2] In each case, new electoral laws were necessary because the old ones typically allowed voters only to vote yes or no on a single candidate or list of candidates. In most instances, the provisional governments established in 1989 went overboard in their efforts to allow representation of all points of view, so the results were often extraordinarily complex voting systems. As the new governments wrestled with their own identities and looked to the West for models, they often adopted electoral systems that were complicated mixtures of the Anglo-American system of plurality voting ("winner takes all"), a majority system of voting in which a candidate had to receive at least half of the votes, and variants of the proportional representation system used in some European states. In Bulgaria, for example, half of the 400 seats in the legislature were allocated by party lists (i.e., proportional representation) and the other half were contested in single-member districts by majority rule. A second round of voting was necessary in those districts in which no candidate received a majority. Hungary's procedures were even more complicated, making it the most complex voting system in Europe.

For all of these elections except the earlier Polish one, the elections were monitored by international observers. By most accounts, and with minor exceptions, they were conducted fairly and were free of major disturbances. Voter turnout was over 90 percent in East Germany, Czechoslovakia, and Bulgaria and over 60 percent in the other countries. The following sections present summaries of the postcommunist political developments in Poland, Hungary, Romania, Bulgaria, and Albania (see Table 4.2). (Germany, Russia, Czechoslovakia, and Yugoslavia were discussed in Chapter 3).

TABLE 4.2 The postcommunist governments of East-Central Europe (as of February 1996)

Country	Presidential term and powers	Type of parliament	Most recent parliamentary elections, % of vote for largest parties (seats in lower house)	Prime minister (party)	President (party), date elected
Bulgaria	Popular election for five-year term	Single-chamber, five-year parliament with 240 seats	12/94, Bulgarian Socialist Party, 44% (125); Union of Democratic Forces, 24% (68)	Zhan Videnov (BSP)	Zhelyu Zhelev (UDF), January 1992
Czech Republic	Chosen by parliament for five-year term	Two-chamber parliament: House, 200 seats, four-year term; Senate, 81 seats, six-year term	6/92, Civic Democratic-Christian Democratic Coalition, 30% (76); Left Bloc, 14% (35)	Vaclav Klaus (Civic Democratic Party)	Vaclav Havel, January 1993
Hungary	Chosen by parliament for four-year term	Single-chamber, four-year parliament with 386 seats	5/94, Hungarian Socialist Party, 33% (209); Free Democrats, 19% (70); Democratic Forum, 12% (37)	Gyula Horn (HSP)	Arpad Goncz (non-party), 1990; re-elected June 1995
Poland	Popular election for five-year term	Two-chamber, four-year parliament: Sejm, 460 seats; Senate, 100 seats	9/93, Democratic Left Alliance, 20% (171); Polish Peasant's Party, 15% (132); Democratic Union, 11% (74)	Wlodzimierz Cimoszewicz (DLA)	Aleksander Kwasniewski (DLA), November 1995
Romania	Popular election for four-year term	Two-chamber, four-year parliament: Chamber of Deputies, 341 seats; Senate, 143 seats	9/92, Democratic National Salvation Front, 28% (117); Democraticd Convention, 20% (82); National Salvation Front, 10% (43)	Nicolae Vacaroiu (Independent)	Ion Iliescu, October 1992
Slovakia	Chosen by parliament for five-year term	Single-chamber, four-year parliament with 150 seats	10/94, Movement for Democratic Slovakia, 35% (58); Left Bloc, 10%; Hungarian bloc, 10%	Vladimir Meciar (MDS)	Michal Kovac (Independent), February 1993

Poland. As we have seen, Poland opened up the whole process of democratization with Solidarity's overwhelming victory in the partly free elections of June 1989.

The new Mazowiecki government moved quickly to stabilize the economy by implementing a plan meant to halt inflation and lay the groundwork for a market economy. The plan, which was spearheaded by Finance Minister Leszek Balcerowicz, was implemented on January 1, 1990, and within a few months had achieved some of its key goals. But here, as in every other country making the transition from plan to market, there were high costs in terms of declining consumer purchasing power, a drop in production (until 1993), and a rapid rise in unemployment. Consequently, by the middle of 1990, the overwhelming early support enjoyed by the Mazowiecki government began to diminish sharply. Walesa himself, as head of a new opposition coalition called the Center Alliance, began to criticize the government. This was not meant to topple Mazowiecki but to prod the government toward a more representative position. In response, Mazowiecki's supporters formed another coalition called Democratic Action.

By the summer of 1990, Poland was in an anomalous and somewhat embarrassing situation: It was the first country in Eastern Europe to establish a noncommunist government, but it had still not experienced completely free parliamentary elections, which by that time had occurred in five other countries. There was increasing irritation in Poland as well about the continued presence of Wojciech Jaruzelski in the presidency because he was another remnant of the roundtable agreements. Bowing to these pressures, Jaruzelski announced in September that he would step down, clearing the way for new elections for the presidency.

The presidential campaign was a strange one, to say the least. The two major candidates were Lech Walesa, the leader of Solidarity, and Tadeusz Mazowiecki, the leader of the Solidarity government. Neither one very clearly defined the issues dividing them, and Walesa mostly banked on popular resentment with the economic reforms and his own charisma. The campaign became even more bizarre with the entry into the race of Stanislaw Tyminski, a Polish-born Canadian businessman who had left Poland twenty years earlier. Making vague promises for rapid economic recovery and relaying even vaguer warnings about anti-Polish conspiracies, Tyminski finished an astonishing second to Walesa in the November elections and forced a runoff two weeks later. Walesa won the runoff, but Mazowiecki, who had won only 18 percent of the vote in the first round, treated the results as a public vote of no confidence, so he and his government resigned.

After Walesa was inaugurated as president, he nominated Jan Krzysztof Bielecki to the post of prime minister. Bielecki, an economist

"The unnecessary can go." Polish local election poster, May 1990. (Author photo.)

and private businessman, was to head up an apolitical government of experts to manage the economic transition. During the first half of 1991, Walesa worked to strengthen the presidency and tried to deflect politics from the Cabinet to his own office. But as the economic reform program continued to inflict hardship on many Poles, the popularity of both Walesa and the Bielecki government declined, just as Mazowiecki's had. When the first totally free parliamentary elections were held in October 1991, voter turnout was just 40 percent. The vote was divided among some 30 parties, and none won more than 12 percent. (Even the semiserious Polish Beer Lovers party won 3.3 percent of the vote and 16 seats in parliament.) A political stalemate prevented the formation of a government for six weeks. The government that finally emerged was short-lived and was replaced five months later first by one weak government and then by another. In May 1993 delegates of the Sejm (the lower house of parliament) representing one of the by-then splintered factions of Solidarity introduced a motion of no confidence, condemning the government for building "capitalism with an inhuman face" (a play on words with the slogan "socialism with a human face" that reform-minded communists

had employed in past years). The government lost by just one vote, leading Walesa to dissolve the legislature and set new parliamentary elections
for September 1993.

The results of those elections were startling for both Poles and Western
governments. The leading vote-getter was the Democratic Left Alliance
(Polish initials SLD), whose main component was the renamed and reformed communist party. Other parties on the left also did well, allowing
the SLD to form a coalition government with the Polish Peasant party
(PSL), which had been an ally of the Polish United Workers' party (PZPR)
in the communist era. Several coalitions and parties affiliated with Solidarity did not even receive enough votes to gain representation in the
parliament. By this time, Lech Walesa was one of the *least* popular politicians in Poland.

Two years later, in November 1995, Poland's electoral "left turn" was
consolidated when Walesa was defeated in presidential elections by Aleksander Kwasniewski of the postcommunist SLD. Kwasniewski, young,
energetic, and telegenic (he did not discourage the media from comparing him to Kevin Costner), appealed to both older voters, concerned
about their living standards, and younger ones, who identified more with
him than with the older, dowdier Walesa. Kwasniewski pledged to main-

A 1994 Solidarity demonstration in Warsaw, with a banner proclaiming "We say
'Enough' to the Growth in the Cost of Living." (Author photo.)

tain the course of democratic and market-oriented reforms. Nevertheless, the victory of the postcommunists, first in 1993 and again in 1995, was a strange turn of events for the country that had created both Solidarity and the first noncommunist government in Eastern Europe. The electoral results, though, were a reflection of the popular concern with the dislocations and hardships of the economic transition; despite renewed economic growth in Poland, in 1995 unemployment remained above 15 percent, inflation was still over 25 percent annually, and both poverty and inequality continued to grow.

Hungary. The parliamentary elections in Hungary took place in the spring of 1990, but the process of political democratization was already well advanced in mid-1989. During 1989, Hungary's National Assembly began to shed its role as a rubber stamp parliament by debating and approving key pieces of legislation that would move the country toward parliamentary democracy. In October, it approved a modified democratic constitution and a new electoral law setting the stage for multiparty elections in early 1990.[3] Newly formed parties proliferated, and by the time of the election in March 1990 more than sixty parties were in the running.

The multitude of parties and the complexity of the voting system may have contributed to a turnout of only 65 percent on the first round of balloting on March 25 and 46 percent in the runoffs a week later. The results of the election were a major victory for parties of the center-right and a major defeat for the parties on the left. The Hungarian Socialist party, the reformed communist party, won only 33 seats out of 386. The rump Hungarian Socialist Workers' party garnered only 3.7 percent of the vote, less than the 4 percent threshold necessary to gain seats in the legislature. The two major parties in the new legislature were the Hungarian Democratic Forum and the Alliance of Free Democrats. Both advocated a free market economy and privatization, though the Free Democrats favored a more rapid transition. The Democratic Forum played a more patriotic and nationalist tune (for example by expressing concern for ethnic Hungarians in Romania), which led some critics to charge the Forum with anti-Semitism. A third party that did well was the Independent Smallholders' party, which had been the largest vote-getter in the last free elections in 1945 and which now wanted state-owned farmlands returned to their pre-1947 owners.

With the charges of anti-Semitism and closet communism, the campaign was lively and sometimes bitter. Anti-Sovietism also came out, especially in many lively and clever political posters. One poster by the Federation of Young Democrats, which limited its membership to those under thirty-five, showed two photographs: one, a slightly disgusting closeup of an aged Leonid Brezhnev giving a hearty full-lip kiss to an

"You choose." Campaign poster of the Hungarian Federation of Young Democrats, 1990. (Author photo.)

aged Erich Honecker; the other of an attractive young couple sweetly kissing on a park bench. The caption, along with the party's slogan, said "You choose." Another poster by the Democratic Forum showed the back of a Soviet soldier with the Russian words: "Comrades, the end."

Partly because of the proportional representation system of voting, no single party won a majority of the seats in the parliament. The Democratic Forum therefore constructed a coalition with the Independent Smallholders' party and the smaller Christian Democratic party. The new government began a program of liberalization and democratization, normalizing relations between church and state, reorienting foreign policy toward the West, and establishing the State Property Agency to supervise the privatization process. But the biggest issues in Hungary, as in most of the region, were economic ones. Despite Hungary's success at attracting foreign investments, many Hungarians were wearied with a declining

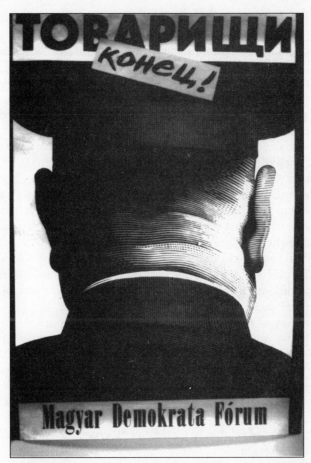

"Comrades: The end." Campaign poster of the Hungarian Democratic Forum, 1990. (Author photo.)

GNP, 12 percent unemployment, inflation rates exceeding 20 percent, and
rising crime. By early 1993, an organization calling itself The Society for
People Living Below the Minimum Standard had collected more than
100,000 signatures calling for early national elections. The petition failed,
but when the next scheduled round of elections were held in the spring of
1994, the results were similar to those in Poland a few months earlier: a
major victory for the Hungarian Socialist Party, the renamed communist
party that had been trounced in the first free elections in 1990.

Romania.   With the overthrow of Ceausescu in December 1989, the government was taken over by the National Salvation Front (NSF), a coalition

of liberal communists. The NSF immediately issued a ten-point program calling for the abolition of one-party rule, the introduction of a democratic and pluralist government, and the holding of free elections. In early 1990, there was a flourishing of new institutions and political parties. The precommunist parties (the Peasant party and the Liberal party) quickly reemerged, though under their earlier leaders who flew back to Romania from long political exiles in Paris and London. By the time of the parliamentary elections in May, about eighty parties competed for seats. Independent trade unions and other associations arose all over the country, and the mass media became more independent and heterodox.

In Romania, however, the Ceausescu era had stifled the development of any independent or opposition groups like that of Poland's Solidarity or Czechoslovakia's Charter 77, so the roots of democracy were very shallow. Furthermore, it became increasingly clear that the NSF was not very different, in either personnel or policy orientation, from the Ceausescu regime. In late January, Romanian President Ion Iliescu was quoted in the Soviet media as saying that political pluralism was not necessarily an option for Romania and that the multiparty system was a model that was "historically obsolete."[4]

The weakness of the opposition and the genuine popular support for the group that threw out Ceausescu contributed to an overwhelming victory for the National Salvation Front in the elections on May 20. The NSF won 66 percent of the votes for the Deputies' Assembly and 67 percent for the Senate; and Iliescu won the presidency with 85 percent of the vote. The elections in Romania had not been as clean as those elsewhere, and there had been frequent reports of intimidation of the opponents of the NSF, but this seemed relatively insignificant, given the National Salvation Front's victory margin.

In the aftermath of the elections, however, the campaign against the opposition intensified. In June, President Iliescu claimed that the regime's opponents had attempted a "fascist" coup d'état and appealed to the population to come to the rescue of the government. As they had done twice before, thousands of miners from the Jiu Valley descended on Bucharest, ransacked the offices of the opposition and the independent press, and beat up several hundred people suspected of being adversaries of the NSF. Six people were killed. The whole incident cast further doubt on the NSF's commitment to liberalization and democratization.

New elections were scheduled for the fall of 1992, and in the period leading up to them there was considerable realignment of political forces. The NSF fragmented, though President Iliescu remained in charge of the dominant, neocommunist faction, which eventually was renamed the Party of Social Democracy. Meanwhile, the weak and scattered opposition united into an umbrella organization, the Democratic Convention of Romania (DCR). But in the elections in September 1992, the DCR was unable to prevail. Iliescu's party won a plurality, with about one-third of the vote and of the seats in parliament, and formed a minority government. Iliescu also won reelection to the presidency. The elections were seen as a mandate *against* market-oriented economic reforms, and they marked a defeat for pro-market forces and prompted the new government to retard liberalizing economic reforms.

Bulgaria. The first round of free elections in Bulgaria came in June 1990, just a day after the Czechoslovak elections. The political landscape of Bulgaria had changed dramatically since the fall of Todor Zhivkov in November 1989, though the change was not as thoroughgoing as in most of the other countries. The leaders who replaced Zhivkov, like the new party leader Petar Mladenov, were liberal communists who had served in Zhivkov's politburo. Nevertheless, there were rapid and significant changes. In January 1990, the Bulgarian Communist party's leading role was deleted from the country's constitution, as was happening all over the region. In April, the Communist party changed its name to the Bulgarian Socialist party (BSP) and pledged itself to democratic socialism. New political parties and movements emerged, including the Union of Democratic Forces (UDF, itself a coalition of sixteen smaller political groups), the Bulgarian Agrarian National Union, and the Movement for Rights and Freedom, which represented the many ethnic minorities in Bulgaria, especially Turks.[5]

In the elections, the BSP (the former communist party) won a solid majority of the seats in the parliament. The strong showing was due to a number of factors: the lack of organization and resources by the opposition parties; the continued support for *some* form of socialism from much of the population; and the absence of strong anti-Soviet (and therefore anticommunist) sentiment within Bulgaria, which had strong ties with Russia from the nineteenth century.

In Bulgaria as elsewhere, though, a strong electoral showing did not guarantee political stability. From 1990 until the end of 1994 Bulgaria went through three parliamentary elections (1990, 1991, and 1994) and six prime ministers. The UDF edged out the BSP in the 1991 elections and governed with an unstable coalition government for three years. But the same economic problems that plagued most of the region—growing unemployment, widespread poverty, high inflation, and stagnant growth—eroded support for the economic reformers and led to the return to power of the Bulgarian Socialist Party after the December 1994 elections under the leadership of thirty-five-year-old Prime Minister Zhan Videnov, a former communist.

Albania. The Albanian party leadership under Ramiz Alia rejected Gorbachev-style reforms all through the 1980s, but by 1989 the revolutionary changes in Eastern Europe had begun to affect even this country, the most economically undeveloped in Europe. In 1989, the government began to move out of its long diplomatic isolationism by restoring contacts with many Western European countries. During 1990, the Alia regime initiated some democratic reforms "from above" as it increasingly felt pressure from below, including an exodus of several thousand refugees in the summer and several rounds of student unrest. By the end of 1990, the government agreed to the formation of a multiparty system and to free elections. In the multiparty elections of March 1991, the communist party won a two-thirds majority and were able to form a government. But with the lid now off, strikes and anticommunist demonstrations accelerated, finally forcing the resignation of the communist government in June 1991.[6] In the March 1992 elections, the opposition Democratic party scored a stunning victory over the socialists, capturing 92 seats in the 140-seat parliament. The next month, parliament elected as president Sali Berisha, a cardiologist who until 1990 had no political experience. Though the economy was near collapse at the time, with almost half of the population unemployed, Berisha and his government managed to restore a modicum of economic and political stability to the country in the next few years. Given the severity of the social and economic conditions, his efforts sometimes bypassed the finer points of parliamentary democracy. As one sympathetic observer noted of the president, although he "has publicly stated that he favors the establishment of a parliamentary republic, he currently makes all major decisions without legislative approval."[7]

THE POSTREVOLUTIONARY POLITICAL PROCESS

The Albanian events marked the fall of the last communist government in Europe. The whole process had taken but two years, beginning with the formation of the Solidarity-led government in Poland in August 1989. After that, the communist governments fell like dominoes, just as many Westerners had feared the *capitalist* countries would fall to communism during the Cold War. The speed and depth of the political transformations in Eastern Europe were startling and exhilarating. But revolutions and free elections did not solve all of the problems of the former communist states, and by the end of 1990 it was becoming clear how enormous were the tasks before the new governments.

The problems included political instability, growing nationalism, and economic deterioration, and all three fed on each other. The collapse of the communist system left a void in the political sphere because there had been no legal alternatives to the political organizations sponsored and controlled by the communists. During or after the 1989 revolutions, incipient political parties began to emerge but without the structures, organizations, rules, or financial resources to make them powerful or decisive. In Poland and Czechoslovakia, where the new governments were founded on broad-based social movements, the solidarity that had been predicated on opposition to the communists began to disintegrate as soon as the common enemy had disappeared. In Bulgaria and Romania, the lack of an effective opposition party allowed the restructured communist party to continue in power, at least temporarily.

In most countries, these political divisions were exacerbated by national or ethnic ones. The most formidable national problems were in Yugoslavia and the Soviet Union. In both, federal and multinational states had been held together for generations by a dominating communist party. As the countries became more open and central controls were lifted, nationalism began to tear them apart. A similar process followed in the multinational states of Eastern Europe, with national republics demanding autonomy in Czechoslovakia and national minorities demanding attention in Romania, Bulgaria, and elsewhere. Anti-Semitism became more visible and aggressive throughout the region, but especially in Poland and Hungary.

Only East Germany escaped most of these political problems by being absorbed by West Germany. But the reunification did not prevent the former East Germany from experiencing the dramatic economic deterioration of the postcommunist states. As each country tried to wrench its economy from plan to market, to cope with huge accumulations of foreign debt, to adjust to the loss of subsidized energy from the Soviet Union, and to reorient trade to the West, their economies went into a tailspin. The general economic malaise left over from the communist era was now compounded with the unpleasant side effects of a market economy: inflation, unemployment, and declining living standards. These problems, of course, put further pressures on the already fragile democratically elected governments, which themselves began to face protests, strikes, demonstrations, and a disconcerting revival of the successor parties of the communists.

In the first rounds of free elections in the postcommunist states, almost everywhere the voters rejected the communist or postcommunist parties. But after the economic difficulties of the transition, many people began to yearn for the welfare states of the communist era, though not for the authoritarianism and repression of that time. Western observers were taken aback when in the second or third rounds of elections, first in Lithuania, then in Poland, Hungary, and Bulgaria, the former communist parties were returned to power (see Figure 4.1). By the middle of 1994, of the

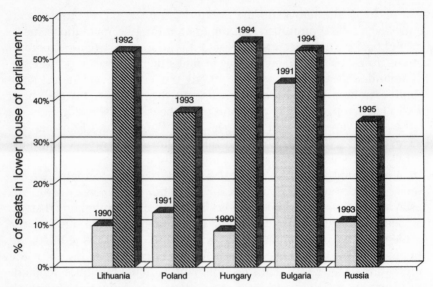

FIGURE 4.1   The left turn in Eastern European elections (% seats won by post-communist parties).

twenty-two states that had emerged from communism in East-Central Europe and the Soviet Union, in only five—Albania, Armenia, the Czech Republic, Estonia, and Latvia—were former communists not in power or sharing power.[8]

Some people, especially in the United States, were concerned that this "left turn" in politics signaled a return to either the authoritarianism or the central economic planning of the communist era. But in most of these countries (more so in East-Central Europe than in the former Soviet Union), the postcommunist parties were by this time thoroughly reformed—committed both to democratic and parliamentary politics and, to greater or lesser degrees, to the development of market economies. By 1995, most of the postcommunist states had new democratic constitutions, genuinely representative legislatures, increasingly organized political parties, and a free press. With few exceptions, they had accomplished these changes with almost no violence—a remarkable achievement. And the return to power of the former communist parties in countries like Poland and Hungary marked an important point in the evolution of democratic politics: the peaceful and routine accession to government of the former "opposition" parties.

THEORIES OF DEMOCRATIZATION

The simultaneous transition of so many states from authoritarian social-ism to democracy provided a wealth of raw material from which social scientists could analyze theories of democracy and democratization and predict the countries or circumstances in which democracy was most likely to flourish or fail. There is a rich social science literature, both theo-retical and empirical, in these areas, and it can help us to understand the problems and prospects of democratization in the former communist states.

The democratization of the postcommunist states faced a daunting number of obstacles: the large number and the complexity of institutions, legal structures, and patterns of behavior necessary for a stable democ-racy; the lack of a democratic tradition in most of these states; the un-precedented nature of the transition from state socialism to liberal democ-racy; and the high degree of ethnic diversity in many of these countries. It is a sobering fact that only about thirty countries in the world have achieved pluralist democracy, and most of those are of quite recent vin-tage and located in a small corner of the globe (i.e., Western Europe).

Democracy means government of the people, from the Greek words meaning "the people rule." The outpouring of popular participation in 1989 would seem to indicate that this condition had been achieved. As Robert Dahl has pointed out in his book *Polyarchy,* however, widespread *participation* must be accompanied by political *competition* for an effective democracy.[9] Dahl and others have identified many procedures and insti-tutions that seem to be necessary to fulfill these two criteria. Dahl posits a "procedural minimum" for democracy that includes secret balloting, uni-versal adult suffrage, regular elections, partisan competition, associa-tional freedom, and executive accountability.[10] In terms of institutions, this requires multiple political parties, representative institutions (such as legislatures) with policy-making powers, and an executive who is ac-countable either to the population (such as the popularly elected U.S. president) or to the legislature (such as the prime minister in the United Kingdom). For all of this to work, there must also be "rule of law," which limits the powers of the government, and legally guaranteed civil liber-ties, which protect individuals from government power and provide the legal space necessary for political activity and organization.[11] In most democracies, the rule of law and civil liberties are provided for in a writ-ten constitution.

The communist regimes in Eastern Europe, which called themselves peoples' democracies, actually possessed many of these democratic fea-tures: elected legislatures, regular elections, and even constitutions that guaranteed many civil rights. There were several important differences, however. The first of these pertains to civil rights. The constitutions of the Soviet Union and Eastern Europe did provide for an extensive array of civil rights, including many social and economic rights (for example, the right to employment) that do not appear in the U.S. Bill of Rights. But whereas the civil liberties guaranteed in the U.S. Constitution are *absolute,* those in the communist party states were *qualified.* The Soviet Constitution, for example, guaranteed the right of free speech, press, assembly, and so on, but only "in accordance with the interests of the people and in order to strengthen and develop the socialist system."[12] Thus, the interests of the people, represented by the state, had priority over the rights of individuals. It was this escape clause that allowed the governments of the region to persecute dissident individuals or organizations whose activities could be viewed as damaging to the interests of the state or of socialism.

The second major difference from democratic principles was the absence in the communist states of plural political parties and independent associations. In some countries, such as the Soviet Union, there was only one legal political party, the communist party, which was guaranteed the "leading role" in society in the country's constitution. In many of the Eastern European countries, there were several other parties in addition to the communist party, but these were subordinate to the communist party, allied with it in a "national front" of some kind, and unable to adopt policy lines independent of the communists. This status led Westerners to refer to these parties as "satellite" or "puppet" parties. In the absence of competitive political parties, there was little competition in the electoral process either. In most cases, voters were simply presented with a list of candidates and asked to vote "yes" or "no" for each. In the 1980s, some Eastern European countries began allowing electoral choice by presenting multiple candidates, but all of the candidates were approved ahead of time by the party authorities. The prohibition of independent political parties was part of a more general pattern of stifling the emergence of *any* associations, political or otherwise, that were not approved by and subordinate to the communist party.

It was these "deficiencies" in liberal democracy (competitive parties and elections and civil rights) that conditioned the early liberalizing actions of the postcommunist regimes. In almost every case, even before the communists had relinquished power, one of the first acts was the elimination of the constitutional provision for one-party dominance. This opened the door to the formation of multiple parties, which then campaigned in truly contested elections. One of the major goals for each of the newly formed governments was the creation of a new constitution that would formalize the new structure of power and insure basic civil liberties.

The early stages of this process followed the patterns of democratization that have been observed in other states in transition from authoritarian rule. A visual representation of such regime change, developed by Stanford political scientist Philippe Schmitter, is presented in Figure 4.2. Schmitter sees five extended and overlapping stages of transition from authoritarian rule to democracy: persistence of authoritarian rule, demise of authoritarian rule, transition to democracy, consolidation of democracy, and persistence of democracy. Along the way, he identifies "indicators of termination" of the old regime, "indicators of initiation" of democracy, and "processes" in the formation of democracy, whose timing is variable.[13] This diagram may seem more deterministic and mechanistic

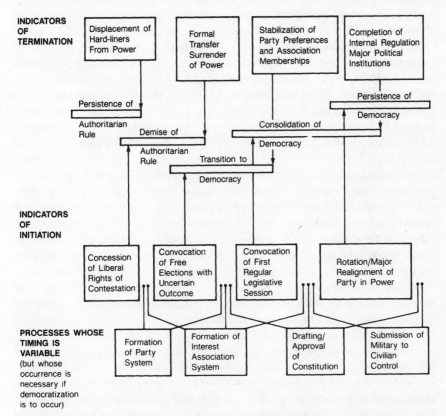

FIGURE 4.2   A visual representation of regime change from authoritarian rule to democracy. Time moves from left to right in this figure, so democratization begins with the phenomena on the left side and progresses through those on the right. (*Source:* Phillippe Schmitter, "The Consolidation of Political Democracy in Southern Europe," unpublished manuscript, 1988. Used by permission.)

than real-life politics; what is important are the indicators and processes (in the boxes) that give a sense of the progress of democratization.

In East-Central Europe, of course, different countries are at different points along this continuum, and some follow Schmitter's process better than others. Nevertheless, the pattern seems to prevail in the region as a whole. During 1989, we saw the displacement of the hard-liners and the concession of rights of contestation with the abolition of one-party dominance. During the same year, most of the communist parties surrendered power, marking an incredibly short demise of authoritarian rule. All of the postcommunist governments then moved into the transition to democracy phase—the emergence of party systems and interest groups, the holding of free elections, and the convening of new legislatures. This also occurred with remarkable alacrity.

The next phase entails stabilization of party and association memberships, the drafting and approval of constitutions, the consolidation of new political institutions, and, to prove the noncommunist parties in power are themselves subject to democratic norms, a rotation out of power by those ruling coalitions. These are time consuming and divisive processes. The party systems in the region at the time were still undeveloped, with dozens or hundreds of parties, on the one hand, and huge integrative social movements (such as Civic Forum), on the other. The parties were often too small and weak and the alliances too large and heterogeneous to effectively aggregate and articulate interest and develop cohesive policies and programs. The constitution-drafting process would be a long and conflictual one, necessitating a spirit of compromise and common purpose that would decline as the revolutions receded. The new political institutions were being overlaid on the old communist ones, complete with many of the communist-era bureaucrats and nomenklatura, many of whom were reluctant reformers. Governments that were trying to revolutionize the political and economic systems might resist efforts to dislodge them, by elections or otherwise, with appeals for law, order, and continuity—a recipe for populism or even benevolent authoritarianism.

Those who have studied democratic transitions in other parts of the world cautioned that the process could take many years or even decades. Philippe Schmitter, for example, wrote that the key to "democratic consolidation" is the full development of parliaments and interest associations. He suggested that it takes three full legislative sessions for a parliament to develop its rules, committees, budgetary routines, and statutes regulating associations and political parties. Given an average term of four years, this would imply that the process would take at least twelve years.[14]

In his book *Polyarchy*, Robert Dahl suggests an even longer time frame, measured in *generations.* From his point of view, the primary task is developing tolerance and a sense of *mutual security* among those participating

"Freedom." *Source: Borba* (Yugoslavia),
date unknown. Reprinted by permission.

in the political system. In the past, most democratizing regimes first made
the system more competitive, within a relatively small elite, and then expanded participation to a broader sector of the population. This was the
case in England, when factions (which later became parties) developed
within Parliament in the eighteenth century, well before the expansion of
the franchise in the following century. Thus, the rules of the political
game, including tolerance of one's opponents, were well established before the political arena was opened up. In the case of the communist
regimes, however, there was widespread (if largely token) political participation without a tradition of competition or political tolerance. Democratization from this starting point is much more difficult, time-consuming,
and "dangerous," Dahl says, because there are so many people and interest groups involved in working out a system of mutual guarantees:

> When conflict erupts, neither side can be entirely confident that it will be safe
> to tolerate the other. Because the rules of the political game are ambiguous,
> and the legitimacy of competitive politics is weak, the costs of suppression
> may not be inordinately high. The danger is, then, that before a system of
> mutual security can be worked out among the contestants, the emerging but
> precarious competitive regime will be displaced by a hegemony ruled by one
> of the contestants.[15]

Dahl was writing about transitions from any "closed hegemony," not just communist regimes. In fact, he did not much address the democratization of those regimes in *Polyarchy*, published in 1971. Many of the concerns that he raised, however, did seem applicable to the postcommunist transitions, in which large numbers of people, parties, and interest groups were suddenly brought into the political arena, and the ground rules of democratic politics were not well established. Despite the historical record of democratization and the cautionary warnings of political theorists, the process has flowed remarkably smoothly and has moved into the final phase of the "persistence of democracy" (from Figure 4.2) in most of the countries of Eastern Europe and some of them in the former Soviet Union. In almost all of Eastern Europe, countries now have new constitutions, newly established institutions, and increasingly stable political parties. While the parliaments in these countries are still working out details of their procedures and still wrangling over important issues like the balance of power between the executive and the legislature, most are now operating in a fairly routine fashion. The "left turn" electoral victories of recent years marked the rotation out of power of ruling coalitions and reflects the sense of tolerance and mutual security that Dahl identified as so important. However, there are disturbing indications of intolerance, **xenophobia** (fear or hatred of foreigners), and demagoguery in some parts of the region. As Dahl and many others have pointed out, ethnic nationalism can be deadly for governments trying to democratize. These problems are particularly evident in the former Yugoslavia and the former Soviet Union. In ethnically diverse states like Croatia and Bosnia, national minorities (such as the Serbs) may not trust guarantees of minority rights and may therefore fear majority rule as potentially deadly. In situations like this, national self-determination supercedes democracy and may make the latter unattainable.

A possible solution to the problem of democracy in heterogeneous states is **consociational democracy.** This form of democracy, developed conceptually by political scientist Arend Lijphart, is possible in societies that are "fragmented" but in which the political elites are able to coalesce and cooperate in the interests of peace and political stability. (If both society and elites are divided, the result is a "centrifugal" form of democracy, which usually deteriorates into political conflict, instability, and immobilism.[16]) So if the *leaders* of a fragmented political culture can agree to share political power, to compromise and bargain, and to distribute public goods more or less proportionately among societal subgroups, democracy can work even in the face of ethnic tensions at the popular level. Consociational democracies have worked in such ethnically heterogeneous states as Holland, Belgium, and Switzerland. But these states have not recently been subjected to the kind of violence that has afflicted

Bosnia, Chechnya, or Nagorno-Karabakh, where there seems to be little immediate hope of such an accommodation.

The rapid democratization of many of the postcommunist regimes may be due to some advantages they have over previous democratizing governments. First, as Dahl points out, democratizing countries in the twentieth century have *models* of democracy and democratization to follow; they do not have to invent political parties, parliamentary politics, or civil rights. Indeed, the new democracies in East-Central Europe have been very attentive to models of democratic politics in Europe and North America. Furthermore, they have received much assistance from Western governments and academics, on a scale exceeding even the U.S. effort to rebuild democratic institutions in Europe after World War II. Second, the postcommunist regimes may have an advantage in that the governments they have replaced are so thoroughly discredited. Although there is some support in these countries for some of the principles and policies of the communist regimes (e.g., full employment), there is almost none for communism as an institution. Thus, the democratizing governments will not have to contend much with those who advocate a restoration of the old order, as earlier democratizing governments have.

Some countries in the region have a better chance than others. Poland, in a way, started democratizing with Solidarity in 1980, though the process was temporarily aborted by martial law. Nevertheless, Solidarity developed an aura of legitimacy as an opposition force, even in the eyes of many people in the communist party. In Hungary too, reform had been under way for some time before the 1989 upheavals, and a group of democratizing liberals had gained a voice within the communist party in 1987 and 1988. Czechoslovakia had some experience of democracy, competition, and cooperation in the years between the two world wars. During the 1970s and 1980s, all three of these countries had experienced the birth of a civil society, which is an essential feature of a mature democratic state. In the Balkans, the prospects were not so bright. In Bulgaria, Albania, and Romania, one-party rule was largely untarnished by dissidence, opposition, or liberalization all the way up to the time of their revolutions in 1989–1991. And the prospects for a stable democratic transition in much of the former Yugoslavia, riven by ethnic hatreds, seemed doomed by violence and civil war.

CONSTRUCTING A MARKET ECONOMY

The task of creating democratic political cultures and institutions is daunting enough but is relatively simple compared to the effort to build market economies. There are, after all, historical precedents and models for countries making the transition from authoritarianism to pluralism; there are no such models for countries moving from state socialism to capitalism. In Gorbachev's first four years of perestroika and democratization in the Soviet Union, there was far more progress in the latter than in the former. In most of Eastern Europe, the political revolutions carried these countries into parliamentary democracies in a matter of months. The economic reorientations would take years, perhaps even generations.

There is an ironic twist to this contrast between political and economic change. Much of Marxist theory was based on the notion that economics were primary in society and that everything else in society was based on the economic "substructure." Only by changing this substructure, Marx contended (and this could only happen through revolution), could the rest of society be transformed. So as Marxism is being rejected throughout Eastern Europe, his observations on this score, at least, are being borne out in practice. This is because the economy touches *everyone's* lives—in a much more direct way than the political system does. In any society, authoritarian or democratic, most people only occasionally come in contact with politics; the most common form of political participation is voting, which happens once or twice a year at most. The structure and health of the economy, however, affect almost everyone on a daily basis: in terms of their employment, the cost of living, the availability of consumer goods, and so forth.

This is the main reason for the more complicated and time-consuming nature of economic transformation. Such a transformation, from state planning to market, affects almost every aspect of political, social, and economic life. It affects employees' jobs, their incomes, and their relationships with their fellow workers and bosses. It creates new institutions (like private banking) and destroys old ones (like planning agencies and ministries). And it affects the country's social structure by creating new classes (entrepreneurs, a middle class) and widening the differences between wealthy and poor.

All of these issues would be imposing enough even for countries with robust economies. In Eastern Europe, however, virtually all of the countries had stagnant economies even before the 1989 revolutions. A Hungarian sociologist referred to the 1980s as a period of "great economic depression" for state socialism, characterized by an exceptionally long period of economic decline, declining real wages and living standards, and an increasing technological gap between them and the Western European economies.[17] Neither a variety of economic reform programs nor an infusion of hard-currency loans from the West in the 1970s had been able to reverse these declines. The Gorbachev-style reforms of the 1980s suffered the same fates.

The newly elected governments of East-Central Europe and the former Soviet Union all committed themselves to a radical shift toward Western-style market economies, though the pace of this change was different in each. The quickest changes occurred in Poland, which in January 1990 began a program of "shock therapy" to initiate movement toward a market system. By freeing prices and tightly controlling the money supply, the government hoped to quickly move through the shock of inflation, end consumer shortages, and lay the groundwork for a rapid transition to the market. In Hungary and Czechoslovakia, the new governments were also committed to radical change, but over a longer period of time. In the countries in which the political transformation was not as thoroughgoing, as in Romania and Bulgaria, the governments pledged to move toward the market but were doing so more slowly.

In all of the countries the problems and plans were similar and involved every aspect of the economy. The major tasks of domestic economic restructuring included price deregulation, monetary and fiscal reforms, the elimination of government subsidies to both consumers and producers, creation of a modern banking system, and a large-scale program of privatization of state enterprises and farmland. For the domestic economies to be more competitive and efficient, they would have to be exposed to world market forces as well, so this required the removal of trade barriers, the "convertibility" of the national currencies, and a drastic reduction of bureaucratic restrictions on foreign trade. These changes would require an enormous amount of legislative work. Czech government officials estimated that creating the legal foundations of a market system would require enacting a new constitution, drafting three thousand new laws, and redefining nearly six thousand rules and regulations.[18] The economic changes would also have to be effected while the government maintained a social safety net to catch the poor, elderly, and unemployed, who would most suffer under the new system.

The Components of Economic Transformation

If the economies of Eastern Europe were to be based on the market rather than a state plan, one of the first tasks was to allow the market to determine prices, which in turn should encourage production based on consumer demand. In the state-socialist economies of Eastern Europe, virtually all prices had been set by government agencies, and prices rarely reflected either the real cost of production or the relationship between supply and demand. In combination with the inefficient system of distribution, this was a major reason for the periodic shortages of consumer goods, for people buying and hoarding goods that *were* available, and for the ever-present lines in front of stores selling meat, liquor, or other scarce commodities.

Currency and Price Reforms. One of the first actions by the new governments in the region, then, was to free prices: to eliminate or reduce the practice of setting prices in government agencies and to allow prices, especially of consumer goods, to be determined by supply and demand. According to the *theory* of supply and demand (though this is not always true in practice), the price for scarce goods will increase until it has reached "equilibrium," a point at which demand has been reduced because of the higher prices and supply has increased because the product now brings in greater profit. At the equilibrium price, consumer demand for the product will be exactly satisfied by the new levels of production and supply. These are considered elemental laws in liberal economic theory, but they had neither been practiced nor well understood in the communist economies of Eastern Europe. Most countries pursued price rationalization in a step-by-step approach, freeing prices in some areas (e.g., "luxury" consumer goods) at first while temporarily maintaining subsidized prices of certain essential goods (like foodstuffs).

This rationalization of pricing was made more difficult by the fact that the national currencies themselves did not have real market value, especially in relation to other foreign currencies. Before 1989, none of the currencies in Eastern Europe or the Soviet Union were "convertible," meaning that they could not be freely exchanged with other currencies. The governments artificially set the value of their currencies, pegging them to foreign currencies like the U.S. dollar or the West German deutsche mark, and prohibited private individuals from buying or selling currencies, except through state-owned banks. This gave rise to a flourishing black market in foreign currencies throughout the region, and in every country there was an unofficial black market rate for each Western currency that was far higher than the official bank rate. A U.S. tourist in Moscow in 1989, for example, would receive less than one ruble for a dollar at the official exchange rate but could easily obtain five or six rubles (illegally) per dollar on the street at the black market rate. By 1991, the black market rate had reached one *hundred* rubles to the dollar.

Currency convertibility, therefore, was necessary for the Eastern European countries to make their own pricing meaningful domestically and in terms of world market prices. The latter was particularly important for their efforts to become more competitive and increase trade in Western markets. So, along with price reform, most of these governments also moved toward international convertibility. Most did so by introducing *partial* convertibility at first (for example, for particular types of transactions) with the intent of pursuing full convertibility in a step-by-step approach.

A new private food store in downtown Warsaw, full of nicely displayed goods— vastly different from the bare shelves and seedy interiors of the communist era. (Author photo.)

Ending Government Subsidies. If freed prices were to have the desired effect of mediating supply and demand, there had to be competition in the marketplace. In the past, there was little such competition in the state socialist economies because most producers were monopolies owned by the state. These monopolies did not, by and large, have to face any domestic competition and were shielded from international competition by their nonconvertible currencies. A firm's monetary incentives were based mostly on *quantitative* indicators set by the state, rather than on any particular concern for quality, consumer satisfaction, or even sales. In the absence of real pricing, it was often difficult to tell whether a firm was efficient. At any rate, efficient and inefficient firms alike were subsidized by the state, which was committed to maintaining full employment.

In this situation, the state subsidized both consumers and producers. Consumer subsidies were delivered through artificially low pricing of particular services and consumer goods, especially for food, housing, and public transportation. This, of course, was consistent with the socialist commitment to assuring all citizens their basic needs, but it was also an enormous drain on the state's resources. In Hungary, for example, housing subsidies alone accounted for 15 percent of the central government's budget.[19] In Poland in the late 1970s, agricultural subsidies were gobbling up a quarter of the government's budget. The price of bread was so low that farmers were using it to feed livestock because feed grains were more expensive. Producers (i.e., firms) were also subsidized in various ways, often with continuing state support to cover a firm's recurring long-term losses. In Poland, for example, such subsidies absorbed about 10 percent of gross domestic product (GDP, the total value of goods and services produced in a society) all through the 1980s.

To encourage firms to become more efficient and competitive, therefore, the new governments resolved to cut drastically the subsidies of consumer prices, businesses, and housing. Over the long run, it was hoped, this would make firms more efficient and more competitive. It would also reduce government spending. In the short run, it would lead to bankruptcies, unemployment, and inflation. These, it was felt, were unavoidable but were to be cushioned with the "social safety net" and other short-term stabilization measures.

With the cuts in government subsidies, firms would have to rely on commercial loans and credits rather than on government handouts, so a commercial banking system was created. Most of the postcommunist countries, consequently, began developing a two-tiered banking system. The central banks were restricted to traditional central bank functions, and the newly established commercial banks were to provide loans, at commercial rates, for housing, investments, new businesses, mortgages, and so forth. Because of the lack of private capital in the Eastern European countries, there were difficult startup problems for these banks. To help fill the need for such capital, foreign banks were invited to set up their own operations.

Privatization and Demonopolization. The core issue in the whole economic reform process, and the most difficult one, was the selling of the state-owned industries and the gradual expansion of the private sector. In the state-socialist societies, of course, virtually all firms were owned and operated by the state (through government ministries), and in all countries except Poland and Yugoslavia, almost all farmland was also state-owned. Transforming all of this to private property was an enormously complicated task that included a number of dimensions: eliminating restrictions on the private sector to allow the formation of new firms; breaking up the large state monopolies into several independent units (demonopolization) to foster increased competition; allowing inefficient state firms to go out of business; selling most of the industrial enterprises in the state sector; and selling (or transferring) state agricultural land to the private sec- tor. These last two tasks were both referred to as **privatization.**

There were all sorts of obstacles and pitfalls to the privatization process. In the case of state enterprises, there was often a question of who actually *owned* them. In Poland and Yugoslavia, for example, where workers' self-management conferred certain rights on the employees of a firm, workers sometimes argued that the firms belonged to them, or at least that the state should transfer formal ownership to them. In some countries, there was a similar problem with the question of land owner- ship in the countryside. In Hungary, for example, the Independent Small- holders' party argued for the return of farmland to the original precom- munist owners or their descendants. In 1991, this issue threatened to bring down the governing coalition.

An even larger problem was: Who would buy large state enterprises, given the dearth of private capital within these countries and the under- developed financial markets? The Stalinist economic legacy meant that most enterprises were very large—too large to be run efficiently from the point of view of most Western investors. In Poland, for example, the aver- age number of employees per individual plant was 378, compared to just 66 in Western economies.[20] Figuring the value of these enterprises was also difficult, both because of the lack of Western-style accounting within state firms and because of the false values of the local currencies. Further- more, few people within Eastern Europe were wealthy enough to pur- chase such firms, and those who did had often accumulated their wealth in ways considered illegitimate by the public. Western investors had the necessary capital, but this raised national sensitivities about selling the national wealth to foreigners. Thus, the process of privatization was inex- tricably linked with the development of a convertible currency, the estab- lishment of a banking system, and the creation of stock markets.

Despite these obstacles, all of the postcommunist governments began privatization as a step-by-step process. Poland, with its fast-paced "shock therapy" plan, began with small-scale privatization, selling state-owned grocery stores and restaurants, for example, while working more deliber- ately on the disposal of the 7,800 large industrial enterprises. First Hun- gary, then Poland, established stock markets to encourage the purchase of shares in newly privatized firms. The opening of the Polish stock market in April 1991 was particularly symbolic and ironic: Brokers wearing red suspenders bartered for stocks in the building that had formerly housed the Central Committee of the communist party.[21]

Foreign Debt and Western Assistance.   The foreign debts of the Eastern Eu- ropean countries, which were already crippling in the early 1980s, contin- ued to grow even after the democratic revolutions. By the end of 1990, total hard currency debts for the region reached $140 billion, with the largest amounts owed by the Soviet Union, Poland, and Hungary. In Poland, the $41 billion hard currency debt was *three times* the size of the country's total annual exports of goods and services, meaning that it was virtually impossible to contemplate ever clearing the debt (see Table 4.3). Some countries simply gave up. Poland had suspended payments on its foreign debt as early as 1981, and Bulgaria stopped honoring its debt payment commitments in March 1990. The debts were not only a drain on government resources but also hurt creditworthiness and therefore deterred foreign investors from injecting urgently needed finance and investment capital.[22]

Recognizing the drag these debts imposed on economic reform, Western governments were willing to reschedule, or even forgive, some of the debts owed to them. There were also substantial commitments of economic assistance to help ease the burdens of the transition. In mid-1989,

From the Budapest magazine *The Hungarian Economy*. Reprinted by permission.

the "G-24" group of twenty-four industrialized countries placed the Commission of the European Community (EC) in charge of coordinating a comprehensive aid program for the economic reconstruction of Eastern Europe. By the end of 1991, these countries, together with the multilateral financial agencies like the World Bank, had pledged about $45 billion in aid to Eastern Europe. A **European Bank for Reconstruction and Development (EBRD)** was established in May 1990 to act with the International Monetary Fund and the World Bank to promote investment in and enhance the competitiveness of the postcommunist states.[23]

The Question of Speed and Timing

These reforms and changes could be implemented in a gradual, step-by-step approach or quickly and simultaneously, through what has been called shock therapy. The advantage of the step-by-step approach is that it allows time for the economy and the population to adjust to each successive change, and it minimizes large-scale economic and social dislocations. The critics of the gradualist approach contend that it prolongs the pain and dislocations and complicates the transition by trying to support the old system (central planning) and the new (the market) at the same time. Poland tried to pursue the path of shock therapy but got bogged down after the initial stabilization measures; Hungary followed the more gradual path. An indication of the tasks involved in such changes, and the likely time frame, appears in Figure 4.3.

TABLE 4.3   Hard currency debt of Eastern European countries

	Net debt at end of 1990 ($ billions)	Ratio of net debt to exports, 1990 (percentage)[a]
Soviet Union	51	150
Poland	41	300
Yugoslavia	9	40
Romania	1	20
Czechoslovakia	6	70
Hungary	20	180
Bulgaria	11	440

[a]The figures in the second column refer to the size of the total foreign debt (from column one) compared to the total value of annual exports of goods and services. For example, Poland's $41 billion debt was 300 percent, or three times the size of its total annual exports.

Source: Rebuilding Eastern Europe (Frankfurt: Deutsche Bank Economics Department, 1991), 86. It should be noted that, as with much economic data from Eastern Europe, estimates of these debts vary widely.

Some Western economists criticized the tendency of Western experts to offer facile and misleading advice to East-Central Europe. In an essay entitled "The Rush to Capitalism," for example, John Kenneth Galbraith condemned those who offered free-enterprise models to these countries when, in fact, these models did not exist even in the West. Advocates of shock therapy were colluding in the imposition of serious and long-term distress on the peoples of the target countries. Those who called for private housing conveniently ignored the millions of homeless in the United States and other countries. Galbraith also pointed out that economic recovery was not likely to be quick or easy: "The return to normal productive activity in Western Europe after World War II, a task less complex than that faced by Eastern Europe and the USSR, took the better part of a decade. In Britain it took some seven years before sterling was fully convertible, and food rationing and associated price controls were similarly continued." What we have in

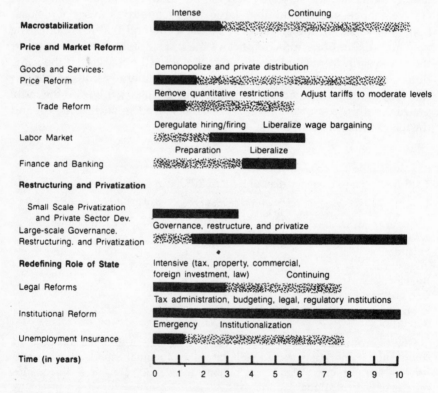

FIGURE 4.3   The phasing of economic reform. (*Source:* Adapted from Stanley Fischer and Alan Gelb, "The Process of Socialist Economic Transformation," *Journal of Economic Perspectives,* 5, no. 4 [Fall 1991], p. 102.)

the West, said Galbraith, was not the "traditional capitalism" that was being sold in the East but "a still imperfect social democracy." The task in both East and West, he counseled, should be "to seek and find the system that combines the best in market-motivated and socially motivated action."[24]

Shock Therapy in Poland

By the time Galbraith's essay appeared, Poland's postcommunist government was well along on the fast track of economic transformation. When Tadeusz Mazowiecki became prime minister in September 1989, Poland's financial situation was among the worst in the world. Inflation was running at 40 percent per month, there were widespread shortages of consumer goods, and the foreign debt exceeded $40 billion. Consumers and politicians alike were fed up with the many prior attempts to remedy economic ills with evolutionary reform programs. Under the leadership of Deputy Prime Minister Leszek Balcerowicz, the new government developed a two-stage program aimed first at curbing inflation and ending shortages and then at attempting to "leap to a market economy" as quickly as possible.[25] Balcerowicz and his economic team were assisted in this planning by a young economics professor from Harvard University, Jeffrey Sachs. Sachs had earlier made a reputation advising the Bolivian government, where his prescriptions helped reduce inflation from 40,000 percent to 15 percent in a matter of months. As the Bolivian planning minister at the time explained, "If you are going to chop off a cat's tail, do it in one strike, not bit by bit."[26]

Consequently, the first stage of the "Balcerowicz plan" was implemented all at once and very quickly, beginning on January 1, 1990, just months after the new government took office. Effective in January, the Polish zloty was made convertible with other currencies, and a new official exchange rate was set at 9,500 to the dollar—about what the black market exchange rate had been. This rate allowed domestic enterprises to purchase foreign currency and thereby import more goods from abroad. It also allowed exporters to easily convert foreign earnings into zlotys. Most trade barriers were eliminated, encouraging more imports, and the government began negotiations for reductions of other countries' restrictions on Polish imports.

Virtually all government price controls were lifted, allowing prices to respond to supply and demand and to thereby reach equilibrium at a realistic level. At the same time, most government subsidies of state enterprises were eliminated, forcing those companies to become profitable or go out of business. The elimination of subsidies helped to reduce the huge government budget deficits and reverse the growth of foreign debt. Anti-inflationary measures included restrictions on wage increases, reductions in the money supply, and sharp increases in interest rates to re-strain credit demand and stimulate savings.

The key element of the leap to the market was the development of private property, especially privatization of state-owned enterprises. Here, however, the government had to move more cautiously for two main reasons: (1) the question of how to dispose of state industries (i.e., to whom and at what price), and (2) the risk of massive unemployment in those industries that could not be sold. The Balcerowicz plan called for rapid small-scale privatization and a more deliberate pace for privatization of major enterprises. Restrictions were lifted on private ownership, and immediately many new private shops and services appeared. Most small state enterprises, especially restaurants and stores, were sold to private owners. Some large enterprises were divided into several smaller units, which were then sold off. During 1990, over 500,000 new private small businesses emerged while nearly 150,000 companies were liquidated. As a result, private industrial production increased by 8.5 percent in 1990, compared to a loss of 25 percent in the much larger state sector.

The privatization of large firms was more difficult. The Balcerowicz team, assisted by foreign consultants, the World Bank, and the European Bank for Reconstruction and Development, worked on the large-scale privatization plan for almost two years before announcing the plan in June 1991. The plan called for the transfer of 400 state enterprises to private hands within six months and giving a stake to every adult citizen by giving them vouchers for control of group stock funds. But the plan unraveled in the fall of 1991 due to both political and economic objections.

In 1993 the government proposed a new privatization plan, designed to sell off 600 state-owned enterprises by creating investment funds and Western managers to oversee the firms and to sell shares in the funds at low cost to Poland's citizens. This bill too, was defeated in the Sejm, with deputies expressing concern both about foreign control over Polish companies and the likelihood of mass layoffs from the privatized companies. This defeat, on centerpiece legislation, weakened the center-right government, which lost a no confidence motion, leading to parliamentary elections in September 1993 that brought the left back into power. The new government, dominated by successors to the communist party, was not nearly as committed to rapid privatization, and the process slowed to a crawl. By the end of 1994, only a quarter of Poland's 8,000 state-owned enterprises had been privatized.

Four years after the introduction of "shock therapy," the results were a mixed bag, though things seemed to be improving. The country's GNP, which had dropped sharply in 1990 and 1991, grew by almost 3 percent in 1992 and even faster in the next three years, marking Poland as the first postcommunist country to generate economic growth. Industrial production, which had also collapsed in the first years of shock therapy, also increased sharply beginning in 1992. While the government had only limited success with the privatization of large state firms, "privatization from below"—the formation of small private companies—boomed, and by the end of 1993 there were some 1.8 million private firms in Poland employing almost 60 percent of the work force. Most of these were small, shoestring operations, but the impact on Polish daily life was substantial. Stores were full of products, often of high quality, and consumers no longer had to wait in lines to buy things. By 1994, the many small shops in Warsaw looked much the same as those in Western Europe.

But not everything was rosy. While consumer inflation *had* been reduced—from almost 2,000 percent in 1989—it still ran at an annual rate of about 30 percent in 1994, much more than expected or planned. Unemployment jumped from 7,000 at the end of 1989 to over 2.8 million four years later—almost 16 percent of the work force. Real wages declined by 32 percent in 1990 and continued to stagnate through 1994, when they were down almost 2 percent from the previous year. A World Bank study released in mid-1994 estimated that about 15 percent of the Polish population was living in poverty. The record was a mixed one, but although the shock was real, the therapy was taking longer than expected.

The Hungarian Model of Evolution

In Hungary, the transition to the market was more measured for two main reasons. First, since the introduction of the New Economic Mechanism (NEM) in 1968, Hungary had made considerable progress in cutting central planning and strengthening the role of the market. Second, the evolutionary nature of *political* change in Hungary in 1988–1989 created an environment less conducive to radical economic reform.

Until the revolutions of 1989, Hungary's New Economic Mechanism had been the most thoroughgoing economic reform effort in the Soviet bloc.[27] The goal of NEM when it was introduced in 1968 was to find an efficient balance of planning and market. On the one hand, by eliminating most mandatory production targets and centralized resource allocation, central planning was sharply restricted. Enterprises were given considerable autonomy in purchasing, production, and sales, and their decisions were to be based primarily on profitability. On the other hand, some of the old constraints were maintained. The NEM did not at first provide for any significant expansion in private economic initiatives, and Hungary continued to be subject to bilateral trade agreements through the Council for Mutual Economic Assistance, or Comecon.

The NEM did produce positive benefits in terms of increased attention to market indicators and improvements in consumer supply. But the in-

Supermarket 1983, 1993. This depiction by the artist Witold Mysyrowicz origi-
nally appeared in the Polish weekly *Nie*. Reprinted by permission.

herent tensions between market and plan led to retreats from NEM during the 1970s. A second round of reforms was begun in the early 1980s,
stimulated by a deteriorating economic situation, a growing external
debt, and pressure from reformers within the party leadership. This time,
people were allowed to set up small private businesses of 2 to 30 employees or "petty cooperatives" with more than 30 people. Several tens of
thousands of new businesses were established, and by the end of the
1980s the private sector's contribution to the economy had doubled, accounting for almost a third of GNP.

Soviet perestroika unleashed an additional intensification of Hungarian economic reform beginning in 1987. The single National Bank was replaced by several competitive banks. New laws allowed for the formation
of joint-stock companies and raised the ceiling on private enterprise employees to 500. In May 1989, Hungary became the first country in Eastern
Europe to privatize a state-run company, and in June 1990 it opened the
first stock exchange in the region.

Until 1990, Hungary had proceeded closer toward the market than any other country in the former bloc. Poland's leap to the market in January 1990 quickly propelled Poland past Hungary, however, and led to demands for faster change within Hungary. By this time, though, public opinion was in favor of a more evolutionary approach. The transitional policies had pinched the Hungarian economy and had caused economic contraction, unemployment, inflation, the largest external debt in the region, and a decline in the standard of living. By 1990, the average Hungary family spent 85 percent of its income on basic living expenses (rent, food, and transportation).[28] Popular concern over the costs of transition was registered in the parliamentary elections in the spring of 1990. The Alliance of Free Democrats had called for a faster pace of economic reform; the victorious Hungarian Democratic Forum, who were for evolutionary change, campaigned under the slogan of a "compassionate transition."[29] The evolutionary approach was still disruptive, however, and fueled the discontent that led to the leftist election victory in 1994.

The Russian Dilemma

The efforts of the Soviet Union and its successor states to move toward a market economy were even more complicated than those of Central Europe for a number of reasons: the lack of *any* modern experience with capitalism; a more established and deep-seated system of central planning and control; popular wariness of the market and its concomitant inequality and unemployment; and the fragmentation and collapse of the Union of Soviet Socialist Republics. These many obstacles did not deter the Gorbachev leadership from pursuing increasingly radical economic reform. Nevertheless, by 1990 there had been few structural changes in the Soviet economy, and the former communist states in East-Central Europe were leapfrogging the Soviet Union toward the market.

The Soviet situation was further complicated by the escalating demands for autonomy by the fifteen constituent republics of the Soviet Union, virtually all of which had declared independence by the summer of 1990. Many local and republican governments had already approved privatization laws far more liberal than the national one. Furthermore, there were disputes between Moscow and some of the republics about who actually owned certain state enterprises and therefore disagreements as to who would be entitled to the proceeds from sales.

It was this prospect of economic and political fragmentation that sparked the conservative coup attempt against Mikhail Gorbachev in August 1991. This attempt occurred on the eve of a meeting at which Gorbachev and the republican leaders would sign a new "union treaty," which would have provided substantially greater political autonomy and economic control for the republics. The failure of the coup discredited the conservative option, ended the dominance of the CPSU, and led to the final dissolution of the USSR.

The final break from communism and the Soviet system facilitated an accelerated move to market economics in Russia and other CIS states. Yeltsin, convinced that the Russian economy needed Polish-style shock therapy, called on the redoubtable Jeffrey Sachs to design a similar program for Russia. As Poland had done two years earlier, in January 1992 Yeltsin freed prices on most products. In many areas, costs soared tenfold. With an average monthly salary of 40 rubles, for example, most people could not afford to buy sausage at 100 to 200 rubles per kilo (2.2 pounds).

But shock therapy in Russia failed both economically and politically. Many factory managers were slow to adapt to market forces and were resistant to laying off workers. The expected large-scale foreign assistance did not materialize. And the Yeltsin government was faced with increasingly hard-line resistance to rapid economic transition, both from the parliament and from the regions constituting the Russian Federation, many of which cut back their tax contributions to Moscow. These tensions culminated in the violent confrontation between Yeltsin and the parliament in the fall of 1993. In the parliamentary elections that followed in December, the reformist parties did badly, signaling the voters' rejection of radical reform.[30] The new prime minister, Viktor Chernomyrdin, abandoned shock therapy for a more gradual approach to economic reform. Even so, the economy continued to slide: In 1995 prices rose by 131 percent; GDP declined by 4 percent; real incomes dropped 8 percent; and the number of unemployed increased by 40 percent. In the December 1995 parliamentary elections, the voters once again showed their discontent: The biggest vote-getters were the Communist Party and the antireform Liberal Democratic Party of Vladimir Zhirinovski.

The problems in Russia affected, in varying degrees, all of the former Soviet republics. Even in tiny Estonia, which had been one of the wealthiest republics in the Soviet Union, independence simply led to a worsening of the economy. As the Estonian minister of economics put it in January 1992, "We lived on cheap oil and cheaper grain [in the Soviet Union]; now we have no oil, no money, no meat, no medicine and no cash. The question is what to do next."[31]

The Social Justice Issue: Capitalism with a Human Face?

In remnants of the Soviet Union especially, but in East-Central Europe as well, the difficulties of economic reform were compounded by some lingering popular distrust of capitalism and its drawbacks. There was much popular concern throughout the region about the possibilities of unemployment and inflation; both had been nonexistent (or at least negligible)

Freedom versus sausage. *Source:* V. Anokhin in *Komsomolskaya Pravda* (Moscow), March 20, 1991. Reprinted by permission.

in the communist era. There was also a strong strand of egalitarianism in these countries, which was often manifested in considerable distrust of the entrepreneurial spirit. This distrust was due in part to the semisuccessful propaganda that led many citizens to accept the key official values and beliefs of their regimes, but it was also a result of the real success of the communist governments in raising the standard of living and assuring most citizens a basic level of security, at least until the 1970s. From the point of view of many citizens of the Soviet Union, and even citizens of the postcommunist states, capitalism may produce wealth, but it also requires hard work, brings uncertainty and insecurity, and fosters inequality. Such perceptions pose a great obstacle to reformers' efforts to move the economy toward competition, market pricing, and greater economic and social differentiation.[32]

Public opinion surveys revealed that this distrust of capitalism (and even support for socialism) was harbored by a significant minority of the population in every country, and perhaps even a majority in the former Soviet Union. In Poland, for example, where antipathy toward communism was stronger than anywhere else in the Soviet bloc, surveys throughout the 1980s showed continuing support for both socialism and egalitarianism. Even in the summer of 1989, after the Solidarity electoral victory, surveys showed real popular ambivalence about the free enterprise system. Though people overwhelmingly supported "full freedom for the private sector" and accepted highly differentiated (unequal) incomes, they even more strongly favored government intervention to ensure jobs for everyone (90 percent support), to control prices (88 percent), and to control wages (73 percent).[33] Attitudes toward privatization also remained ambivalent through mid-1991: Whereas only 9 percent thought that privatization would *not* be beneficial for the Polish economy, less than half (42 percent) thought that it *would* be.[34] This was less than a ringing endorsement for a key element of the reforms. Public opinion from other countries in the region showed similar patterns: People basically supported the *idea* of the free enterprise system but resisted many of the policies and consequences of that system.

These same concerns about the free enterprise system were raised from a very different quarter with Pope John Paul II's 1991 encyclical "Centseimus Annus" (the hundredth year). The pope, a Pole and a strong supporter of the Solidarity movement during the 1980s, addressed some of the economic issues raised by the revolutions of 1989 and by Eastern Europe's transition to the market. The pope's support for the free market, like that of public opinion, was measured. The free market, he said, was "the most efficient instrument for utilizing resources and effectively responding to needs." But, at the same time, "There are many human needs which find no place on the market." He also raised concerns about private enterprise and the role of profit: "In fact, the purpose of a business firm is not simply to make a profit, but is to be found in its very existence as a community of persons who in various ways are endeavoring to satisfy their basic needs, and who form a particular group at the service of the whole of society. Profit is a regulator of the life of a business, but it is not the only one; other human and moral factors must also be considered." The pope also expressed concern about consumerism, "destructive competitiveness," and alienation in Western capitalist societies. Asking whether the Eastern Europeans should pursue a market economy in the aftermath of communism, he said, "The answer is obviously complex."[35] The economic, social, and political complexity of the economic transition was matched by the moral complexity.

A Report Card on the First Phase of the Transition

By 1994, five years after the revolutions in East-Central Europe, the record of the economic transition was mixed and varied widely across countries.

In almost all of the postcommunist states the new governments had managed to dismantle most of the old system of central economic planning, set free prices, introduce the market forces of supply and demand, and create currencies of real value (though not all of them were fully convertible with Western ones). The hyperinflation of the early years of the transition was generally brought under control. "Small-scale" privatization occurred everywhere, allowing the emergence of private shops and restaurants that vastly expanded the availability and variety of consumer goods and services. Large-scale privatization (i.e., of industry) proceeded more slowly but steadily. Increasingly large proportions (e.g., 40 percent in Russia by mid-1994) of the work force were employed in the private sectors of the economy. The countries were increasingly looking like typical Western consumer societies.

The good news was often overwhelmed by the bad, however. In every country in Eastern Europe and the former Soviet Union, industrial production and GNP declined sharply through 1993 and beyond (see Table 4.4). Only in Poland and Hungary did industrial production begin to recover (in 1992 and 1993, respectively), but in almost all countries the levels of industrial output in 1994 were still well below those of 1990. Layoffs and bankruptcies in industry led to spiraling unemployment in countries that had not experienced this phenomenon under communism and toward double-digit levels in most of them. Inflation rates, while reduced from earlier years in some countries, remained high everywhere, eroding real wages and purchasing power, especially for elderly people on pensions.

Although consumer goods were more widely available, many people could not afford them, and though some people benefited from the new capitalism, in almost all of the postcommunist states the vast majority of the populations told pollsters that they were worse off economically than they had been in the communist era.[36] Increasingly large portions of the populations were falling into absolute poverty. In Poland, for example, the percentage of the population living in poverty jumped from 25 percent in 1989 to 44 percent in 1992—almost half of the population—and those in "extreme poverty" from 6 percent to 15 percent of the population. These figures were typical for other countries in the region. A 1994 UNICEF study of the region found that the economic changes had "provoked a deterioration of unparalleled proportions in human welfare" and a "health crisis" marked by rising incidences of infectious diseases, stress, malnutrition, and alcoholism.[37]

The costs of the transition were high in all of the postcommunist states, but some were hit much harder than others. Generally, the East Europeans fared better than the successor states of the Soviet Union, though within each grouping there were dramatic differences. As is apparent from Table 4.4, the Czech Republic had the smoothest sailing, with rela-

TABLE 4.4   The economics of the transition

	Industrial production (annual rates of change) (%)			Unemployment rates (%)			Inflation rate of consumer prices (%)			Private sector share of GDP (%)
	1992	1993	1994	1990	1992	1994	1990	1992	1994	1994
Bulgaria	−16	−7	4		13.2	16.3[a]	50	79.4	122	40
Czech	−14	−5	2	1.2	3.1	3.3	14	11.1	10.0	65
Hungary	−9	4	10	2.0	10.7	11.3	29	23.2	18.9	55
Latvia	−35	−38	−9		1.1	6.3	10	951	35.9	55
Poland	4	6	12	7.0	12.9	16.4	800	45.3	33.2	55
Romania	−22	−4	3		6.2	11.0	20	210.4	136.8	35
Russia	−18	−14	−21		0.4	1.7	10	2509	215.4	50

[a]Figure is for 1993

Sources: Organization for Economic Cooperation and Development, Short-Term Economic Indicators: Transition Economies 2/1995 (Paris: 1995) and 1/1996 (Paris: 1996); World Bank, Transition: The Newsletter About Reforming Economies 6 (April 1995); Ben Slay, "The Polish Economy Six Years After," paper presented at the annual convention of the American Association for the Advancement of Slavic Studies, Washington, D.C., October 1995.

tively low levels of inflation and unemployment. The Czechs had, like Poland and Russia, pursued the path of shock therapy but seemed to have weathered the shock much better than other countries in the region. Because of its relative success with the domestic economy, the Czech Republic was relatively successful in attracting foreign aid and investments and seemed to have the best chance at early entry into the European Union and perhaps even NATO. All of this contributed to the country's political stability and inoculated the republic from the electoral "left turn" that affected so many other countries.

On the opposite end of the spectrum were many of the successor states of the former Soviet Union. The most visible though by no means the worst difficulties were in the big countries of Ukraine and Russia. In both of these, the economies contracted sharply and steadily through 1995, by which time economic output in both countries was only about half the level of 1989. Economists estimated that the transition from central planning to the market did more damage to Russia than the Great Depression had done to the industrial West.[38] In Russia, prices rose tenfold in 1993, fourfold in 1994, and by 130 percent in 1995. In mid-1995, the real rate of unemployment (as opposed to *registered* unemployed) was 13–17 percent and was expected to rise to 20 percent. A committee report from the Duma (the legislature) reported that 10 percent of all Russians did not have enough to eat and that 30 percent lived in poverty[39]. These economic problems were compounded by (or perhaps contributed to) dramatic declines in health and health care and sharp increases in alcoholism, drug abuse, and crime, especially violent crime. Organized crime became a dominant factor in the Russian economy, collecting protection money from 80 percent of the country's banks and private enterprises, leading one Western expert to characterize the "Russian mafia" as the "largest, busiest, and possibly meanest collection of organized hoods" in the world.[40] With all of these social and economic problems, it is no wonder that Russia was also experiencing political instability.

THE REEMERGENCE OF NATIONALISM IN EUROPE

Complicating the already difficult processes of political and economic transition was the rising force of nationalism in Eastern Europe and the former Soviet states. As we saw in Chapter 3, nationalism was a major factor in the unification of Germany and the breakup of the Soviet Union, Yugoslavia, and Czechoslovakia. But the impact of nationalism went beyond these dramatic events, affecting every postcommunist state in one way or another, and in the worst cases leading to violence on a scale not seen in Europe since World War II.

Nationalism is difficult to define. Many social scientists and historians have addressed the issue, but there is no consensus definition or interpretation of the phenomenon. Perhaps we should begin by distinguishing a "state," which is defined primarily by territory that has a government, from a "nation," which is "a group of people who feel themselves to be a community bound together by ties of history, culture, and common ancestry."[41] Anthony Smith, in his *Theories of Nationalism,* suggests that "nationalism fuses three ideals: collective self-determination of the people, the expression of national character and individuality, and finally the vertical division of the world into unique nations, each contributing its special genius to the common fund of humanity."[42] There are many forms that these ideals and expressions may take, however, which gives nationalism its amorphous character.

Nationalism often emerges when the nation does not coincide with the boundaries of the state—when many nations (or ethnic groups) inhabit one state (e.g., in Yugoslavia and Bosnia), or when a single national group is divided between two states (e.g., the Germans before unification). The first instance can lead to separatism or civil war; the second to **irredentism**, the claim by one state for territory belonging to another. Often, the darker side of nationalism is manipulated by political leaders striving to win support or to deflect popular attention from economic or other problems. This was the case, for example, with President Milosevic in Serbia, stirring up nationalism and chauvinism among Serbs within Serbia but also in Croatia and Bosnia after those republics declared independence from Yugoslavia.

In the nineteenth century, nationalism was a powerful force in Europe in shaping the nation-states and the cultures of the continent. The nation became a focus of identity and unity that helped monarchs to forge national states by breaking the power of feudal lords and that later helped nations to break away from multinational empires. With the first unification of Germany and Italy, most of the western half of Europe was formed into nation-states by the end of the nineteenth century. By that time, nationalism had also become a driving force in the eastern part of the continent. Poles, Czechs, Magyars, Serbs, and others struggled to achieve national recognition and carve out national states from the empires that dominated the region: the Russian, the Austro-Hungarian, and the Ottoman. In this national movement, writers and intellectuals played a major role by developing national cultures (through literature, art, and music), by reinforcing national languages, and by helping to create a sense of national history, community, and identity.

World War I brought an end to the European empires and initiated the creation of a host of new or revived nation-states in Central Europe. "National self-determination" was one of the principle postwar goals of U.S.

President Woodrow Wilson (one of his Fourteen Points) and of most of the Allied leaders at the postwar conferences that established the new world order and a new map of Europe. Despite the proclamations and good intentions, however, most of the new Eastern European borders did not coincide very well with national divisions, and most of the new states contained large ethnic minorities. The positive side of nationalism, which had helped create the new states, was now replaced by its negative aspects: ethnic chauvinism, xenophobia, anti-Semitism, fascism, and irredentism. This divisiveness made Eastern Europe easy prey for Hitler and his "national" socialism during World War II. All of the states in the region were either occupied by Nazi Germany or fascist Italy or were allied with them.

After World War II, nationalism seemed to have retreated from the European stage. The United Nations was founded in 1945 on a new spirit of "universalism" that seemed to bridge even ideological divides. Hundreds of new intergovernmental organizations (IGOs) emerged to link countries together in common efforts to eliminate disease, regulate trade, enhance academic cooperation, and so forth. The rapid expansion of international trade in the postwar period also fostered ties and interdependence among nations. In Western Europe, the early successes of economic cooperation and integration through the European Coal and Steel Community (ECSC) and the European Economic Community (EEC, later evolving into the European Community and then the European Union) led to hopes of *political* integration and even of the creation of a "United States of Europe."

Many of these forces operated on Eastern Europe as well, but there were additional constraints on nationalism imposed on those countries by the Soviet Union and the communist ideology. The governing principle of interstate relations in the bloc was "socialist internationalism," which required individual states (at least those in Eastern Europe) to subordinate national interests to international socialist ones. It was this principle that was invoked by the Soviet Union to justify intervention in Czechoslovakia in 1968—the famous Brezhnev Doctrine. Thus, during the communist era in Eastern Europe, states were enjoined from making national or territorial claims on other "fraternal socialist" states, and reports of ethnic tension *within* these countries were prohibited by the censors. Furthermore, any criticism of other socialist states in good standing, and especially of the Soviet Union, was ruled out. So although there may have been ethnic and national tensions in the region, they were largely hidden and repressed.

First with glasnost, then with revolutions, these nationalist passions, deeply imbedded and long repressed, burst out into the open. The constructive side of nationalism, the sense of community, identity, and common purpose, was a major force in driving out the communist governments. For many people in the region, communism was seen as an alien force, brought in on Soviet bayonets. With the departure of the communist governments and Soviet troops and the dissolution of the bloc's alliance system, nationalism turned in other directions and became divisive and destructive. Many intellectuals from the region, particularly those who yearned for the reintegration of the whole of Europe, expressed concern about the revival of nationalism. Adam Michnik, one of the founders of Poland's KOR, defined nationalism as "the articulation of provincialism and particularism, a basis for xenophobia and intolerance." In Michnik's view, "nationalism always leads to egoism and self-deception. To egoism, because it allows one to ignore the injuries suffered by other nations and disregard other peoples' values and ways of seeing. To self-deception, because by focusing on one's own injuries, nursing the memory of those injuries, nationalism allows one to ignore the injuries one has also inflicted."[43]

This negative nationalism took many forms, but affected every country in the region. The problem was the worst in the multinational states of the USSR and Yugoslavia, where ethnic tensions and separatism caused national disintegration, violence, and civil war. In Czechoslovakia, there was a revival of the old tensions between Czechs and Slovaks. In Bulgaria, the large Turkish minority came under increased pressure from the government, and in Romania the Hungarian minority was increasingly an issue for both governments. Even in Poland, the most ethnically homogeneous country in the region, there was a revival of anti-Semitism and a lingering spirit of Russophobia.

Fragmentation and Nationalism in the Former Soviet Union

Along with the liberalization of perestroika and glasnost, the Soviet Union was plagued by nationalism, separatism, and fragmentation both before and after the collapse of the state. These problems were perhaps inevitable, given the USSR's great size and ethnic heterogeneity. Each of the country's fifteen constituent republics represented a different nationality, and the Russian republic alone contained over 100 nationalities (see Figure 4.4). Most of these people were brought into the Russian Empire over centuries of territorial expansion and were then prohibited from leaving the newly created communist state that replaced the empire after World War I. The Soviet Union was always somewhat of an anomaly in the post–World War II era as the last remaining multinational empire. The nationalism that swept the Third World in this period was dampened in the Soviet Union by the strong central controls and by the homogenizing efforts of the Communist Party of the Soviet Union.

Ethnic Composition of Former Soviet Republics

Each of the constituent republics was named for the predominant ethnic group. Charts show the size of the majority (white), proportion of ethnic Russians (black) and other significant minorities (shaded).

1 Ukraine
73%
21% Russian
1% Jewish
5% Other

6 Russia
84%
4% Ukrainian
12% Other

11 Uzbekistan
69%
11% Russian
4% Tajiks
16% Other

2 Belarus
80%
12% Russian
4% Polish
4% Other

7 Moldova
64%
13% Russian
14% Ukrainian
9% Other

12 Kazakhstan
40%
40% Russian
6% Ukrainian
14% Other

RUSSIA
MONGOLIA
CHINA

3 Estonia
66%
28% Russian
3% Ukrainian
4% Other

8 Georgia
69%
8% Russian
9% Armenian
14% Other

13 Tajikistan
58%
11% Russian
23% Uzbek
7% Other

4 Latvia
49%
38% Russian
5% Belorussian
8% Other

9 Turkmenistan
69%
13% Russian
9% Uzbek
9% Other

14 Armenia
90%
3% Russian
6% Azeris
1% Other

5 Lithuania
80%
9% Russian
8% Polish
3% Other

10 Azerbaijan
78%
8% Russian
8% Armenian
6% Other

15 Kyrgyzstan
48%
26% Russian
12% Uzbek
14% Other

Note numbers may not equal one hundred due to rounding

AP/T Dean Caple

FIGURE 4.4   Ethnic composition of the former Soviet republics. (*Source:* Updated from Wide World Photos. Reprinted with permission.)

As these controls were weakened in the Gorbachev era, nationalism flourished in each of the fifteen republics and in many of the smaller national groups as well. The 1989 revolutions in Eastern Europe intensified nationalism in the Soviet Union, leading all fifteen republican parliaments to declare sovereignty or independence by the end of 1990 and subsequently to the disintegration of the USSR.

The nationalities problem was a multilayered one: There were disputes not just between Moscow and the breakaway republics but within republics as well. This was particularly the case within the Russian republic, which in the Soviet era contained sixteen Autonomous Soviet Socialist Republics (ASSRs), five Autonomous Regions, and ten National Areas, each based on a different non-Russian national minority. So while the Russian republic was attempting to extract some measure of independence from the USSR, legislatures in the Karelian, Tatar, and Yakutian ASSRs and in the Komi National Area were declaring independence from the Russian Republic, which, in turn, rejected those declarations. Other republics had similar problems. After the Moldavian Soviet Socialist Republic (SSR) declared independence in June 1990 and renamed itself Moldova, the Russian minority in the region attempted to form an independent Russian Dnester Republic and the Turkic minorities to create a Gagauzi Republic. Both efforts were rebuffed by the Moldovan government, whose crackdown on the two regions led to bloodshed and tensions that continued through 1995.

Indeed, the scale of violence among non-Russian nationalities was far greater than Moscow's anti-independence crackdowns. The worst violence took place in the Caucasus, where Armenians and Azeris clashed over the Autonomous Region of Nagorno-Karabakh, which belonged to the Azerbaijan SSR but whose population was 75 percent Armenian. Armed clashes and pogroms killed thousands of people. In Georgia, the elected president, Zviad Gamsakhurdia, exploited nationalist and religious intolerance to persecute the republic's Muslim minorities. When the South Ossetian Autonomous Region declared independence from Georgia in early 1991, the violent Georgian crackdown on the region resulted in fifty deaths and hundreds of wounded. Over 80,000 Ossetians fled to the North Ossetian Autonomous Republic within the Russian Federation. Altogether, ethnic conflict in the USSR had by mid-1991 produced some 700,000 internal refugees.[44]

Many of these nationalities problems persisted, and new ones emerged, after the collapse of the Soviet Union, both within and between the new post-Soviet states. Some people have called this phenomenon "matryoshka nationalism," referring to the traditional Russian painted nested dolls: As you open the largest doll, you find another inside, and then another inside that, and so on as the dolls get smaller and smaller. The nationalities problem in the former Soviet Union has been variegated and complex, ranging from restrictive citizenship laws directed against Russians living in the Baltic states (especially Estonia), to an ethnically and religiously based civil war in Tajikistan. (See the Suggested Readings for this chapter.)

For Russia, the most protracted, violent, and disruptive national conflict involved Chechnya, a mostly Muslim region on the northern slopes of the Caucasus mountains in southern Russia. Chechnya, like Tatarstan, declared independence from Russia in 1991 and refused to sign the Federation Treaty that united the various components of the Russian Federation following the collapse of the Soviet Union in December 1991. When the president of Chechnya, Dzhokhar Dudayev, first declared independence in 1991, Russia sent troops, but Chechen fighters blocked the airport at Grozny, the capital, and the Russians had to retreat. In December 1994 the Russian military and security services launched a major assault on the region in an effort "to restore constitutional order." The Chechens again resisted, leading to a bloody conflict that by mid-1995 had caused some 40,000 deaths, over 100,000 refugees, and the virtual destruction of Grozny.

In June 1995 a group of Chechen fighters took the war into Russian territory, occupying a hospital in the southern Russian city of Budennovsk, taking and killing some hostages, and resisting an attack by Russian security forces. The crisis was resolved when the Russian government agreed to a safe escort for the Chechens back to Chechnya and to resume negotiations with the Dudayev government over the status of the region. The Russian public was so horrified by the whole incident that the legislature voted no confidence in the Yeltsin government, almost bringing it down.

For Russia, Chechnya was important strategically, due to its location and rich oil deposits, but even more important symbolically. If Chechnya succeeded in becoming an independent state, so might Tatarstan, or Yakutia, or Bashkortostan, three of Russia's twenty-one ethnic republics, threatening the unraveling of the Russian Federation, or at least the control of the regions by Moscow.

Nationalism Elsewhere in the Region

Of the many nationalities problems in the area, those in the former Soviet Union and Yugoslavia were the most dramatic and acute. Nevertheless, nationalism was on the rise all over the region, and it took different forms in different countries (see Table 4.5).

In Bulgaria, the country's largest ethnic minority, Muslim Turks, faced a rising tide of popular nationalism. During the communist era, the regime had tried to force assimilation on the Turks by prohibiting Turkish-

"My sovereign hut—my castle." *Source: Argumenty I Fakty* (Moscow), no. 34, August 1991, p. 1. Reprinted by permission.

TABLE 4.5   Nationalities in East-Central Europe (total population in 1994 and nationalities as a percentage of total)

Albania (3.4 million)		Hungary (10.3 million)	
Albanian	95.0	Hungarian	89.9
Greek	3.0	Gypsy	4.0
		German	2.6
Bosnia-Herzegovina (4.7 million)		Serb	2.0
Muslim	44.0	Slovak	0.8
Serb	31.0	Romanian	0.7
Croat	17.0		
Other	8.0	Poland (38.7 million)	
		Polish	97.6
Bulgaria (8.8 million)		German	1.3
Bulgarian	85.3	Ukrainian	0.6
Turkish	8.5	Belarussian	0.5
Gypsy	2.6		
Macedonian	2.5	Romania (23.2 million)	
		Romanian	89.1
Croatia (4.7 million)		Hungarian	8.9
Croat	78.0	German	0.4
Serb	12.0		
Muslim	0.9	Slovakia (5.4 million)	
Hungarian	0.5	Slovak	85.6
Slovenian	0.5	Hungarian	10.8
		Gypsy	1.5
Czech Republic (10.4 million)		Czech	1.1
Czech	94.4		
Slovak	3.0	Yugoslavia (Serbia and Montenegro)	
Polish	0.6	(10.8 million)	
		Serb	63.0
		Albanian	14.0
		Montenegrin	6.0
		Hungarian	4.0

Source: Central Intelligence Agency, *The World Factbook 1994* (Washington, D.C., 1994).

language schools, instruction, and media. The postcommunist government reversed these policies, but Bulgarian nationalists opposed that decision and mounted large-scale protests throughout the country. When the government introduced the teaching of Turkish in schools with large Turkish populations, Bulgarian nationalists occupied or picketed schools in some areas. This narrow sense of Bulgarian citizenship was disturbingly widespread; a late 1989 public opinion poll showed almost half the population believing that elective offices in the country should be filled only by people of "pure Bulgarian descent."[45] Some political parties (especially the former communist party) capitalized on this sentiment in electoral campaigns in 1991 and 1992, using anti-Turkish slogans and propaganda.

Another potential explosive issue was the fate of the three million ethnic Hungarians who lived in neighboring countries. Emerging nationalist movements in Romania, Serbia, and Slovakia made them targets of verbal and physical attacks, and some 35,000 sought refuge in Hungary from "ethnic cleansing" by the Serbs in the former Yugoslavia. The Hungarian government's response to these problems was to advocate substantial local autonomy for Hungarians in these other countries, which in turn were alarmed by what they saw as steps by Hungary to restore its former larger borders at their expense.

Perhaps the most disturbing aspect of nationalism was the revival, or the increasing openness, of anti-Semitism in the former Soviet Union and East-Central Europe. In Russia, Gorbachev's glasnost allowed the more open expression of democratic ideas, but also nationalist and anti-Semitic ones. Often nationalism and anti-Semitism were combined, as with the right-wing group "Pamyat" (Memory) and in the pages of a number of conservative, nationalist, and even literary magazines and newspapers. Many Russian nationalists hold Jews responsible for past and present problems. The popular Russian nationalist writer Valentin Rasputin told a U.S. reporter that "Jews here should feel responsible for the sin of having carried out the Revolution, and for the shape that it took [and] for the terror that existed during the Revolution and especially after the Revolution."[46] And the right-wing nationalist politician Vladimir Zhirinovski weaved anti-Semitic remarks into his campaigns.

In Poland, where only 7,000 Jews remain from the prewar population of over 3 million, the revival of Polish national pride was accompanied by often blatant anti-Semitism. Publications of right-wing groups and parties accused "the left Jewish intelligentsia" of "having led Poland into the war with Hitler."[47] Others identified the Jews with the communists, blaming Poland's past problems on both. During the local election campaign in Warsaw in May 1990, someone had plastered posters around the university with a crude caricature of a Jew saying: "A vote for [one of the political parties] is a vote for me."

Romania experienced similar phenomena. In April 1991, the editor of the country's largest weekly publication, *Romania Mare*, wrote that he had nothing against Jews as long as they "leave this country alone" and he complained that Parliament and the government were "full of Jews." Later that month, the Romanian Parliament rose in a minute of silent tribute to Marshall Ion Antonescu, the wartime dictator of Romania who had ordered pogroms and deportations to death camps that claimed the lives of a quarter million Jews and who was later executed as a war criminal. No one opposed the parliamentary motion honoring Antonescu.[48]

Nationalism, Democracy, and Economic Reform

Nationalism, more than any other phenomenon in East-Central Europe, had the potential to disrupt both democratization and economic liberalization. As we have seen, nationalism was a positive force in helping the Eastern European states emerge from the shadow of the Soviet Union. But extreme nationalism can also erode the tolerance and compromise necessary for democracy to work. This is particularly a problem in new states, as Robert Dahl has pointed out, where "nationalism does not so much encourage toleration of dissent and opposition as it provides a ready and acceptable justification for intolerance and repression."[49] These problems are all the more likely in East-Central Europe as these new states struggle with the burdens of economic transition. Such an environment often stimulates the search for scapegoats. In the national patchwork of the region there are always ethnic minorities to pick on.

The dangerous combination of minorities and nationalism posed a special dilemma for the changing governments of the region. The central governments had to be loose enough to allow the free expression of ideas, including nationalist ones, but also strong enough to protect minorities. This was part of the genius of the U.S. constitutional system with its division of authority between federal government and states, and a strong federal judiciary capable of protecting civil rights. But the U.S. Constitution was written for a new country that was relatively homogeneous ethnically and linguistically. The former Soviet Union and the states of East-Central Europe may require a different type of arrangement—thus the frequent discussion in the waning days of the Soviet Union, Yugoslavia, and Czechoslovakia of the possibility of a *con*federal system. (Indeed, the new Commonwealth of Independent States looked very much like a confederal arrangement.) In such a system, almost all government powers are held by the states (or republics), leaving the central government with minimal authority in defense, foreign affairs, foreign trade, and so forth. The problem with this solution is that it deprives the central governments of the very tools they need for managing the drastic economic changes from communism to capitalism.

Nationalism and separatism in East-Central Europe was also working against the contrary tendency of globalization and integration in the rest of Europe. As Harvard political theorist Michael Sandel put it:

The challenge confronted by the multinational states of Eastern Europe and the Soviet Union is that they are at once too large and too small. If Slovenia or Azerbaijan want to break off, they are too small to compete economically in a global economy. After all, even France and Germany prefer to be members of a larger economic unit, the European Community. But Yugoslavia and the Soviet Union are also too large to give full expression to the national identities of their constituent communities. So economics is pulling them toward bigger units and culture is pulling them toward smaller units.[50]

Many intellectuals in East-Central Europe were also concerned about the corrosive effects of nationalism and the problems it posed for reintegrating the East into Central Europe. Adam Michnik put the dilemma this way: "One road leads to border wars, the other to minimizing borders, reducing them to little more than road signs; one road leads to new barbed-wire fences, the other to a new order based on pluralism and tolerance; one road leads to nationalism and isolation, the other to a return to our 'native Europe.'"[51]

CONCLUSION

The aftermath of the 1989 revolutions showed mixed results. The task of rebuilding the political and economic orders was not nearly as exhilarating or satisfying as the overthrow of the old communist order. The opening up of the political system revealed tensions and conflicts that had been papered over in the more centralized and closed communist system. And the transformation from central plan to market in the economy turned out to be more complicated and disruptive than most people expected. The changes in East-Central Europe also had consequences that went far beyond their national borders, especially affecting East-West relations and the international alliance system.

In the political sphere, the countries in the region experienced reasonable success, with all of them holding free (or mostly free) elections and reconstituting their legislatures and with the gradual emergence of competitive political parties and a free press. By 1991 the wave of democratization had spread even to tiny, isolated Albania and to the center of the communist world, the Soviet Union. But the process in the region was not without problems. The unleashing of interest groups and political parties brought out tensions and conflicts that had not been so apparent before. The broad-based opposition movements that had created such solidarity in confronting the communists now had to deal with the multitude of interests and orientations within the opposition. Under the old system of one-party rule and democratic centralism, the spirit of tolerance and compromise had languished; these characteristics were now much needed.

The biggest of such problems was nationalism, which had so tormented the region in the past but which had been largely suppressed under the communist ideology of "internationalism." National fears and animosities had plunged Yugoslavia into civil war and had fractured the Soviet Union. Anti-Semitism revived, as did old animosities between Croats and Serbs, Romanians and Hungarians, and Russians and Ukrainians, Estonians, Tatars, and others, causing political instability and even violence. Even in Germany, there were tensions between easterners and westerners and a revival of Nazism.

In the economic sphere, the problems were even more daunting. In terms of democratization, at least, it was fairly clear what a country needed to do to move from authoritarianism to pluralism. In economics, there were no precedents for a transition from a state-owned, centrally planned economy to a market system based on private property. Furthermore, the reorientation of an economic system affects almost everyone in the society in a direct way. At the macro level, economists considered it necessary to end government subsidies, free prices, and open the domestic market to world prices and competition. At the micro level, however, this often meant that firms went bankrupt, employees were laid off, and household incomes declined. No matter what policies the government pursued, there would be a difficult transition between the old system and the new. It was hoped that a quick transition would minimize the pain and that when the market began to take over, employment, production, and incomes would be revived. The problem was with the short term, and nobody knew how long this would last. In 1991, the World Bank estimated it would take five to ten years for the Central European countries to recover from the contractions of 1989–1991 and decades for them to reach the per capita income levels of the industrial countries.[52]

It was an open question whether the fragile democracies could survive belt-tightening for that long. All governments are to some extent dependent on the economy for popular support. In the communist era this was particularly the case, as in the communist governments' last decades economic stability and growth were about their only source of legitimacy. The populations came to expect governments to deliver the goods. So the tendency of citizens to identify the government with the economy was probably stronger in the postcommunist states than in most democracies. If the economic transition was too long and too painful, the populations were likely to reject their governments. The resulting political uncertainty and instability would make it even more difficult for the governments to make the difficult economic decisions.

The lessons of history were not very favorable for these new governments. There were, however, some mitigating circumstances. For one thing, they could rely on the past experience of other states, especially in terms of models of democracy, and could look to each other for assistance, advice, and common experience. All of them had a similar past and similar goals, so there was much room for cooperation. Even more important, perhaps, was the international environment. The Western democracies expressed their willingness to assist the transition in the Eastern states, if not with the same level of support as the postwar Marshall Plan for Western Europe, at least with loans, trade, and technical assistance. And with the end of the Cold War, there should have been more opportunity and more resources for such cooperation and assistance. This leads to the topic of the next chapter, which addresses the impact of the Eastern European revolutions on the rest of the world and how the international environment is likely to affect East-Central Europe.

FIVE

□ □ □

The Postcommunist Era
in International Politics

The collapse of communism in East-Central Europe not only revolutionized the societies of the region, but also revolutionized international
politics. For four decades the international political environment was
dominated by the Cold War and the conflict between communism and
capitalism. Postwar U.S. foreign policy, throughout the ups and downs of
U.S.-Soviet relations, was dictated by the containment of communism. An
extended arms race between the Soviet Union and the United States led to
the deployment by the superpowers of over 50,000 nuclear weapons,
haunting the world with the specter of nuclear holocaust. Through most of
the postwar period, U.S. military spending consumed about a quarter of
the federal budget and reached $300 billion in the late 1980s. This drained
money away from domestic needs and contributed to annual budget
deficits of hundreds of billions of dollars and an accumulated national
debt of over $3 *trillion*. In the Soviet Union, with a much smaller economy
to begin with, the strain of defense spending was even greater.

With the disappearance of the communist threat, so disappeared the rationale for containment and the basis of the Cold War. The events in East-
Central Europe and the Soviet Union seemed to open up a new chapter in
European history and world politics and to provide an opportunity to move
beyond the tension and conflict of the postwar era. Even before the disappearance of the Soviet Union, Gorbachev spoke of global interdependence
and the settling of disputes by diplomacy rather than arms. In the United
States, there was discussion of an economic "peace dividend" and the possibility of construction of a "new world order." Much of this early euphoria
disappeared with the massive U.S. military intervention in the Persian Gulf
in early 1991 and the growing problems of nationalism and economic decay
in the former Soviet Union and East-Central Europe. Nevertheless, a major
transformation of world politics was under way, affecting Europe, East-
West relations, the Third World, and the global political environment.

REVISING THE ALLIANCE SYSTEMS

The collapse of communism in East-Central Europe also meant the collapse of the network of alliances that had bound the communist countries together, and this led to a rethinking and restructuring of the Western alliances in the region. Part of the process of economic liberalization in East-Central Europe was an effort to integrate the countries into the world economy. This involved a reorientation of trade: away from the protected and artificial environment of the Council for Mutual Economic Assistance (Comecon or CMEA); increased trade with the Western capitalist countries; and efforts by the former communist states to join Western economic institutions.

Council for Mutual Economic Assistance

Comecon had been founded in 1949 by the USSR, Bulgaria, Czechoslovakia, Hungary, Poland, and Romania. Later, it was joined by East Germany, Mongolia, Cuba, and Vietnam. The countries involved in this bloc conducted much of their trade with each other: 40 to 80 percent of each country's foreign trade was within Comecon. Payments in intra-Comecon trade were made by means of an artificial currency, the transferable ruble, which was neither convertible nor genuinely transferable. The transferable ruble, like the national currencies, bore no real relationship to world currencies, so Comecon prices did not reflect world prices or economic realities.

Despite these artificialities, or rather because of them, the Eastern Europe countries substantially benefited from their trade with the Soviet Union. Comecon prices were artificially low for energy sources, including oil, and other raw materials, which were the principal Eastern European imports from the Soviet Union. These low prices for imports were set against relatively high intra-Comecon prices for machinery, plant, and consumer goods, which were the main exports from Eastern Europe to the Soviet Union. The balance constituted an implicit Soviet subsidy of Eastern Europe, which the Soviet Union was willing to bear for a largely *political* reason—to keep the Eastern European countries closely tied to the Soviet Union.[1] In the short run, this arrangement was advantageous for the Eastern European economies. In the long run, however, it insulated them from competitive pressure to produce quality goods and discouraged adaptation and reform.

The purpose of Comecon disappeared with the revolutions in East-Central Europe. The postcommunist states no longer *wanted* to be tied to the Soviet Union, which, in turn, was no longer inclined to press the issue. Furthermore, the new governments' reorientations toward the domestic and international markets led to a sharp decline in intrabloc trade, by some 30 percent in 1990. In 1991, there was an even sharper decline in trade between Eastern Europe and the Soviet Union due to the latter's accelerating economic and political collapse and to Moscow's decision, effective January 1, 1991, to convert all foreign trading (including Comecon) to world market pricing and hard currency payments.

This decision was a major blow to the economies of the smaller Eastern European countries, which now lost both the implicit Soviet subsidy and, increasingly, the Soviet market. It was also the death knell for Comecon, which was formally dissolved in 1991.

The Warsaw Treaty Organization

If economic liberalization in East-Central Europe killed Comecon, political liberalization doomed the WTO (or the Warsaw Pact). The Warsaw Pact was formed in 1955 as a response to West Germany's entry into NATO that year, and it comprised the Soviet Union, Poland, East Germany, Czechoslovakia, Hungary, Romania, and Bulgaria. Albania withdrew from the pact in 1961. Like NATO, the Warsaw Pact facilitated command and control of the militaries in the alliance, but the pact was more centralized, more dominated by the superpower, and more standardized in terms of military formations and equipment than was the Western alliance. The pact also provided legal justification for the stationing of Soviet troops in Eastern Europe and for the occasional Soviet interventions in the region. Soviet intervention in Czechoslovakia in 1968, for example, was formally a collective action by the Warsaw Pact.

At the time of the Eastern European revolutions, the Soviets had about 565,000 troops in Eastern Europe. The bulk of these (380,000) were stationed in East Germany, with smaller numbers in Poland, Czechoslovakia, and Hungary, the main buffer states against NATO. With the formation of noncommunist governments in each of these countries (and Germany's unification), these troops became increasingly anachronistic, so each of the new governments began to negotiate with the Kremlin for their withdrawal. The last Soviet troops were pulled out of Hungary and Czechoslovakia in June 1991 and from Poland in September 1993. As discussed in Chapter 3, the September 1990 treaty on the final settlement of Germany allowed Moscow to keep troops in the eastern part of Germany until 1994.

Like Comecon, the Warsaw Pact became increasingly irrelevant as the postcommunist governments realigned their foreign and military policies and as Soviet troops withdrew from the region. Furthermore, the East German armed forces, which had been the largest non-Soviet contingent of the pact, were taken out of the pact and absorbed by the Bundeswehr (the Germany army) after unification. In January 1991, the foreign ministers of Poland, Hungary, and Czechoslovakia issued a joint statement in Budapest demanding the phasing out of the Warsaw Pact by March 1992. Bulgaria and Romania subsequently aligned themselves with this position. As on so many other issues, the Gorbachev leadership conceded the point. At the organization's last meeting in Prague in July 1991, the Warsaw Pact was formally dissolved. Czechoslovakia's President Vaclav Havel noted the symbolism of ending the Pact in his country, which was "once the victim of the Warsaw Pact."[2]

THE RESTRUCTURING OF EUROPE

In November 1990, the leaders of thirty-four European and North American states met in Paris to declare the end of the Cold War and to launch a new era of cooperation in Europe. Meeting under the auspices of the **Conference on Security and Cooperation in Europe (CSCE)**, the participants signed a "Charter for a New Europe," which committed the signatories to the principles of free elections, free markets, respect for human rights, and the rule of law. The parties agreed to refrain from the threat or use of force. The charter also established the first CSCE organizations, with a small permanent CSCE secretariat in Prague, a Conflict Prevention Center in Vienna, and an organization in Warsaw to observe and monitor free elections. To reflect this more institutional nature, in 1995 the CSCE was renamed the **Organization for Security and Cooperation in Europe (OSCE).**

Immediately before the CSCE conference, the sixteen member nations of NATO and the six Warsaw Pact nations signed a far-reaching disarmament agreement, the Treaty on Conventional Forces in Europe (CFE) that sharply limited the number of tanks, artillery pieces, armored vehicles, and aircraft in a region extending from the Atlantic Ocean to the Ural Mountains in the Soviet Union. The treaty established a comprehensive verification system and provided detailed procedures for the destruction of military equipment. Although the Soviet Union remained the single largest military power in Europe, the CFE treaty effectively eliminated its ability to mount a surprise attack on Western Europe. This treaty was the last important activity of the Warsaw Pact, which was formally dissolved the following year.

The disintegration of the Warsaw Pact and the subsequent collapse of the Soviet Union itself created an oddly unbalanced security system in Europe. NATO had been created in 1949 to counter the threat of a Soviet attack on Europe. This possibility had now disappeared. These changes in the East, then, occasioned discussion in the West about new security arrangements and perhaps new roles for existing ones such as NATO and

CSCE. Many participants at the Paris summit envisioned a greatly expanded role for the CSCE process. The CSCE had the advantage of comprehensiveness, in that it included virtually every state in Europe, plus the United States and Canada. Many of the new democracies in East-Central Europe saw CSCE as their entrée into Europe and favored strengthening the security dimensions of the CSCE process. They and some of the smaller European states saw in CSCE a way to achieve a more pluralistic Europe and to reduce the domination of the superpowers. CSCE had drawbacks, however. Until the Paris summit it was a *process*, not an institution, and it had no permanent institutional structure. It emerged out of the Helsinki summit in 1975 and was meant mostly to convene periodically to monitor compliance with the accords that were signed in Helsinki. Most of the conference discussions had been devoted to human rights issues; it was not a collective security organization. In fact, this was one of the reasons why CSCE was so popular with the new Eastern European democracies. Many of their new leaders had benefited earlier from the CSCE spotlight on human rights in Eastern Europe.

But the role of the CSCE continued to be redefined and debated. At the 1992 Helsinki summit meeting of the fifty-three-member CSCE, the group agreed to take a more active role in managing and preventing crises in Europe. Subsequently, it helped to coordinate the enforcement of United Nations sanctions against Yugoslavia and sent small missions to try to ease tensions in Ukraine, the Baltic republics, Tajikistan, Georgia, Moldova, and the former Yugoslav republic of Macedonia. In 1994 the conference recommended sending a 3,000-member multinational peacekeeping force to Nagorno-Karabakh (the Armenian enclave within Azerbaijan), though this idea was opposed by the Russians, who wanted a dominant role for their own forces in such an operation. Nevertheless, Moscow continued to press for an expanded security role for OSCE, while Washington remained concerned about OSCE's overshadowing NATO.

NATO

With the dismantling of the Warsaw Pact and the withdrawal of the last Soviet troops from Czechoslovakia and Hungary, the Soviet Union called for the dissolution of its Western counterpart, NATO. Moscow may have been counting on a short life span for NATO when it finally countenanced NATO membership for a reunified Germany. The United States, however, was committed to retaining NATO. It continued to view NATO as its primary link to Western Europe and the major forum for crisis prevention in Europe. Furthermore, the United States had a predominant role in NATO, which it did not have in the more egalitarian CSCE.

The United States agreed, however, that NATO had to be transformed and made into more of a political than a military instrument. In early 1991 NATO decided on a sweeping reorganization of its forces in Europe that included a reduction by half of the 320,000 U.S. troops in Europe. The new NATO force structure was to be based on smaller, more mobile units that could respond quickly to small-scale crises on the continent. This was based on the assumption that a direct frontal attack on NATO from the East was unlikely but that instability in the Soviet Union and East-Central Europe was a continuing possibility. In a reversal of its Cold War orientation, NATO also threw a protective blanket over its former Warsaw Pact adversaries in Central Europe, declaring that any "coercion or intimidation" aimed at those countries would be considered a matter of "direct and material concern" to the sixteen members of NATO. This declaration, in June 1991, occurred at a time when some of the postcommunist states were expressing concern that instability in the Soviet Union might provoke a return of hard-liners in Moscow, who might, in turn, attempt to reassert control in East-Central Europe.

Some of the East European states, however, wanted an even closer relationship to NATO, and this potential eastward expansion of the organization provided a new rationale for the continued existence of NATO in the post–Cold War era. In early 1994, President Clinton proposed a "**Partnership for Peace**" (**PFP**) to bring the former communist countries (indeed, *all* European states) into closer cooperation with NATO through joint military planning, training exercises, peacekeeping, and crisis management. By April 1995, twenty-six nations had joined the Partnership, including all of the former Warsaw Pact nations and their successor states, excepting only Tajikistan (see Table 5.1).

The formation of the PFP naturally led to questions about potential full membership in NATO for some of the PFP members. After a study of the idea, the United States and NATO agreed to prepare for the enlargement of the alliance with the addition of some of the new eastern democracies on a "case-by-case basis" through a process that would be "gradual, deliberate, and transparent."[3] This policy raised alarms, however, both in Russia and in some of the less developed East European states, and concerns in the United States and Western Europe as well. Many Westerners wondered, for example, whether the United States and NATO were really prepared to go to war to defend countries so deep within the Russian sphere of influence.

Though the Russians signed on to the PFP, they were alarmed by the prospect of NATO, their former adversary, expanding to the very borders of the Russian state. They were also concerned that bringing only some Eastern European countries into NATO (the most likely prospects were Poland, the Czech Republic, Hungary, and possibly Slovakia) would effectively exclude the others from European security decision making.

Criticizing NATO's plans for expansion, President Yeltsin warned that in the aftermath of the Cold War "Europe is in danger of plunging into a cold peace."[4] The Russian government argued that the OSCE, not NATO, should have the overriding responsibility for maintaining peace and stability in Europe.

Differences among the East European states on this issue were apparent in a Washington panel of East European ambassadors sponsored by the Atlantic Council[5] in June 1995. The Czech ambassador, Michael Zantovsky, argued for a "differentiated" approach to NATO membership, knowing that such an approach would favor early NATO entry for countries like his that were well along the path of democratization and capitalism. On the other hand, the Romanian ambassador, Mihai Botez, worried that it would be destabilizing for Romania internally if Hungary, for example, were admitted to NATO before Romania, and that such an event would strengthen the hand of "extremists" in Hungary. His concern reflected the widespread sense in Washington that countries like Romania, Bulgaria, and Albania had little chance of joining NATO early, or ever.

As noted earlier, NATO's transformation included the creation of smaller, more flexible, and more mobile forces. In 1993 and 1994, NATO adopted a new mission that would allow the use of such forces "out of area"—outside the territory of NATO members—though only under a mandate from another organization such as the United Nations or the OSCE. This provision allowed the UN to request NATO assistance during the Bosnian crisis in enforcing sanctions against Serbia, establishing a naval blockade in the Adriatic Sea, and, in 1994 and afterwards, bombing Serbian positions in Bosnia and Croatia in retaliation for Serb attacks on UN and NATO forces. These marked NATO's first combat action in its forty-five-year history and raised a number of questions in the United States about the commitment of U.S. forces to Bosnia, the subordination of U.S. or NATO forces to the United Nations, and the role of NATO in European security.

NATO's role and visibility increased sharply with the Dayton agreement on Bosnia at the end of 1995. That accord (discussed in Chapter 3), which called for a cease-fire and the creation of a confederal Bosnian state, was to be enforced by 60,000 NATO peacekeeping troops led by an American general. The primary mission of this NATO force was to oversee the withdrawal of warring factions from a buffer zone along the cease-fire line. Its secondary missions included removing land mines, providing security for relief agencies, and insuring safe passage for refugees returning home.[6] They were also authorized to defend themselves and respond to threats with "immediate and decisive force"—a mandate that the UN forces did not have. The whole operation was a delicate and dangerous one, and casualties were to be expected. The mission would severely test U.S. commitment both to NATO and to peacemaking in the Balkans.

TABLE 5.1 Membership in European organizations, 1995

Country	NATO	PFP	EU	WEU	OSCE
				Membership in	
Albania		X			X
Armenia		X			X
Austria		X	X		X
Azerbaijan		X			X
Belarus		X			X
Belgium	X		X	X	X
Bulgaria		X			X
Canada	X				X
Czech Republic		X			X
Denmark	X		X	O	X
Estonia		X			X
Finland		X	X		X
France	X		X	X	X
Georgia		X			X
Germany	X		X	X	X
Greece	X		X	X	X
Hungary		X			X
Iceland	X			A	X
Ireland			X	O	X
Italy	X		X	X	X
Kazakhstan		X			X
Kyrgyzstan		X			X
Latvia		X			X
Lithuania		X			X
Luxembourg	X		X	X	X

	NATO	PFP	EU	WEU	OSCE
Macedonia		X			O
Moldova		X			X
Netherlands	X		X	X	X
Norway	X			A	X
Poland		X			X
Portugal	X		X	X	X
Romania		X			X
Russia		X			X
Slovakia		X			X
Slovenia		X			X
Spain	X		X	X	X
Sweden		X	X		X
Tajikistan		X			X
Turkey	X			A	X
Turkmenistan		X			X
Ukraine		X			X
United Kingdom	X		X	X	X
United States	X				X
Uzbekistan		X			X

NATO: North Atlantic Treaty Organization; PFP: Partnership for Peace; EU: European Union; WEU: Western European Union; OSCE: Organization on Security and Cooperation in Europe; O: Observer status; A: Associate members of WEU.

Source: *The Defense Monitor*, 24, no. 2 (Washington, D.C.: Center for Defense Information, 1995).

A United Europe?

The fall of the iron curtain and the unification of Germany raised once again the possibility of a whole Europe integrated and at peace. In the 1960s, French President Charles de Gaulle had raised the idea of a Europe "from the Atlantic to the Urals." Mikhail Gorbachev revived this notion in 1985 with his evocation of a "Common European Home."

From Moscow's point of view, this concept was meant to insure a place for the Soviet Union in the continent. With the increasing affiliation of the East-Central European states with Western Europe and the new power and influence of the unified Germany, the Soviet leadership no doubt feared that the Soviet Union would be isolated or consigned to Asia. The country's desperate need for Western trade, aid, and capital meant that Moscow had to maintain a presence in Europe. All of these concerns carried over into Russia and the other states of the new commonwealth.

The postcommunist states of Europe were also scrambling to affiliate with Western Europe and its multilateral institutions. As discussed in Chapter 1, the development of the idea of "Central Europe" by East European intellectuals was part of an effort to leverage their countries out of the Soviet orbit. Because of their democratic revolutions and the collapse of the Eastern European alliances, there was no longer any *political* barrier, at least, to Eastern Europe becoming part of Europe. The new governments in East-Central Europe, consequently, applied for membership in NATO and the European Community, and they and the commonwealth states requested assistance from the World Bank, the International Monetary Fund, and the new European Bank for Reconstruction and Development, or EBRD. All of them tried to attract Western investments and to reorient trading patterns toward the West.

Assistance from the multilateral financial institutions, however, could be two-edged. The World Bank, the IMF, and the EBRD were all dominated by the Western industrialized nations, and all of them were primarily interested in opening up the new Eastern European states to Western trade and investment. In some cases, as we have seen earlier, this meant wrenching readjustments in these societies. The IMF and the World Bank, for example, sponsored the programs of shock therapy in Poland, Czechoslovakia, and then in Russia. In early 1992, the IMF pressured the Russian government of Boris Yeltsin to raise petroleum prices by ten to fifteen times and to cut government spending. This may have made good sense from an economic perspective, but it also resulted in increased unemployment, a reduction in social programs, and dramatic increases in the prices citizens paid for home heating oil.

Despite the almost universal desire for a "Europe Whole and Free" (President Bush's phrasing), there were substantial obstacles to the near-term fulfillment of this vision. Economically, the economies of East-

Central Europe were well behind those of the West, and the transition from plan to market would set them back even further in the short run. They, therefore, could not expect early admission into the European Community. The political transition would also be slow and disruptive, and there was no guarantee that all of the postcommunist states would emerge as liberal democracies. Even in terms of culture, there were reasons to doubt Central Europe's identity with Western Europe, despite the arguments of Milan Kundera and others (see Chapter 1). Although Eastern Europe did share some historical and cultural experiences with Western Europe, there were also many differences: the stronger role of the state in the East; the weaker development of civil society; the greater social and ethnic divisions; and the more widespread sense of collectivism. Historically and culturally, as a British political scientist has argued, "East European society's participation in the European experience was only partial."[7]

The European Community

The European Community was founded in 1957 as the European Economic Community, consisting of only six member-states. By 1986 it had grown to a membership of twelve states with a total population of 347 million. By 1990, the community's members had a combined GNP of almost $6 trillion, compared to $5.5 trillion for the United States and $3 trillion for Japan. It was a powerful economic bloc and was evolving toward closer economic integration and political alliance. In the mid-1980s, the EC governments had approved an ambitious new plan to create a single, integrated market by the end of 1992 within which there would be free movement of people, goods, services, and capital. With the revolutions of 1989 and the reunification of Germany, many observers expected a slowdown in the move toward "1992," but instead the community seemed to have gained both momentum and stature. The EC's 1992 "Maastricht" Treaty (named after the Dutch city where it was signed) transformed the EC into a **European Union** (EU) committed to full economic and monetary union, including a common currency, by the end of the decade and moved toward a Common Foreign and Security Policy among its members. In January 1995 Austria, Finland, and Sweden joined the EU, bringing its membership to fifteen. (See Map 5.1.)

The EC was well positioned to fill the vacuum left by the decline of the Soviet Union and the diminished U.S. influence in Europe. The community was not fundamentally a Cold War institution, as both NATO and the Western European Union were, and it had generally avoided playing a partisan role in a divided Europe. With the emergence of democracies in East-Central Europe, the EC played a leading role in assisting their economic transitions, coordinating economic assistance to the region, and helping constitute the European Bank for Reconstruction and Develop-

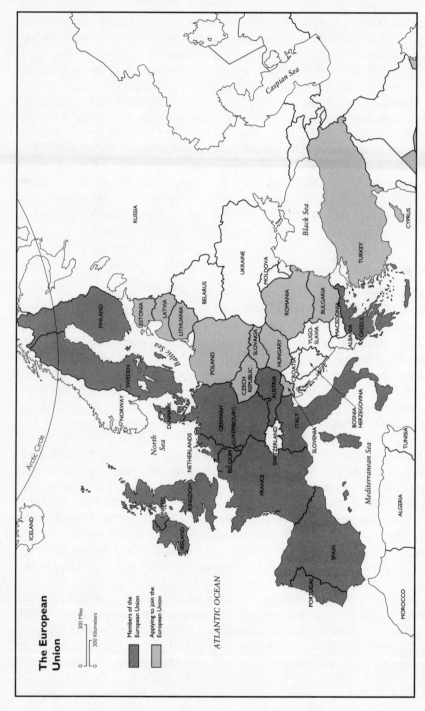

MAP 5.1   The European Union (as of June 1996).

ment. The postcommunist states, especially Poland, Czechoslovakia, and Hungary, were more anxious to join the EC than any other multilateral institution. As the Czechoslovak foreign minister, Jiri Dienstbier, put it:

> The association with and eventual full membership in the EC of Czechoslovakia, Hungary and Poland is a basic precondition for stability and security in Central Europe. This is not just a matter of economic and financial assistance. Rather, the principal objective is to integrate the economies and particularly the societies of Central Europe into an economic, social, cultural, and political environment that by its very nature is conducive to the adoption of European standards and norms.[8]

The issues facing the EU, however, were complicated enough without the addition of countries with little experience in either democracy or capitalism. The Maastricht plans for further economic and political integration within the existing community ran up against both political and economic obstacles. Even the seemingly innocuous issue of a common EU currency became a source of national misunderstandings. The Maastricht Treaty decreed that the currency should be called ecu, short for European currency unit. But many Germans balked at this, since in German "ein Ecu" sounds like "eine Kuh," or cow, hardly the image for a new-age Europe. Furthermore, in 1995 Europe was mired in a two-year-old recession, with the unemployment rate in the EU states averaging 11.5 percent, posing additional burdens on EU resources. There were also other complicated issues facing the EU: its relationship to NATO; the increased vulnerability (with newly open borders) to smuggling and terrorism; and the Bosnian crisis.

Settling these problems would be made more difficult even with the addition of prosperous and democratic states (like Austria, Finland, and Sweden), simply because greater numbers make for a more complicated decision-making process. Membership for the postcommunist states raised additional problems because of their weakly developed market structures and legal systems and because of sensitive political and security considerations. Most EU members, for example, were also members of the **Western European Union (WEU),** which was designated at the Maastricht summit as the defense component of the EU. But the WEU is also closely tied to NATO, so there were both hopes (e.g., in Eastern Europe) and concerns (e.g., in Russia) that EU membership could provide a "back door" to NATO membership through the WEU.

Thus the EU made it clear to the postcommunist states of Eastern Europe, almost all of which sought membership in the organization, that they were not likely to be accepted for full membership before the end of the decade. However, the EU did attempt to accommodate the postcommunist states in other ways, such as by providing over half of all the foreign aid received by the East European states. By mid-1995, the EU had also concluded "association agreements" with six East European states (Poland, Hungary, the Czech Republic, Slovakia, Bulgaria, and Romania) and the three Baltic states (Estonia, Latvia, and Lithuania), giving them trade and cooperation deals afforded certain Mediterranean countries (Turkey, for example). These associate countries are required to be constitutional democracies with multiple parties and free elections and to have an economy based on market principles; some countries in East-Central Europe were more prepared for this than others. The associate status, however, would give them access to EU markets and would pave the way for full membership, perhaps after five or ten years.

In the short run, then, the leaders of the new postcommunist governments were likely to be frustrated in their efforts to achieve early entry into the European Union. In the long run, perhaps over a decade, the EU held promise of developing into a powerful regional bloc representing much of Europe. Furthermore, the EU had the potential to develop truly supranational governing institutions. In 1987, the EU heads of government implemented the Single Europe Act (SEA), which replaced unanimity with majority voting of the twelve members on many economic and social issues. The SEA gave an important boost to 1992 by eliminating the right of a single country to veto progress.[9] The decisions of 1990 presaged the extension of supranationalism into the political arena as well. Thus during the 1990s, the EU was likely to expand both its power and its membership. The EU, more than any other institution, had the potential to make real the dream of a Common European Home.

THE IMPACT ON EUROPE OF THE COLLAPSE OF THE SOVIET UNION

The dissolution of the USSR in December 1991 left in its stead fourteen new states plus the Russian Federation (itself a multinational state), most of which were loosely associated through the Commonwealth of Independent States (CIS). The CIS was created, in large measure, to stave off the even worse economic disaster that would occur if each of the former Soviet republics went its own way. But the end of communism and the Soviet Union did not mean the end of political and economic problems for the peoples and governments of the former union. As we have seen, the economic problems promised to worsen, at least in the short run, and new conflicts of pride and national identity threatened the harmony of both the commonwealth and the Federation.

The disintegration of so large a country would have dramatic consequences outside the commonwealth as well. It would entail a redrawing of the former country's western borders. It would mean yet another redrawing of the map of Europe with the emergence of new, small and vulnerable states. It would further complicate the efforts of the states in East-Central Europe to align and integrate themselves with the West. The multitude of new, poor states in the commonwealth would additionally stretch the financial aid resources of the industrialized countries and would probably reduce those available to the ECE states outside the commonwealth. It would also pose a host of new issues for the West: those concerning economic aid and trade, new security arrangements, political stability, and membership in the UN, EU, NATO, and other multilateral institutions.

Like so many other changes in East-Central Europe, the decline of the Soviet Union was two-edged in terms of its impact on other states. On the one hand, the Eastern European revolutions were made possible by Moscow's turn inward and its efforts to reverse its own long economic decline. On the other hand, the economic decline and political fragmentation of the USSR posed new problems for its postcommunist neighbors. The biggest of these problems was the economic one.

Under the old system of intrabloc trade coordinated by Comecon, goods were traded with little consideration for quality or cost, and transactions were conducted with the "transferable ruble," an artificial currency that was of less value than even the ordinary Soviet ruble. A joke in Poland described this system of exchange as "one dead dog for two dead cats." The system was not very efficient, perhaps, but it did promote high amounts of trade among the European communist states; goods that might not have been marketable in the West could be sold to other bloc states.

This whole system, however, was destroyed with the dissolution of Comecon and with the Soviet decision, effective in January 1991, to conduct all foreign trade on a hard currency basis and to sell its own products (especially energy) at world market prices. This was part of the Kremlin's effort to rationalize its own foreign trade and to integrate the Soviet economy more closely with global trade. Nevertheless, the impact on East-Central Europe was immediate and negative and worked in both directions. From the Soviet side, now that they were buying with hard currency there was no advantage to buying inferior goods from their former Comecon partners. For the countries of East-Central Europe, the new rules meant that Soviet oil and natural gas, which they had previously purchased at subsidized prices, were now much more expensive and were available only for scarce hard currency. Furthermore, the galloping economic collapse of the Soviet Union and then of the commonwealth states drastically reduced their own abilities to trade. Consequently, the postcommunist governments, while struggling to revive their domestic economies, suddenly lost their most lucrative export markets. In the first quarter of 1991, Poland's exports to the Soviet Union declined 80 percent from the year before and was responsible for a quarterly trade deficit of $300 million. In the same three months Czechoslovakia's exports to the Soviet Union declined by 36 percent and Hungary's by 85 percent.[10] The loss of Soviet markets meant the closure of many industries in those countries, exacerbating the already difficult problem of unemployment. The new governments in East-Central Europe were expecting a reorientation of their trade to the West, but they had been hoping that the reduction in Soviet trade would be more gradual. This sudden thrust out of the nest and into the global market was an important test of their ability to survive on their own. It would also make them even more dependent on Western largess.

The Soviet decay and collapse most immediately affected its neighbors in the economic sphere, but it also raised national security concerns in East-Central Europe. The new governments in the region were delighted to remove themselves from Soviet domination and gladly cooperated in the dismantling of the Warsaw Pact. Extricated from this Eastern alliance, but unable to join NATO, the postcommunist states found themselves without alliances or solid security guarantees. Even before the disappearance of the Soviet Union, there was concern in the ECE states about instability in that country. Some feared that efforts by Soviet republics to leave the union would allow the return of a hard-line and authoritarian leadership in Moscow. Such a situation almost materialized with the August coup attempt. There was also concern over the possibility of civil war or ethnic conflicts that could possibly spill over into East-Central Europe.

None of these concerns disappeared with the termination of the Soviet Union; indeed, many new problems and potential threats emerged. Some of the former Soviet states, now independent, had the same concerns about Russian power that the ECE countries did. Tensions emerged (or, more correctly, continued) between Russia and Estonia over the status of Russians within Estonia; between Russia and Ukraine over the disposition of the Soviet Black Sea naval fleet and Soviet nuclear weapons on Ukrainian territory; and between Russia and Moldova over the status of Russian army units in the separatist "Trans-Dniester Republic." East European sensitivities were sharpened by statements from Russian nationalist politician Vladimir Zhirinovski, who advocated the restoration of the old Soviet Union (i.e., including Estonia, Ukraine, and Moldova, among others).

The breakup of the Soviet Union also had less apocalyptic consequences for the ECE countries. The combination of the economic breakdown and the relaxation of emigration restrictions in the former Soviet Union led to a huge new flow of migrants to both Eastern and Western Europe from the Soviet successor states. These came on top of the already substantial population flow from Eastern to Western Europe (especially Germany), which contributed to the rise of right-wing xenophobia in Germany, France, and elsewhere, and even led Germany to revise its constitution to restrict the influx of immigrants. All of these concerns intensified the efforts of the ECE governments to seek closer association and assurances from the West and from NATO.

THE END OF THE COLD WAR

The Cold War had been based on mutual fear; the United States feared aggression by the Soviet Union and therefore created a huge military establishment, which in turn intimidated the Soviet Union and led it to fortify its defenses. This vicious circle of distrust and suspicion spun off an arms race, with each side fearful of falling behind the other. In nuclear arsenals in particular, this led to an enormous "overkill" capacity on both sides. The United States, for example, had enough strategic nuclear weapons to strike every large- and medium-sized Soviet city *forty times*—enough "to make the rubble bounce."

The accelerating decline of Soviet power and the Gorbachev regime's commitment to new thinking sharply reduced the Soviet threat to the United States and the West, which in turn reduced its belligerent stance toward the Soviet Union. The vicious circle of threats and distrust was replaced by a new spiral of trust and reassurance. At first, many Westerners did not put much faith in Gorbachev's new thinking, insisting that rhetoric alone did not justify a lowering of Western defenses. Over time, however, the actions did match the words as the Soviet Union reduced its armaments, withdrew its troops from Afghanistan, and cut its commitments to leftist movements and regimes in the Third World. The major test of new thinking, however, was in Eastern Europe, the region of primary strategic concern to the Soviet Union. Here too, Moscow's actions followed its rhetoric. When Poland's communist government fell apart after the elections of June 1989, Moscow reacted with equanimity and promises of support for the new government of Tadeusz Mazowiecki. It was now apparent that the Brezhnev Doctrine was no longer in force. The Polish precedent gave heart to reformers and revolutionaries elsewhere in the region as one communist regime after another began to fall apart. The Moscow leadership watched its empire collapse and did nothing, and eventually even the Soviet Union fell apart. The Cold War started in Eastern Europe and it ended there.

The U.S. Response

In the United States, the collapse of communism in Europe and the end of the Cold War initially brought a sense of euphoria, exhilaration, and optimism. Some felt that the United States had "won" the Cold War, and now it faced no obstacles to the spread of Western institutions and ideas. Others saw in the collapse of the Soviet threat an unprecedented opportunity to rethink U.S. national security policy and to reshape domestic priorities. There was much discussion of a peace dividend that could be realized from reductions in defense spending. Savings from the huge defense budget could be committed to pressing domestic needs: education, the environment, poverty, drug abuse, and medical care.

The disappearance of the communist threat, however, left the United States in a "conceptual vacuum." The Cold War had always provided a framework for U.S. foreign policy and had dictated its foreign, military, and national security policies. In terms of U.S. relationships with other states, that policy was governed primarily by a country's orientation toward communism. The United States supported governments or movements that opposed communism and opposed those that did not. The most important U.S. allies were usually also democratic, but in many cases the U.S. effort to contain communism led the country to support governments that were repressive or dictatorial (e.g., South Vietnam, Taiwan, South Africa, El Salvador) or to subvert governments that were leftist but freely elected (the Dominican Republic in 1965, Chile in 1973, Nicaragua in the 1980s).

With containment of communism no longer necessary after 1989, the United States lost this conceptual framework for its foreign policy. There were many voices that suggested a rethinking of U.S. foreign and national security policy. Theodore Sorensen, a former adviser to President Kennedy, argued for redefining national security around two major goals: the preservation of the country's economic effectiveness and the peaceful promotion of democracy around the world. In his view, this would entail reduced efforts to project U.S. military power and greater attention to reducing the country's trade deficit and debt, to strengthening its global economic competitiveness, and this would also mean increased foreign aid for fledgling democracies. Sorensen was concerned, however, that without strong executive leadership a rethinking of U.S. priorities would be lost in a "mishmash of political considerations." Military budget reductions, for example, would "reflect not actual needs but log-rolling among the services as well as pressures on the Congress from local defense plants and bases."[11]

In the United States, the Reagan and Bush administrations struggled to fill the conceptual vacuum left by the waning threat of communism. President Reagan frequently evoked terrorism as the new global threat and accused Libya's President Muammar Khadafy of being a major sponsor of terrorism. In April 1986, Reagan ordered an air raid on Libyan military installations, hoping in the process to kill Khadafy himself. Khadafy survived, but his adopted infant daughter perished in the air attacks. President Bush identified yet another global threat in international drug traffickers. He also employed military force, sending U.S. Marines to take over Panama in December 1989. The major target was Panamanian strongman Manuel Noriega, whom the United States accused of supporting drug shipments to the United States. But these were shadowy and elusive enemies that did not evoke the unanimity and fear in the American public that communism had. As Congressman Les Aspin put it, "The old world was good guys and bad guys. The new world is gray guys."[12] There was no basis here for a new U.S. foreign policy.

President Bush developed a bolder and more visionary approach in September 1990 when he announced to a joint session of Congress his concept of a "new world order," which was strikingly similar to Gorbachev's vision of global interdependence and peaceful resolution of disputes. This new framework seemed to work well in the face of the threat posed by Iraq's invasion of Kuwait in August 1990. Meeting with President Bush in Helsinki in early September, President Gorbachev expressed strong support for the U.S. position, denounced the Iraqi invasion, and called for Iraq's unconditional withdrawal from Kuwait. The Soviet Union also backed the successive resolutions of the United Nations Security Council that imposed an embargo on Iraq and, by November, authorized member states "to use all means necessary" to effect Iraq's withdrawal from Kuwait. This behavior led Secretary of State Baker to characterize the Soviets as "very reliable partners" in the Persian Gulf crisis.[13] For the first time since World War II, the superpowers were working together rather than against each other in a major Third World crisis.

This easy condominium began to erode, however, as the Bush administration increasingly escalated its demands on Iraq and steadily moved toward a military solution. The Soviet leadership was uncomfortable with Bush's unstated but clear intention to eliminate Iraq as a major power in the region—a goal that went far beyond the UN resolutions calling simply for the removal of Iraq from Kuwait. The Soviet military, especially, became increasingly alarmed as the United States massed a half million troops in the Persian Gulf, only 500 miles from the southern borders of the Soviet Union. Gorbachev and his advisers repeatedly attempted to negotiate a peaceful settlement of the issue. Gorbachev's adviser, Yevgeniy Primakov, visited the Gulf three times. But the Bush administration was strongly opposed to these efforts and insisted on Iraq's full compliance with all UN resolutions. In the absence of any concessions from Saddam Hussein, the United States unleashed a furious aerial bombardment of Kuwait on January 15, softening up the Iraqi forces for a massive U.S.-led ground assault six weeks later. Operation Desert Storm lasted just 100 hours and resulted in a humiliating surrender by Saddam Hussein and the death of as many as 200,000 Iraqis.

The war was also a humbling experience for Gorbachev. The outbreak of the war increasingly marginalized the Soviet Union, especially because Gorbachev continued to strive for a negotiated settlement. During the combat, the Kremlin leadership looked on as superior U.S. weaponry outclassed and destroyed Iraqi materiel, much of which had been supplied by the Soviet Union. The war strengthened the voice and the hand of the antiperestroika conservatives in Moscow, who complained of the eclipse of Soviet power and influence in world affairs. In December, on the eve of the air war, foreign minister Eduard Shevardnadze tendered his resignation and warned of a possible right-wing coup d'état in the country. The conservative newspaper *Sovetskaia Rossiia* contended that Moscow's participation in the U.S.-led alliance against Iraq "ended the U.S.S.R.'s existence as a superpower."[14] This perception almost certainly contributed to the coalition of military and security forces that attempted to oust Gorbachev from power in the failed coup of August 1991.

The war also seemed to place the new world order on the back burner. The furious attack on Saddam Hussein's forces seemed to belie Bush's dedication to a world of diplomacy and peaceful settlement of disputes. The predominance of the United States in the anti-Iraq coalition and in the combat operations raised questions about the U.S. commitment to multilateral diplomacy, especially as far as the other "superpower" was concerned. However, it was clear by the end of the war, if not before, that there now was only one superpower. Both friends and foes of the United States began to talk of the replacement of the "bipolar" world with a "unipolar" one. The Gulf War also did nothing to slow U.S. military spending; the Bush administration asked Congress for $291 billion for the Pentagon in 1992, compared to $286 billion in 1991, and this did not include a $15 billion "supplemental" request to cover part of the Gulf War costs. The Center for Defense Information, a coalition of retired U.S. military officers, argued that a military budget of $200 billion would suffice in the post–Cold War era.[15] But the U.S. fascination with the high-tech weapons of the Gulf War and the Bush administration's preoccupation with foreign affairs over domestic seemed to offer little hope to those who expected an early "peace dividend."

Bill Clinton's presidency seemed to suggest a change in approach. Both during the 1992 presidential campaign and early in his administration, Clinton focused more on domestic issues than foreign policy, suggesting a scaling back of U.S. global involvement and assertiveness. On the one hand, Clinton pledged to maintain the country's global leadership, especially in efforts to enlarge the community of free-market democracies. In a speech to the Polish parliament in July 1994, for example, Clinton pledged that "we will not let the Iron Curtain be replaced with a veil of indifference."[16] On the other hand, in other contexts Clinton cautioned against U.S. overcommitment, and especially against military commitments that could entangle the United States in other countries' problems and lead to the loss of U.S. soldiers. Speaking in Berlin a few days after his speech in Warsaw, Clinton noted that "trade, as much as troops, will increasingly define the ties that bind nations in the twenty-first century."[17]

Thus, the Clinton administration was much more wary of using military force than most of its predecessors had been and more committed to multilateral approaches to international problems through the United Nations, NATO, and the OSCE. When U.S. troops were sent to Somalia in December 1992 (just before Clinton took office), the purpose was simply to facilitate humanitarian relief efforts. When the situation deteriorated and U.S. troops were increasingly endangered, Clinton brought them home and turned over the relief efforts to United Nations troops. The role of U.S. troops was similarly circumscribed and coordinated with the UN in the 1994 intervention in Haiti to restore to office Jean-Bertrand Aristide, the democratically elected president who was ousted in a military coup in 1991.

This minimalist foreign policy came under particular attack in the United States, however, over the Bosnian crisis. The Clinton administration contended that the war between Muslims and Serbs could not be resolved by U.S. military intervention without a large-scale and long-term commitment of U.S. troops to the area. Critics from both the left and the right argued that the United States or NATO had to use military force, or at least air power, to respond to aggressive Serb military attacks on Muslim positions.

When NATO air power finally was employed, in mid-1995, in combination with renewed offensives by Croatian and Bosnian forces, the Serbs were forced to retreat and were brought to the negotiating table. In Dayton, Ohio, the Clinton administration was able to wrest a settlement from the belligerents, but only with a guaranteed commitment of NATO and U.S. peacekeeping forces to supervise the implementation of the Dayton accords (see Chapter 3). President Clinton then faced opposition to the commitment of U.S. troops to Bosnia, often from the same people (especially many congressional Republicans) who had criticized him for *not* employing force earlier. In a televised Oval Office address at the conclusion of the Dayton agreements, the president sought support for the U.S. troop commitment, but his speech once again acknowledged the limits of U.S. power in the post–Cold War world: "America cannot and must not be the world's policeman," he said. "We cannot stop all war for all time. But we can stop some wars. We cannot save all women and all children. But we can save many of them. We cannot do everything. But we must do what we can do. There are times and places where our leadership can mean the difference between peace and war."[18]

This speech was a far cry from the universalist commitment to freedom and democracy made by President Wilson after World War I and President Truman after World War II. But it reflected both the complexities of the era and the limits of U.S. power.

Western Aid to the Postcommunist States

The economic transformation and recovery of the East-Central European states and the Soviet successor states depended in large measure on increased trade with and aid from the West. At the same time, the potential for expanded trade with the postcommunist states was *the* major attraction of the region for Western governments and corporations. As discussed in Chapter 4, the ECE states all hoped to accelerate their transition to a market economy by opening their economies to the competitive environment of the world market. The hope was that increased exports to the West would stimulate internal growth and that increased imports from the West would stimulate internal consumption. There was much room for growth in East-West trade (as it used to be called). In 1989, Eastern Europe and the Soviet Union accounted for less than 3 percent of trade by the countries of the Organization for Economic Cooperation and Development (OECD), which includes most of the industrialized countries. Exports from the industrialized countries to Eastern Europe and the Soviet Union, with a combined population of 410 million, were only slightly higher than exports to the two city-states of Hong Kong and Singapore, with only 8.5 million residents.[19] The potential for increased trade and new export markets in East-Central Europe was particularly tantalizing for Western firms.

The obstacles to such trade, however, were imposing. By 1990, all of the states in the region had developed huge foreign debts, which limited their creditworthiness and deterred foreign investors. Their Comecon ties had isolated them from world markets, and many of their exports were of low quality and not competitive with Western products. The January 1991 transition to world market pricing among the former Comecon partners particularly hurt the smaller countries of East-Central Europe. Soviet exports (especially energy and raw materials) to the region were now more expensive, and the Soviet Union no longer gave preference to the purchase of lower-quality, high-priced goods from Eastern Europe. As the terms of trade between the Soviet Union and ECE deteriorated, ECE debts grew even larger, contributing to their problems of economic recovery.

Western governments and banks were reluctant to extend new loans to these countries without evidence of progress toward both the market and political stability. Poland, Hungary, and the Czech Republic were thus much more attractive candidates for loans and investments than Bulgaria, Romania, or Albania. The former Soviet states and Yugoslavia, plagued by internal fragmentation and even civil war, were even more difficult cases. In the first two years after the revolutions of 1989, by far the largest amount of Western economic assistance to the region went to Poland and Hungary. In March 1991, for example, the United States forgave 70 percent of Poland's accumulated government-to-government debt.

Very limited Western assistance was forthcoming for the Soviet Union and its successors, whose economic problems were especially dire. Germany was by far the largest contributor of aid to the former Soviet Union. Of the $80 billion in assistance pledged in late 1990 and in 1991, 57 percent came from Germany, and another 18 percent from the other EC countries. The U.S. contribution was only 6.5 percent.[20] But in early 1992, the German government announced that it was scaling back on assistance to the CIS because it was concerned about the rising financial and political risks there. The Germans wanted other Western states to assume more of the burden. But in the face of a major economic recession in the United States and other Western countries, large-scale assistance seemed unlikely. Western aid to the commonwealth was expected to amount to only about $30 billion a year. This *was* an expensive proposition, but it was minuscule compared to the $88 billion in public transfers from western to eastern Germany with a population one-fifteenth that of the commonwealth.[21]

U.S. economic assistance to the postcommunist states, in particular, was insubstantial. Although many Americans believed that foreign aid was the largest single item in the U.S. budget, in fact it represented just 1 percent,[22] and the largest chunks of U.S. economic assistance went to Israel, Egypt, and other Third World countries rather than to Eastern Europe. Most of the U.S. aid to the postcommunist states was actually channeled through multilateral financial institutions like the World Bank, the International Monetary Fund, and the European Bank for Reconstruction and Development, and some of these funds did more to help U.S. companies than poor East Europeans. For example, the largest portion of U.S. assistance to Poland was allotted to a capital investment fund that would provide insurance for American companies that invest in Poland.[23]

Arms Control

The reduced international profile of Russia and the end of the Cold War created major new opportunities for the superpowers to reduce their vast stockpiles of nuclear and conventional weapons. Since the early 1970s, the United States and the Soviet Union had made almost no progress in arms control, apart from the 1979 Strategic Arms Limitation Treaty (sometimes called SALT II), which, however, was never ratified by the United States Senate. Only with the advent of Mikhail Gorbachev did this logjam open, and in 1987 the two powers signed the Intermediate-Range Nuclear Forces Treaty (INF Treaty), which provided for the dismantling of all Soviet and

U.S. medium- and short-range nuclear missiles. This treaty left untouched, however, the longer-range and more powerful strategic nuclear arsenals.

Negotiations on strategic weapons were resumed by the Bush administration in June 1989 in the midst of the Eastern European revolutions, and they concluded with a Strategic Arms Reduction Treaty (START) in July 1991. Unlike the SALT I (1972) and SALT II (1979) treaties, this was the first to call for actual reductions in the number of nuclear weapons rather than ceilings. The treaty would cut the U.S. strategic nuclear arsenal by about 15 percent and the Soviet one by 25 percent over a period of 7 years. Ballistic missile warheads, the most powerful and accurate weapons, would be reduced by 35 percent and 50 percent, respectively. The treaty was a major accomplishment, though it would still leave the United States with over 10,000 warheads and the Soviets with 8,000 warheads, numbers which seemed superfluous and anomalous in the post–Cold War era. This anomaly became even more apparent after the dissolution of the USSR. In June 1992, at a Washington summit meeting, Presidents Bush and Yeltsin agreed to a second START agreement (START II) that would reduce strategic nuclear warheads to 3,000 for Russia and 3,500 for the United States—about half of the levels established by START I.

By this time, however, there was a further complicating factor, since the former Soviet nuclear forces were now located on the territory of *four* states: Russia, Belarus, Kazakhstan, and Ukraine. There was considerable trepidation in the West at first over the possibility of the world's gaining three new nuclear powers. The United States made the ratification of START II contingent on Belarus, Ukraine, and Kazakhstan's signing on to both START I and the 1968 nuclear Non-Proliferation Treaty (NPT) committing them not to become nuclear powers. Fortunately, all three states agreed to transfer all of their nuclear weapons to Russia, and by the end of 1994 all three had ratified both START I and the NPT. This potential crisis was solved remarkably quickly and easily.

The end of Cold War tensions also allowed reductions in conventional (nonnuclear) forces. As mentioned above, the members of NATO and the Warsaw Pact agreed in late 1990 to the Treaty on Conventional Forces in Europe that sharply restricted conventional armaments from the Atlantic to the Urals. With the collapse of the Warsaw Pact shortly thereafter, NATO planned a radical reorganization of its forces in Europe that would lead to a 50 percent cut in U.S. forces on the continent and smaller cuts for the alliance as a whole. The European members of NATO also initiated defense cutbacks of their own. In July 1991, the British Defense Secretary announced that Britain planned to reduce its armed forces by 20 percent over 3 years. The same month, France scrapped plans to build a new system of mobile nuclear missiles. Further cutbacks, at least in Europe, seemed likely following the crumbling of the USSR.

The collapse of communism in Europe and the disintegration of the Soviet Union finally put an end to the Cold War, which had dominated East-West relations and U.S. foreign policy for half a century. It allowed for a reorientation of U.S. policy, both domestic and foreign, and a reduced emphasis on nuclear deterrence and global containment of communism. The United States reacted cautiously to the new global environment, however, and President Bush warned against "actual and potential despots around the world."[24] The United States seemed determined to maintain a global role, even a global military one, in spite of the changed international environment. It seemed more likely, however, that the dominant role played by the United States during the Cold War would fade. In the past, much of the world had looked to the United States as a counterweight to Soviet power and international communism. With the withering of communism and of Soviet power, United States power became increasingly irrelevant. The Europeans were no longer dependent on the United States either economically or militarily. After 1992 especially, the European Community would be the focus of attention and economic growth in Europe, and the United States was not a part of that community. And with the dissolution of the Warsaw Pact and the Soviet Union, the role of NATO was cast into doubt. In the Third World, many countries had relied on the United States simply because it was a less threatening power than the Soviet Union. With the world now a "unipolar" one, the United States itself was likely to be perceived as the major threat to smaller and weaker states. In the short run, the United States would dominate the new unipolar world. But because U.S. power had been so closely and fatally linked to Soviet power, over the long run U.S. dominance would fade as well.

THE IMPACT ON THE THIRD WORLD

The revolutions of East-Central Europe and the Soviet Union had an impact that went beyond Europe and East-West relations. They began to affect the Third World as well. In part this was due to the dramatic reorientation of Soviet foreign policy and Moscow's lowered profile in the Third World. As discussed in Chapter 2, as early as 1987 Soviet officials and academics were claiming that the Soviet Union could no longer afford large-scale assistance to, or involvement in, the Third World. The Soviet Union would not even necessarily continue to support socialist governments in the Third World. Indeed, it was argued, socialism may not always be the appropriate path for economic development in all countries. The shift in the Kremlin's rhetoric was matched by changes in policy as the Soviet Union began to scale back its financial commitments to Third World countries and to reduce its diplomatic and military presence as well. The most dramatic example was Afghanistan, from which Moscow withdrew the last of its troops in early 1989.

In southern Africa, the Marxist government of Angola was also a victim of the changes in Soviet foreign policy and the end of the Cold War. That country had been plagued by sixteen years of civil war between the governing Popular Movement for the Liberation of Angola (MPLA), supported by Cuba and the Soviet Union, and the rebel National Union for the Total Independence of Angola (UNITA), backed by the United States and South Africa. The reduction of Cold War tensions allowed these parties to agree in 1988 to a settlement of the conflict. By mid-1991 the last of the 50,000 Cuban troops had left Angola, the MPLA had abandoned its commitment to Marxism, and the country moved toward its first multiparty elections in 1992. Fighting between the government and UNITA continued sporadically, though without the Cold War overtones and foreign involvement.

The changes in Angola left Ethiopia as the last Soviet client state in Africa. Consistent with the Kremlin's new thinking, however, Moscow imposed sharp reductions in military and economic aid to the government of President Mengistu Haile Mariam, culminating in a nearly complete cutoff in December 1990. This was a fatal blow to the government, which, like Angola, was mired in a costly civil war. The termination of Soviet assistance eroded the capabilities and morale of the Ethiopian army, and by May 1991 the rebels had ousted Mengistu. Moscow, which had supported Mengistu for sixteen years, made no move to save him.

The collapse and discrediting of communism in Europe reverberated throughout the Third World. Marxist regimes were transformed or voted out in Benin and Mozambique in Africa and Nicaragua in Central America. By the end of 1991, there were only a handful of Marxist governments left in the Third World including, most importantly, Cuba, Vietnam, and North Korea. With the collapse of the Soviet Union, these countries lost an important source of support and assistance. Fidel Castro's Cuba was especially vulnerable. The country was in desperate economic straits and was heavily dependent on subsistence from the Soviet Union. It seemed only a matter of time before Cuba followed the Eastern European pattern.

The Eastern European revolutions had an apparent demonstration effect on Third World authoritarian states on the right as well as the left. In the aftermath of the Eastern European events, for example, the central African country of Congo experienced a velvet revolution of its own. A series of Solidarity-style strikes and demonstrations in the fall of 1990 practically closed down the country and forced the Marxist government of President Sassou-Nguesso to call a national conference to chart the country's future. The conference, held in June 1991, looked much like the Eastern European roundtables and brought together representatives of the government, trade unions, and opposition. In the end, the conference forced the president to dismiss the cabinet, rewrite the constitution, and schedule the nation's first free elections. It also changed the country's national anthem and flag, and removed the word "people's" from the country's name, the People's Republic of Congo. All of this seemed to be scripted from the Eastern European experience. Furthermore, as in Eastern Europe, there was a demonstration effect within Africa. Opposition leaders in more than a dozen other African countries said they hoped to use the Congo conference as a model for democratic change.[25] By 1994, more than half of the forty-eight countries south of the Sahara had held or promised multiparty elections.

The most startling, sweeping, and heartening changes occurred in the Republic of South Africa, where a small white minority had for forty years dominated the black majority politically and economically through its policy of "separate development" of the races, called **apartheid.** In 1989, the same year as the East European revolutions, Frederick de Klerk assumed the presidency of South Africa and almost immediately initiated a "perestroika" of his own: ending the ban on the African National Congress (ANC), the principal antiapartheid organization, and freeing ANC leader Nelson Mandela after twenty-seven years of imprisonment. Negotiations between the government and the ANC led to agreement on a new majority-rule constitution and, in 1994, to democratic elections that resulted in a massive victory for Mandela and the ANC.

If the revolutions of East-Central Europe had stimulated democratization in the Third World, they also seem to have accelerated economic reform and privatization in those countries. In its 1991 *World Economic Development Report,* the World Bank observed a "powerful new economic pragmatism" sweeping the Third World as many countries reduced government controls of the economy, privatized state-owned firms, and opened their economies to free trade and foreign investments. Such reforms were being adopted, for example, in Chile, Ghana, India, Indonesia, South Korea, Mexico, Morocco, and Turkey. The World Bank saw this pattern as a trend away from the economic nationalism and protectionism that had characterized economic policy in many Third World countries since they had achieved independence.[26] The more open posture toward the rich capitalist countries encouraged the latter to increase trade and investments in reforming Third World countries and to renegotiate more favorable terms on loans and debt repayments. With many countries now viewing private investment as a catalyst to growth, such investments increased substantially, especially in East Asia and Latin America.

There was, however, a darker economic side of this equation. As we have seen, "new thinking" in the Soviet Union had led to sharp cutbacks in Soviet aid to Third World countries, and the collapse of the Soviet Union meant even further reductions. At the same time, after 1989 much of the Western countries' attention, aid, and investment was being redirected toward the new democracies and markets in East-Central Europe. This was likely to be drawn at the expense of the needier countries in the Third World—especially away from those countries that were *not* embarking on market-oriented reforms. In the United States, in particular, the foreign aid pie was not very big to begin with—less than 5 percent of the defense budget—and there seemed to be no particular inclination to expand it. The economic recession of the early 1990s, affecting all of the developed countries, also discouraged major new expenditures of foreign assistance.

Even when economic assistance was forthcoming, the results were not uniformly beneficial. Aid provided by the International Monetary Fund and the World Bank, for example, was almost always tied to a "structural adjustment" program on the part of the recipient country designed to foster free-market enterprise and minimize government interference. These programs, similar to those being pursued in the transitional economies of Eastern Europe, often entailed currency devaluations, cutbacks in government subsidies, even for food, and restrictions on wage increases. The consequences, in the short run at least, were increased unemployment and declining standards of living, which especially hurt the poor. It also meant that the IMF and the World Bank, founded after World War II to serve the needs of the industrialized world, had become "the overlords of Africa in the 1990s."[27]

The end of the Cold War offered the hope that the Third World would no longer be the battleground of the superpowers. Throughout the postwar years, Third World countries had functioned as proxies for the superpowers and their strategic and ideological conflict, for example in Korea, Vietnam, Angola, Nicaragua, Afghanistan, Cuba, and the Middle East. Conflicts in these areas provided a rationale for huge transfers of weapons from north to south. In the postwar period, there were over 170 wars and conflicts worldwide, mostly involving countries that relied on foreign suppliers for their military needs. In the 1980s alone, for example, the United States provided over $128 billion in weaponry and military assistance to 125 of the world's 169 countries.[28]

With the end of the Cold War, it seemed less likely that the major powers would be so readily drawn into local or regional conflicts in the Third World. The Soviet Union, at least, had disappeared as a major power, and Russia did not seem positioned to replace it as a global actor. And for the United States, the major rationale for military involvement in the Third World, the containment of communism, had also disappeared. But U.S. military intervention in Panama in 1989 and the Persian Gulf in 1991 demonstrated that the United States would exercise its military power in the Third World even without the threat of communism. Furthermore, U.S. arms sales and military assistance actually increased during the early 1990s, just as communism was collapsing.

U.S. policy toward the Third World, as toward Europe and the remains of the Soviet Union, faced a conceptual void in the aftermath of the collapse of communism. With the rejection of the communist model in the second world, that model became less and less attractive in the Third World. For the United States and other Western countries, communism was no longer an important threat anywhere in the world. Because the United States no longer needed to fight a perceived communist threat in the Third World, it was in need of a new conceptual framework for its foreign policy. Inasmuch as the containment of communism was no longer necessary, U.S. support for right-wing authoritarian regimes would have to be reexamined. If Washington supported democratization and pluralism in Central and Eastern Europe, it would also have to do so in Taiwan, South Korea, Singapore, Guatemala, and Chile. Regime changes in such countries might well result in a loss of U.S. influence, military bases, investments, and markets. Whether the United States would tolerate such changes *away* from the U.S. model rather than toward it would be an important test of the new international environment.

THE NEW GLOBAL ORDER

Early in his tenure, Mikhail Gorbachev began discussing "new thinking" in Soviet foreign policy and his vision of global cooperation and interdependence. In 1990, George Bush proclaimed his vision of "a new world order" with similar themes. By the fall of 1991, however, history had passed beyond both of these men. Gorbachev was fatally weakened as a result of the failed putsch in August and was left without a country to govern by the end of the year. Bush's vision, although couched in lofty and optimistic tones, by 1991 seemed curiously anachronistic and rooted in the Cold War. On the one hand, his speech before Congress had called for a world in which "the rule of law supplants the rule of the jungle" and where "the strong respect the rights of the weak." On the other hand, this speech, made during the Persian Gulf crisis, was both belligerent and militaristic. The United States was strong and resolute, rather than "kinder, gentler" as he had earlier called for. The president frankly recognized that our "vital economic interests" in the Persian Gulf were a possible cause for war. This was a different vision of interdependence than the less self-interested one of Gorbachev and, certainly, was not what many had hoped for in the post–Cold War era. As it had in Korea, Vietnam, Angola, Chile, Grenada, and Panama, the United States was declaring its vital interests at stake in the Persian Gulf. U.S. economic interests were indeed far-reaching, and they still needed to be protected by military force.

The world had changed enormously since World War II, but the U.S. presidents had not changed much. Every U.S. president from Dwight Eisenhower to George Bush was part of the same generation, born in the first quarter of this century and coming of age during the rise of Hitler in Germany. (President Bush, for example, was born only seven years after John Kennedy, who was inaugurated twenty-eight years earlier.) Hitler was the dominant enemy of that generation, so it is perhaps not surprising that all of the postwar presidents tended to identify their enemies, whether in Korea, Vietnam, Nicaragua, or Iraq, with Hitler. Although it was communism that was usually the threat, the enemy was often personified with these references to the fascist dictator. Bill Clinton, twenty-two years younger than his predecessor, was the first president born after World War II. His worldview was shaped more by the Vietnam war than by World War II, and his foreign policy was less ideological and nuanced than that of his predecessors. As president, he wanted to focus on what he saw as the *domestic* threats to the American way of life (e.g., deteriorating health care and education, crime) and was reluctant to employ military force to solve international problems. The collapse of communism seemed to afford him that opportunity. Over time, however, especially as the crisis in Bosnia worsened, he was criticized for being indecisive and waffling. It was not easy being president in a world where the old enemies were gone, the new ones ill-defined, and the rules in flux.

Almost everyone, inside the communist countries and out, was surprised by the sweep and pace of the collapse of the communist regimes and then by the rapidity with which many of the postcommunist states established themselves as democracies. In Eastern Europe in 1989, as in the Soviet Union in 1991, revolutionary fervor fed on itself until the old orders had been swept away. A prudent person, therefore, would not hazard detailed predictions about the future of East-Central Europe, the Soviet successor states, or international politics. Nevertheless, there were indications that the world had changed in fundamental ways and that a new global order was likely to emerge.

The Decline of Ideology

The biggest change was likely to be the diminished role of ideology in international politics. The conflict between capitalism and communism had been an important factor in global affairs since the Russian Revolution of 1917 and had dominated international politics since World War II. In the early decades of the Cold War, this ideological conflict had split the world into two camps, creating a "bipolar" world in which neutrality was barely recognized by the superpowers. This bipolar world was eroded somewhat with the emergence of a large number of newly independent and nonaligned states in the 1960s, especially in Africa. But even as those states refused to take sides in the East-West conflict, they were often objects of ideological competition between the superpowers.

With the collapse of communism in Eastern Europe and the Soviet Union, and the subsequent erosion of the Marxist alternative in the Third World, the ideological element in international politics faded away. Even in the Western European countries, the communist parties had mellowed and become domesticated. By the 1970s, most of them had already abandoned the more authoritarian Leninist elements of Marxism-Leninism. Communist parties remained in power in China and Cuba, but after 1989 neither of these countries seemed interested in or capable of playing a major role in international politics or of pressing their "models" on other states. In a controversial article entitled "The End of History," a U.S. State Department official proclaimed "the end of mankind's ideological evolution and the universalization of Western liberal democracy as the final form of government."[29] This assessment was overly simplistic and optimistic, but in the United States it reflected the widespread view that the United States had "won" the Cold War. Whether or not this was the case, there certainly seemed to be a decline in ideological conflict worldwide, and the major international crises in the early post–Cold War period were mostly nonideological, involving territory and resources in Iraq, ethnicity in Bosnia and Rwanda, famine and anarchy in Somalia. Political scientist Samuel Huntington argued in an article entitled "The Clash of Civilizations?" that ideological struggles are being replaced by *cultural* conflicts between Western and Orthodox Christianity and Western and Islamic civilizations. "The Velvet Curtain of culture," Huntington wrote, "has replaced the Iron Curtain of ideology as the most significant dividing line in Europe."[30]

The Decline of the Superpowers

If this was the end of the Cold War and of the East-West ideological struggle, what now would be the role of the United States in the world arena? Since World War II, the United States had been the major champion worldwide of liberal democracy and the most important counterweight to communism. With the disappearance of the communist threat, other countries would not need to rely so heavily on the United States and would therefore be less likely to be accommodating to U.S. interests and demands. As we have seen above, the U.S. role in Europe was likely to be diminished both with the erosion of NATO and the growth of the European Union. If U.S. influence declined in Europe, it would almost certainly decline in other parts of the world too, for the same reasons. Countries near the old Soviet Union would no longer need to depend on the

United States for military protection, so U.S. influence was likely to decline in the Middle East, South Asia, and East Asia. In 1991, for example, the United States was having difficulty renegotiating leases for important military bases in the Philippines, which had always been a key strategic outpost for U.S. forces, and eventually relinquished them. In other parts of the Third World, governments would no longer be able (or willing) to raise the threat of communism as an excuse for U.S. aid or intervention. Indeed, with internal or external communism no longer such a threat to these governments, they were now more likely to be wary of the United States, the lone remaining superpower. This was most likely to be the case in Latin America, where the U.S. presence was so large to begin with.

Paradoxically, then, the United States faced a decline in world power just at the time of the collapse of its major adversaries. Even before the collapse of communism in Europe, this was a scenario that had been predicted by the historian Paul Kennedy in his book *The Rise and Fall of the Great Powers*.[31] Over the last five hundred years, Kennedy found, major powers tended to overextend themselves strategically and militarily and then to spend so much on national security that their domestic economies were weakened. If, he argued, "too large a proportion of the state's resources is diverted from wealth creation and allocated instead to military purposes, then that is likely to lead to a weakening of national power over the longer term."[32] Kennedy believed this was happening to both the USSR and the United States even in 1987, before the great revolutions of 1989–1991. The economic decay and political collapse of the Soviet Union seem to confirm this theory for that superpower. The serious economic problems faced by the United States—for example, the national debt increasing geometrically in the 1980s and 1990s (from 33 percent of GNP in 1980 to 68 percent in 1993)—suggested that the United States also faced eventual decline as a world power. The changes in Europe and the Soviet Union were likely to accelerate that process.

The Resurgence of Nationalism

If the conflict between capitalism and communism was fading from global politics, nationalism was taking its place. As discussed in Chapter 4, nationalism had played a major role in shaping the modern international system but had been muted in the postwar period, at least in Europe. In Eastern Europe and the Soviet Union, nationalism had been suppressed by the highly centralized political systems and the enforced bonds of socialist internationalism. In Western Europe, national tensions were overshadowed by the larger issues of the Cold War and softened by the region's economic growth and prosperity. The collapse of communism in the East would rouse the ghosts of nationalism all over the continent.

Communism … nationalism. *Source:* Emanuel Jakub in *Novy Dikobraz* (Czechoslovakia) April 25, 1990, p. 12. Used by permission.

This was most apparent and most dangerous in the former Soviet Union where the communist party had held nationalism in check in one of the world's most ethnically heterogeneous states. As the party withered away and central authority evaporated, the voices of nationalism became more strident. There were multiple layers to the nationalities problem; the issue was not as simple as independence for the fifteen constituent republics, though this itself would be disruptive enough. Although each of the republics was based on a dominant nationality, each also included large numbers of other nationalities. In Ukraine, for example, 21 percent of the population was Russian, and this led to some tension between the two republics as they each proposed to go their own way. Russians constituted over a quarter of the populations in Kazakhstan, Latvia, Estonia, and Kirghizia (now named Kyrgyzstan). The Russian Federation itself was highly heterogeneous; it contained thirty nationalities represented in autonomous republics, autonomous oblasts, and autonomous districts. As the USSR fell apart in 1991, some of these non-Russian components of the Russian Federation began lobbying for more autonomy. A separatist leader in the Tatar Autonomous Republic told the *New York Times:* "The big empire has collapsed. . . . The Russian federation will be more difficult, but I think it is inescapable that this empire will also collapse."[33]

In East-Central Europe the strains of national and ethnic tensions were also reemerging. By the fall of 1991, the civil war in Yugoslavia had already become the bloodiest conflict in Europe since World War II. Nevertheless, the breakup of the state would not end the national problems in the Balkans. Albania had claims on the one million Albanians in the Kosovo region of Yugoslavia, and both Greece and Bulgaria had historical claims to Macedonia, which opted out of Yugoslavia in 1992.

There were several sad ironies to this renewal of national conflicts in Europe. First, they came at a time when many of the most bedeviling and protracted postwar international issues were being resolved—the end of apartheid in South Africa, and peace talks between Israel and the Palestine Liberation Organization and between the British government and Catholic separatists in Northern Ireland. Almost certainly, these changes were due in part to the new thinking initiated by Gorbachev and to the restructured international environment caused by the collapse of communism. Yet those same forces also opened the Pandora's box of nationalism in Europe and elsewhere.

The other irony was that the disintegrating forces of nationalism, separatism, and ethnic conflict were occurring in the face of *integrative* forces moving in precisely the opposite direction: the expansion of the European Union; the enhanced role of the United Nations; the increasing scope, power, and influence of transnational corporations; and the communications and information revolutions that so facilitated contact among people in different countries. All of these tendencies suggested that the nation-state was being superseded by larger, more global forces and institutions. Yet at the same time, Tatars, Chechens, and Slovaks were struggling for identity in *smaller* political units.

The end of the ideological divisions of the Cold War raised hopes of a revitalization of international peacekeeping institutions, especially the United Nations. That organization, after all, had been formed at the end of World War II to cope with the irredentism of the 1930s that seemed to be on the rise again in the 1990s. The organization had been largely paralyzed by the unexpected ideological tensions of the Cold War. The new possibilities for the United Nations were indicated by its broad cooperation in backing U.S. military operations against Iraq in Operation Desert Storm. (This action, however, did demonstrate once again the domination of the United Nations by the major powers.) The United Nations also deployed peacekeeping forces in Cambodia in 1991, Somalia in 1992, and Yugoslavia in 1992. The number of UN peacekeeping forces around the world increased from 15,000 in 1991 to 72,000 (in fourteen countries) in

1994, reflecting the increasing activity of the UN in the post–Cold War era. But these operations also revealed the limits of UN influence. In Somalia, neither a U.S. nor a UN presence was able to solve the deep-seated problems of poverty, starvation, and political factionalism. In Bosnia, the UN presence was unable to prevent Serbian forces from seizing Muslim territory and shelling cities designated by the UN as "safe areas." So the UN, at least as presently constituted, was also no panacea for nationalism and ethnic conflict.

CONCLUSION

The changes in East-Central Europe had a powerful impact on international relations and especially on the European alliance system. With the collapse of communist governments in Eastern Europe, the Warsaw Pact and Comecon slipped into oblivion. The postcommunist states all began to look and turn westward, for both trade and security, and with hopes of assistance from the IMF and the World Bank and for membership in the European Union and even NATO. This created a whole new environment in Europe, with the continent no longer divided by ideology or iron curtain. It suggested the possibility of a truly united Europe. It also brought into question the continued relevance of some of the *Western* alliances, including NATO.

The collapse of communism brought both peril and promise to Europe and the world. It destroyed the old structures of politics, economics, and diplomacy; the efforts to rebuild these were fraught with difficulties and dangers. The collapse of ideology brought with it the reemergence of nationalism, which could not only build states but also destroy them. This new world had many dark corners. But there were hopeful signs as well. Most of the new governments in Europe were intent on creating societies that were both pluralist and humane. The end of the Cold War created an unprecedented opportunity for the major powers to reduce armaments and redirect their resources to human needs. The end of the ideological struggle would allow international cooperation to rebuild shattered societies and to attend to such global problems as hunger, disease, and environmental degradation. This would mean a major reorientation of politics and foreign policy in the United States and an adjustment to the new global environment. The United States would have to change, too.

□ □ □

Discussion Questions

CHAPTER ONE

1. How did the U.S.-Soviet alliance during World War II deteriorate into the Cold War? Who was to blame? Was it avoidable or inevitable?

2. Describe the institutions of rule, domestic and international, in Eastern Europe in the 1950s and 1960s. How did the Soviet Union exercise influence over Eastern Europe?

3. What factors led to the decay of communism in the 1970s?

4. Why were *ideas* so important in East-Central European politics? Identify some of the ideas that helped shape the region.

5. How did attempts at reform in Hungary in 1956, Czechoslovakia in 1968, and Poland in 1980–1981 foreshadow the events of 1989?

6. Discuss the dilemma of conformity versus diversity in Eastern Europe and how it affected the policies of the Soviet leadership and the Eastern European party leaders.

CHAPTER TWO

1. Mikhail Gorbachev's progressive reforms of 1985 can be classified into four main categories: perestroika, glasnost, democratization, and new thinking. Because these reforms did not have the power to work on their own, they were interrelated. How?

2. How did Gorbachev's reforms in the Soviet Union affect Eastern Europe?

3. The changes in Eastern Europe in 1989 resulted in a domino effect. How did changes in each country build on and, in turn, influence further changes in neighboring countries?

4. The revolutions in Eastern Europe were relatively smooth save some very real problems, particularly in Romania. How did these revolutions differ from previous attempts at change and from previous revolutions? Why?

5. To what extent do theories of social movements and revolutions contribute to our understanding of the Eastern European revolutions? Which features of these theories best explain these developments? Is there a particular theory that is especially helpful?

CHAPTER THREE

1. Given the long-standing Soviet concerns about a strong and united Germany, why was it that German reunification occurred so quickly, and with the apparent blessing of Moscow?

2. The eastern German transition to democracy and the market was facilitated by the fact of unification. What does the experience of eastern Germany tell us (if anything) about the fate of the political and economic transitions in the rest of East-Central Europe?

3. How did the revolutions in Eastern Europe contribute to the collapse of the Soviet Union? What other factors were involved?

4. Try to devise a solution (including a new map of the area) to the Bosnian crisis, then discuss the elements of your proposal that would be supported or opposed by the affected parties.

5. Why was it that Czechoslovakia broke apart, even though most people in both parts of the country opposed the breakup? In retrospect, was this solution a good thing for Czechs and Slovaks?

6. In your view, what are the long-term consequences for international politics of the unification of Germany, the collapse of the Soviet Union, and the breakup of Yugoslavia?

CHAPTER FOUR

1. This chapter argues that the transition in Eastern Europe in many ways was more difficult than efforts at democratization and economic liberalization in other parts of the world. Do you agree with this assessment? In what ways were the problems similar to, or different from, other such historical transformations?

2. What was the typical pattern of political change in East-Central Europe after their revolutions? Why was it that each of these countries followed a similar pattern? In your view, could democratization have been pursued in a different way?

3. How do you account for the revival and success of the postcommunist political parties in Eastern Europe and the former Soviet Union? Is this good or bad for the development of democracy in the region? Why?

4. Why was it that each of the ECE governments was so anxious to establish capitalist economic systems? Do you think this was the right choice for them? Do you think that they will be successful in this transformation? What are the factors that are working for and against them?

5. Discuss the relationship between economic reform and political change in the postcommunist states. In what ways do these two processes work together and work against each other?

6. What do past theories of democratization tell us about the prospects and timetables for democracy in East-Central Europe? Are these theories applicable to the region, or are there special circumstances that make East-Central Europe unique?

7. In your view, which is the best approach to a market economy in East-Central Europe: shock therapy or evolution? What are the pros and cons of each?

8. What accounts for the revival of nationalism in Europe? Is this just a transitory phenomenon, or is it likely to remain a long-term problem in the continent? How is it likely to affect international political developments in Europe?

CHAPTER FIVE

1. Discuss the changed role of Germany in Europe. Why is it that some Europeans are concerned about the growth of German power and influence? Is this concern justified?

2. In your view, what is the likely future of NATO? Should some of the former communist states be brought into the organization? If they are, how will this affect the role of NATO and the European security system?

3. Given the collapse of the Cold War and the dramatic restructuring of alliances in Europe, what new security institutions or structures are likely to emerge in the postcommunist environment? Will the balance of power be replaced by collective security?

4. Does the death of communism in Eastern Europe mean the end of communism and/or socialism worldwide? What is the likely impact of the collapse of the Soviet Union on communist regimes in the Third World and on socialist parties in the first world?

5. What should the U.S. response be to these dramatic changes in the communist world? Does the United States need to restructure its foreign or domestic policies?

6. Why are the ECE states so anxious to join the European Union? What are the obstacles to such membership? In your view, which will be the first postcommunist states to join, and what will be the consequences (on trade, security, the EU) of this expansion of the EU?

7. In your view, what should be the role of the world community, especially the United States, the UN, and NATO, in the Bosnian crisis? Should the United States play a more active role in trying to settle this crisis?

□ □ □

Notes

INTRODUCTION

1. This formulation suggested to the author by Robin Remington.

CHAPTER ONE

1. The Yalta Agreements and the Balkan percentages agreement (which was re-counted in Churchill's memoirs) appear in Gale Stokes, ed., *From Stalinisn to Pluralism: A Documentary History of Eastern Europe Since 1945* (New York: Oxford University Press, 1991), 13–32.

2. For a sampling of this debate, see Thomas G. Paterson, ed., *The Origins of the Cold War*, 2d ed. (Lexington, Mass.: D. C. Heath, 1990).

3. "The Sources of Soviet Conduct" (published under the pseudonym "X"), *Foreign Affairs*, 25, no. 4 (July 1947):566–582.

4. The Truman Doctrine is reprinted in Stokes, ed., *From Stalinism to Pluralism*, 35–37.

5. Zhdanov's speech is reprinted in Stokes, ed., *From Stalinism to Pluralism*, 38–42.

6. See John Michael Montias, *Central Planning in Poland* (New Haven, Conn.: Yale University Press, 1962), 6.

7. Joseph Rothschild, *Return to Diversity: A Political History of East Central Europe Since World War II* (New York: Oxford University Press, 1989), 93.

8. From Khrushchev's speech to the Twentieth Congress of the Communist Party of the Soviet Union (CPSU) in February 1956; cited in Rothschild, *Return to Diversity*, 132.

9. Quoted in Rothschild, *Return to Diversity*, 136.

10. The suggestion to "roll back" communism and "liberate" Eastern Europe was first articulated by Dulles in a 1952 article in *Life* magazine, entitled "A Policy of Boldness." See *Life*, 32 (May 19, 1952):146–148.

11. Ghita Ionescu, *The Breakup of the Soviet Empire in Eastern Europe* (Harmondsworth, England: Penguin, 1965).

12. *Pravda*, September 26, 1968.

13. The play *Dziady* (Forefathers' eve) was written by Adam Mickiewicz, the Polish national poet.

14. David S. Mason, *Public Opinion and Political Change in Poland, 1980–1982* (Cambridge: Cambridge University Press, 1985), 148.

15. Adam Michnik, "Does Socialism Have Any Future in Eastern Europe?" *Studium Papers,* 13, no. 4 (October 1989):184.

16. Paul Marer, "The Economies and Trade of Eastern Europe," in William E. Griffith, ed., *Central and Eastern Europe: The Opening Curtain?* (Boulder, Colo.: Westview Press, 1989), 50.

17. See Marer, "The Economies and Trade of Eastern Europe," 51–52.

18. Western currencies are convertible in that they can be freely traded at market rates. The Soviet ruble and the Eastern European currencies were not convertible in this way and were therefore unacceptable as payment by most Western firms and governments.

19. Milovan Djilas, *The New Class* (New York: Praeger, 1967).

20. Peter Hauslohner, "Gorbachev's Social Contact," *Soviet Economy,* 3, no. 1 (1987):54–89; Lena Kolarska-Bobinska, "Poland Under Crisis: Unreformable Society or Establishment?" in Roger Clarke, ed., *Poland: Economy in the 1980s* (White Plains, N.Y.: Longman, 1989), 131–132.

21. Krzysztof Jasiewicz, "Kultura Polityczna Polakow: Miedzy Jednoscia a podzialem," *Aneks,* no. 48 (1988):70.

22. The title of Part VII of the Final Act of the Conference on Security and Cooperation in Europe, signed in Helsinki in 1975 and reprinted in part in Stokes, ed., *From Stalinism to Pluralism,* 160–162.

23. See Robert Sharlet, "Dissent and the Contra-System in East Europe," *Current History,* 84, no. 505 (November 1985):353–355.

24. Sharlet, "Dissent and the Contra-System in East Europe," 355–356.

25. For a penetrating and enlightening discussion of both concepts, see Timothy Garton Ash, "Does Central Europe Exist?" in T. G. Ash, *The Uses of Adversity: Essays on the Fate of Central Europe* (New York: Vintage, 1990), 179–213. This essay first appeared in *New York Review of Books* in October 1986.

26. Vaclav Havel, *The Power of the Powerless* (London: Unwin Hyman, 1985); reprinted in part in Stokes, ed., *From Stalinism to Pluralism,* 168–174.

27. Stokes, ed., *From Stalinism to Pluralism,* 171; emphasis in the original.

28. See his 1976 essay on "The New Evolutionism," in Adam Michnik, *Letters from Prison and Other Essays* (Berkeley, Calif.: University of California Press, 1985), 135–148.

29. Gyorgy Konrad, *Antipolitics* (New York: Harcourt Brace Jovanovich, 1984); excerpted in Stokes, ed., *From Stalinism to Pluralism,* 175–180.

30. Cited in Ash, "Does Central Europe Exist?" 184.

31. This essay first appeared in English in *New York Review of Books,* April 26, 1984.

32. A joke frequently heard in Poland tells of two gentlemen traveling by train; one from Moscow to Paris and the other from Paris to Moscow. Each disembarks in Warsaw, thinking he has reached his destination.

CHAPTER TWO

1. Quoted in Kevin Ruane, *The Polish Challenge* (London: British Broadcasting Corporation, 1982), 180.

2. Quoted in Richard Sakwa, *Gorbachev and His Reforms 1985–1990* (New York: Prentice-Hall, 1990), 1.

3. Axel Lebahn, "Political and Economic Effects of Perestroika on the Soviet Union and Its Relations to Eastern Europe and the West," *Aussenpolitik*, 39, no. 2 (1988):107.

4. *World Military Expenditures and Arms Transfers, 1987* (Washington, D.C.: U.S. Arms Control and Disarmament Agency), 12.

5. *Moskovskiye Novosti,* August 21, 1988, 12; translated in Current Digest of the Soviet Press (hereafter CDSP), October 26, 1988, 27.

6. For a discussion of this point, see Gail W. Lapidus, "Gorbachev and the Reform of the Soviet System," *Daedalus,* 116, no. 2 (Spring 1987):6, 16.

7. *Pravda,* January 28, 1987; cited in Werner Hahn, "Electoral Choice in the Soviet Bloc," *Problems of Communism,* 36, no. 2 (March–April 1987):29.

8. *Pravda,* August 2, 1986; see discussion in Lapidus, "Gorbachev and the Reform," 11.

9. See Alice Gorlin, "The Soviet Economy," *Current History,* 85 (October 1986): 325–328; and Paul Hofheinz, "Gorbachev's Double Burden: Economic Reform and Growth Acceleration," *Millennium: Journal of International Studies,* 16, no. 1 (Spring 1987):21–31.

10. *Wall Street Journal,* March 27, 1987, 11.

11. For useful discussions of glasnost, see Lapidus, "Gorbachev and the Reform"; Archie Brown, "Gorbachev and Reform of the Soviet System," *Political Quarterly,* 58, no. 2 (April–June 1987):139–151; and Ellen Jones and Benjamin Woodbury, "Chernobyl and Glasnost," *Problems of Communism,* 35, no. 6 (November–December 1986):28–39.

12. The Novosibirsk Report was not published in the Soviet Union in the 1980s but did appear in English in *Survey: A Journal of East and West Studies,* 28, no. 1 (Spring 1984):83–108.

13. *Pravda,* February 6, 1987.

14. *Moskovskiye Novosti,* November 23, 1988; cited in Sakwa, *Gorbachev and His Reforms,* 94.

15. *Pravda,* November 24, 1989; cited in Sakwa, *Gorbachev and His Reforms,* 98.

16. For a discussion of the emergence of such groups, see S. Frederick Starr, "Soviet Union: A Civil Society," *Foreign Policy,* no. 70 (Spring 1988):26–41.

17. Cited in Brown, "Gorbachev and Reform," 148.

18. "A New Philosophy of Foreign Policy," *Pravda,* July 10, 1987, 4; translated in CDSP, August 12, 1987, 1–4.

19. *Pravda,* July 26, 1988, 4; translated in CDSP, August 24, 1988, 13–14.

20. V. I. Dashichev in *Komsomolskaya Pravda,* June 19, 1988, 3; translated in CDSP, July 27, 1988, 29.

21. *Izvestia,* November 18, 1988, 5; translated in CDSP, December 14, 1988, 1.

22. *Pravda,* April 11, 1987, 1–2; stress added.

23. For a review of the impact of perestroika in 1987–1988 on each country in Eastern Europe, see David S. Mason, "Glasnost, Perestroika and Eastern Europe," *International Affairs* (London), 64, no. 3 (Summer 1988):431–448.

24. From Gorbachev's speech at the Twenty-seventh Party Congress in February 1986.

25. *Pravda,* April 11, 1987; translated in CDSP, May 13, 1987.

26. Wiktor Kulerski quoted in the underground publication *KOS,* April 22, 1988; translated in *East European Reporter,* 3, no. 3 (Autumn 1988):36.

27. Survey cited in Radio Free Europe Research (hereafter RFER), Background Report 119, June 28, 1988, 20.

28. *Izvestia,* April 7, 1989; translated in Foreign Broadcast Information Service (hereafter FBIS), *Daily Report: Soviet Union,* April 12, 1989, 35.

29. For a discussion of the rehabilitation and reburial of Nagy, see Timothy Garton Ash, *The Magic Lantern: The Revolution of '89 Witnessed in Warsaw, Budapest, Berlin and Prague* (New York: Random House, 1990), 47–60.

30. Quoted in Ash, *The Magic Lantern,* 59.

31. *Stern,* April 8, 1987.

32. *Washington Post,* June 10, 1987.

33. Gorbachev reportedly said this to Honecker in a private meeting, but it was then reported in the media. *New York Times,* October 9, 1989, A6.

34. For an account of these events and of the fall of the Berlin Wall, see Ash, *The Magic Lantern,* 61–77.

35. Jaroslav Sabata quoted in *Christian Science Monitor,* August 17, 1988, 9.

36. For the roots of the Czechoslovak revolution, see William H. Luers, "Czechoslovakia: Road to Revolution," *Foreign Affairs,* 69, no. 2 (Spring 1990): 77–94.

37. This quip was first suggested to Havel by the British journalist Timothy Garton Ash, who provides an eyewitness account of the velvet revolution in *The Magic Lantern,* 78–130.

38. Vladimir Tismaneanu, "The Revival of Politics in Romania," in Nils H. Wessell, ed., *The New Europe: Revolution in East-West Relations* (New York: Academy of Political Science, 1991), 85–87.

39. Quoted in "Chronology 1989," *Foreign Affairs,* 69, no. 1 (1990):229.

40. Jeane J. Kirkpatrick, "Dictatorships and Double Standards," *Commentary,* 68, no. 5 (November 1979), 34–45; reprinted in her *Dictatorships and Double Standards* (New York: Touchstone, 1982), 23–52.

41. Early works in this genre included Michel Tatu, *Power in the Kremlin: From Khrushchev to Kosygin* (New York: Viking, 1967); Robert Conquest, *Power and Policy in the U.S.S.R.: The Struggle for Stalin's Succession 1945–1960* (New York: St. Martin's, 1961); and Carl Linden, *Khrushchev and the Soviet Leadership 1957–1964* (Baltimore, Md.: Johns Hopkins University Press, 1966).

42. For example, H. Gordon Skilling and Franklyn Griffiths, eds., *Interest Groups in Soviet Politics* (Princeton, N.J.: Princeton University Press, 1971).

43. Wendell King, *Social Movements in the United States* (New York: Random House, 1956), 27.

44. James C. Davies, "Towards a Theory of Revolution," *American Sociological Review*, 27 (February 1962):5–19; and Ted Robert Gurr, *Why Men Rebel* (Princeton, N.J.: Princeton University Press, 1970).

45. Denton Morrison, "Some Notes Toward a Theory of Relative Deprivation, Social Movements and Social Change," *American Behavioral Scientist*, 14 (May/June 1971):675–690.

46. Samuel Huntington, "Social and Institutional Dynamics of One-Party Systems," in Samuel Huntington and Barrington Moore, eds., *Authoritarian Politics in Modern Society* (New York: Basic Books, 1970), 18.

47. For example, John McCarthy and Mayer Zald, "Resource Mobilization and Social Movements: A Partial Theory," *American Journal of Sociology*, 82 (May 1977), 1212–1241.

48. J. C. Jenkins, "Resource Mobilization Theory and the Study of Social Movements," *Annual Review of Sociology*, 9 (1983):530.

49. Mancur Olson, *The Logic of Collective Action* (New York: Schocken, 1965).

50. Jadwiga Staniszkis, *Poland's Self-Limiting Revolution* (Princeton, N.J.: Princeton University Press, 1984).

51. Crane Brinton, *Anatomy of Revolution* (New York: Prentice-Hall, 1952).

52. Charles Tilly, *From Mobilization to Revolution* (Reading, Mass.: Addison and Wesley, 1978).

53. Theda Skocpol, *States and Social Revolutions* (New York: Cambridge University Press, 1979).

54. Cited in *Survey*, 26 (Autumn 1982).

55. These patterns are described by Rex Hopper in "The Revolutionary Process," *Social Forces*, 28 (March 1950):270–279.

CHAPTER THREE

1. *New York Times*, July 17, 1990, A8.

2. *New York Times*, September 13, 1990.

3. "Treuhand in Action: The Privatization of East Germany," *Transition: The Newsletter About Reforming Economies*, 2, no. 5 (May 1991):3–5.

4. *New York Times*, September 20, 1990.

5. Martin Malia, "The Soviet Union Has Ceased to Exist," *New York Times*, September 4, 1990.

6. *Washington Post*, December 30, 1991, A10; cited in Carol Barner-Barry and Cynthia A. Hody, *The Politics of Change: The Transformation of the Former Soviet Union* (New York: St. Martin's, 1995), 101.

7. See, for example, Richard Rose and Christian Haerpfer, *New Russia Barometer II: The Results* (Glasgow: University of Strathclyde, 1994).

8. See Robin Alison Remington, "Bosnia: The Tangled Web," *Current History* (November 1993):364–369; and "The Republics of the Former Yugoslavia," in Minton F. Goldman, *Russia, the Eurasian Republics, and Central/Eastern Europe*, 5th edition (Guilford, Conn.: Dushkin, 1994).

9. Quoted in the *New York Times*, November 1, 1995, A1.

CHAPTER FOUR

1. *Vademecum Partii I Ugrupowan Politycznych* (Handbook of political parties and groups) (Warsaw: Polska Agencja Prasowa, 1990).

2. Much of this section is drawn from Vladimir V. Kusin, "The Elections Compared and Assessed," *Report on Eastern Europe* (published by Radio Free Europe/Radio Liberty), July 13, 1990.

3. For a review of Hungary's transition in 1989 and 1990, see Alfred Reisch, "Hungary in 1989: A Country in Transition," *Report on Eastern Europe,* January 5, 1990, 19–23; and Judith Pataki, "Major Political Change and Economic Stagnation," *Report on Eastern Europe,* January 4, 1991, 20–24.

4. Michael Shafir, "Romania: Promises and Reality," *Report on Eastern Europe,* January 4, 1991, 35.

5. For a review of developments in Bulgaria in 1990, see Rada Nikolaev, "Bulgaria: Between Hope and Hunger," *Report on Eastern Europe,* January 4, 1991, 5–10.

6. *New York Times,* June 5, 1991, 1.

7. Elej Biberaj, speaking at The Woodrow Wilson Center on East European Studies and reported in the Center's *Meeting Report* of March-April 1994, p. 5.

8. Adrian Karatnycky, "The Return of the Former Communists," *Indianapolis Star,* July 14, 1994.

9. Robert A. Dahl, *Polyarchy: Participation and Opposition* (New Haven, Conn.: Yale University Press, 1971), 1–10.

10. Robert Dahl, "Procedural Democracy," in P. Laslett and J. Fishkin, eds., *Philosophy, Politics and Society* (Oxford: Basil Blackwell, 1979), 97–113.

11. Some scholars posit even more extensive requirements for a liberal democracy. Valerie Bunce, for example, mentions five characteristics: rule of law, extensive civil liberties guaranteed by law, representative government, Weberian bureaucracy, and some dispersion of economic resources. She sees the fourth as necessary to make the bureaucracy accountable to the public and the fifth to avoid excessive concentration of resources in the hands of the government. Valerie Bunce, "The Struggle for Liberal Democracy in Eastern Europe," *World Policy Journal,* 7, no. 3 (Summer 1990):399.

12. Article 50 of the Constitution of the Union of Soviet Socialist Republics, adopted in 1977.

13. Philippe Schmitter, "The Consolidation of Political Democracy in Southern Europe," unpublished manuscript, 1988.

14. Schmitter, "The Consolidation of Political Democracy," 26.

15. Dahl, *Polyarchy,* 38–39.

16. Arend Lijphart, "Consociational Democracy," *World Politics,* 21 (1969) and *Democracy in Plurals Societies: A Comparative Exploration* (New Haven, Conn.: Yale University Press, 1980). See also a useful summary of these ideas in B. Guy Peters, John C. Doughtie, and M. Kathleen McCulloch, "Do Public Policies Vary in Different Types of Democratic Systems," in Paul G. Lewis, David C. Potter, and Francis G. Castles, eds., *The Practice of Comparative Politics* (London: Longman, 1978), 73–75.

17. Ivan Szelenyi, "Eastern Europe in an Epoch of Transition: Toward a Socialist Mixed Economy," in V. Nee and D. Stark, eds., *Remaking the Economic Institutions of Socialism* (Stanford, Calif.: Stanford University Press, 1989), 208–233.

18. Grzegorz Ekiert, "Prospects and Dilemmas of the Transition to a Market Economy in East Central Europe" (Paper presented at the annual convention of the American Political Science Association, San Francisco, Calif., August 1990), 11.

19. Paul Marer, "Roadblocks to Economic Transformation in Central and Eastern Europe and Some Lessons of Market Economies," in Dick Clark, ed., *United States–Soviet and East European Relations: Building a Congressional Cadre* (Queenstown, Md.: Aspen Institute, 1990), 24.

20. Jeffrey Sachs and David Lipton, "Poland's Economic Reform," *Foreign Affairs*, 69, no. 3 (Summer 1990):49.

21. "Warsaw Turns on the Stock Tickers," *New York Times*, April 17, 1991.

22. *Rebuilding Eastern Europe* (Frankfurt: Deutsche Bank Economics Department, 1991), 86.

23. *Rebuilding Eastern Europe*, 87–90.

24. John Kenneth Galbraith, "The Rush to Capitalism," *New York Review of Books*, October 25, 1990, 51–52.

25. Sachs and Lipton, "Poland's Economic Reform," 48.

26. Sachs and Lipton, "Poland's Economic Reform," 56.

27. The following discussion of Hungary's reforms is based primarily on Tamas Bauer, "Reforming the Planned Economy: The Hungarian Experience," *Annals of the American Academy of Political and Social Science*, 507 (January 1990):103–112.

28. *Rebuilding Eastern Europe*, 52.

29. Marer, "Roadblocks to Economic Transformation in Central and Eastern Europe and Some Lessons of Market Economies," 20.

30. Padma Desai, "Aftershock in Russia's Economy," *Current History* (October 1994):320–323.

31. *New York Times*, January 24, 1992, A5.

32. See David S. Mason and Svetlana Sydorenko, "Perestroyka, Social Justice, and Soviet Public Opinion," *Problems of Communism*, 39 (November–December 1990):34–43.

33. This survey was based on a large representative national sample and was conducted between June and September 1989; reported in Witold Morawski, "Reform Models and Systemic Change" (Paper presented to the Fourth World Congress for Soviet and East European Studies, Harrogate, England, July 1990).

34. Centrum Badania Opinii Spolecznej, "Opinia Publiczna o Prywatyzacji: Komunikat z badan" (Public opinion on privatization: Research communique), Warsaw, May 1991.

35. "Excerpts from the Pope's Encyclical: On Giving Capitalism a Human Face," *New York Times*, May 3, 1991, 1, 7.

36. Summer 1994 Gallup polls reported in the *New York Times*, September 30, 1994; the "New Democracies Barometer" of the Paul Lazarsfeld Society of Vienna survey results from late 1993 and early 1994 reported in the World Bank's *Transition*, July–August 1994.

37. *Crisis in Mortality, Health and Nutrition,* Regional Monitoring Report No. 2 (Florence, Italy: UNICEF International Child Development Center, 1994).

38. *New York Times,* April 20, 1995, p. C2.

39. From the "Jamestown Monitor" (electronic newspaper), June 8, 1995.

40. From Clair Sterling, *Thieves' World* (Simon and Schuster, 1994); quoted in World Bank, *Transition,* April 1994, 6.

41. James G. Kellas, *The Politics of Nationalism and Ethnicity* (London: Macmillan, 1991), 2.

42. Anthony D. Smith, *Theories of Nationalism* (London: Duckworth, 1971), 23–24.

43. Adam Michnik, "Notes on the Revolution," *New York Times Magazine,* March 11, 1990, 44.

44. Astrid S. Tuminez, "The Soviet Union's 'Small' Dictators," *Christian Science Monitor,* May 3, 1991, 19.

45. National survey conducted in November 1989; reported in Galin Gornev and Pepka Boyadzhieva, "Characteristics of the Perception of Justice in Contemporary Bulgaria," unpublished manuscript, June 1990.

46. As told to Bill Keller of the *New York Times* and quoted in Hedrick Smith, *The New Russians* (New York: Avon Books, 1991), 405.

47. Cited in Abraham Brumberg, "Poland: The Demise of Communism," *Foreign Affairs,* 69, no. 1 (1990):83.

48. *New York Times,* June 19, 1991.

49. Dahl, *Polyarchy,* 44.

50. Quoted in the *New York Times,* June 30, 1991, sec. 4.

51. Michnik, "Notes on the Revolution," 45.

52. *Transition: The Newsletter About Reforming Economies,* 2, no. 5 (May 1991):7.

CHAPTER FIVE

1. *Rebuilding Eastern Europe* (Frankfurt: Deutsche Bank Economics Department, 1991), 93.

2. Quoted in the *New York Times,* July 2, 1991.

3. U.S. Department of Defense, *United States Security Strategy for Europe and NATO* (Washington, D.C.: June 1995).

4. *New York Times,* December 6, 1994, A4.

5. The Atlantic Council, based in Washington, D.C., sponsors a number of excellent educational and informational programs on Atlantic community issues for faculty and students of affiliated universities.

6. *New York Times,* November 22, 1995, A7.

7. George Schopflin, "The Political Traditions of Eastern Europe," *Daedalus,* 119, no. 1 (Winter 1990):61.

8. Jiri Dienstbier, "Central Europe's Security," *Foreign Policy,* no. 83 (Summer 1991):127.

9. Leigh Bruce, "Europe's Locomotive," *Foreign Policy,* no. 78 (Spring 1990):82.

10. *New York Times,* May 6, 1991, C3.

11. Theodore C. Sorensen, "Rethinking National Security," *Foreign Affairs*, 69, no. 3 (1990):6–7.

12. *New York Times*, January 12, 1992, E3.

13. Quoted in "Chronology 1990," *Foreign Affairs*, 70, no. 1 (1991):230.

14. Cited in Graham E. Fuller, "Moscow and the Gulf War," *Foreign Affairs*, 70, no. 3 (1991):67.

15. "A New Military Budget for a New World," *Defense Monitor*, 20, no. 2 (1991).

16. *New York Times*, July 8, 1994.

17. *New York Times*, July 12, 1994.

18. *New York Times*, November 28, 1995.

19. *Rebuilding Eastern Europe* (Frankfurt: Deutsche Bank, 1991), 97.

20. *New York Times*, January 23, 1992, A4.

21. *New York Times*, January 24, 1992, C2.

22. *New York Times*, April 30, 1995, E4.

23. *New York Times*, July 8, 1994.

24. President George Bush in his speech to a Joint Session of Congress; printed in the *Washington Post*, September 12, 1990, A34.

25. *New York Times*, June 26, 1991.

26. *New York Times*, July 8, 1991.

27. John Darnton, "In Decolonized, Destitute Africa, Bankers Are the New Overlords," *New York Times*, June 20, 1994.

28. *Defense Monitor*, 20, no. 4 (1991).

29. Francis Fukuyama, "The End of History?" *National Interest*, no. 16 (Summer 1989):3.

30. Samuel P. Huntington, "The Clash of Civilizations?" *Foreign Affairs*, 72 (Summer 1993):22–49.

31. Paul Kennedy, *The Rise and Fall of the Great Powers: Economic Change and Military Conflict from 1500 to 2000* (New York: Random House, 1987), xvi.

32. Ibid.

33. *New York Times*, September 8, 1991, 1.

□ □ □

Suggested Readings

CHAPTER ONE

Ash, Timothy Garton. *The Polish Revolution: Solidarity.* New York: Scribner's, 1983.

Ash, T. G. *The Uses of Adversity: Essays on the Fate of Central Europe.* New York: Vintage, 1990.

Brzezinski, Zbigniew. *The Grand Failure: The Birth and Death of Communism in the Twentieth Century.* New York: Scribner's, 1988.

Brzezinski, Zbigniew. *The Soviet Bloc: Unity and Conflict,* rev. ed. Cambridge, Mass.: Harvard University Press, 1971.

Crampton, R. J. *Eastern Europe in the Twentieth Century.* New York: Routledge, 1994.

Djilas, Milovan. *The New Class.* New York: Praeger, 1967.

Havel, Vaclav. *Living in Truth.* New York: Faber and Faber, 1987.

Lewis, Paul G. *Central Europe Since 1945.* New York: Longman, 1994.

Michnik, Adam. *Letters from Prison and Other Essays.* Berkeley: University of California Press, 1986.

Paterson, Thomas G. *The Origins of the Cold War,* 2d ed. Lexington, Mass.: D. C. Heath, 1974.

Rothschild, Joseph. *Return to Diversity: A Political History of East Central Europe Since World War II,* 2d ed. New York: Oxford University Press, 1993.

Seton-Watson, Hugh. *The East European Revolution.* New York: Praeger, 1956.

Skilling, H. Gordon. *Charter 77 and Human Rights in Czechoslovakia.* London: Allen and Unwin, 1981.

Stokes, Gale, ed. *From Stalinism to Pluralism: A Documentary History of Eastern Europe Since 1945.* New York: Oxford University Press, 1991.

CHAPTER TWO

Ash, Timothy Garton. *The Magic Lantern: The Revolution of '89 Witnessed in Warsaw, Budapest, Berlin, and Prague.* New York: Random House, 1990.

Brinton, Crane. *Anatomy of Revolution.* New York: Prentice-Hall, 1952.

Brinton, William M., and Alan Rinzler, eds. *Without Force or Lies: Voices from the Revolution of Central Europe in 1989–90.* San Francisco: Mercury House, 1990.

Davies, James C. "Towards a Theory of Revolution." *American Sociological Review* 27 (1962):5–19.

Dawisha, Karen. *Eastern Europe, Gorbachev, and Reform.* Cambridge, Eng.: Cambridge University Press, 1988.

Echikson, William. *Lighting the Night: Revolution in Eastern Europe.* New York: William Morrow, 1990.

Glenny, Misha. *The Rebirth of History: Eastern Europe in the Age of Democracy.* London: Penguin, 1990.

Gorbachev, Mikhail. *Perestroika: New Thinking for Our Country and the World.* New York: Harper and Row, 1987.

Graubard, Stephen R., ed. *Eastern Europe . . . Central Europe . . . Europe.* Boulder: Westview Press, 1991.

Gurr, Ted Robert. *Why Men Rebel.* Princeton: Princeton University Press, 1970.

Sakwa, Richard. *Gorbachev and His Reforms, 1985–1990.* New York: Prentice-Hall, 1990.

Skocpol, Theda. *Social Revolutions in the Modern World.* Cambridge, Eng.: Cambridge University Press, 1994.

Smith, Hedrick. *The New Russians.* New York: Avon Books, 1991.

Stokes, Gale. *The Walls Came Tumbling Down: The Collapse of Communism in Eastern Europe.* New York: Oxford, 1993.

CHAPTER THREE

Burg, Steven, and Paul Shoup. *Ethnic Conflict and International Intervention: The Crisis in Bosnia-Herzegovina, 1990–1993.* White Plains, N.Y.: M. E. Sharpe, 1994.

Cohen, Lenard J. *Broken Bonds: The Disintegration of Yugoslavia.* 2d ed. Boulder: Westview Press, 1994.

Dallin, Alexander, and Gail W. Lapidus, eds. *The Soviet System: From Crisis to Collapse.* Boulder: Westview Press, 1994.

Daniels, Robert V., ed. *Soviet Communism from Reform to Collapse.* Lexington, Mass.: D. C. Heath, 1995.

Denber, Rachel, ed. *The Soviet Nationality Reader: The Disintegration in Context.* Boulder: Westview Press, 1992.

Hall, Brian. *The Impossible Country: A Journey Through the Last Days of Yugoslavia.* Boston: David R. Godine, 1994.

Hamalainen, P. K. *Uniting Germany.* Boulder: Westview Press, 1994.

Lieven, Anatol. *The Baltic Revolution: Estonia, Latvia, Lithuania, and the Path to Independence.* New Haven: Yale University Press, 1993.

Malcolm, Noel. *Bosnia: A Short History.* New York: New York University Press, 1994.

Pond, Elizabeth. *Beyond the Wall: Germany's Road to Unification.* Washington, D.C.: Brookings, 1993.

Remnick, David. *Lenin's Tomb: The Last Days of the Soviet Empire.* New York: Random House, 1993.

Twining, David T. *The New Eurasia: Guide to the Republics of the Former Soviet Union.* Westport, Conn.: Praeger, 1993.

Woodward, Susan. *Balkan Tragedy: Chaos and Dissolution After the Cold War.* Washington, D.C.: Brookings, 1995.

CHAPTER FOUR

Aslund, Anders. *How Russia Became a Market Economy.* Washington, D.C.: Brookings, 1995.

Berglund, Sten, and Jan Dellenbrant, eds. *The New Democracies in Eastern Europe: Party Systems and Political Cleavages.* 2d ed. Aldershot, Eng.: Edward Elgar, 1994.

Brown, J. F. *Hopes and Shadows: Eastern Europe After Communism.* Durham, N.C.: Duke University Press, 1994.

Bugajski, Janusz. *Nations in Turmoil: Conflict and Cooperation in Eastern Europe.* 2d ed. Boulder: Westview Press, 1995.

Crawford, Beverly, ed. *Markets, States, and Democracy: The Political Economy of Post-Communist Transformation.* Boulder: Westview Press, 1994.

Dahl, Robert A. *Polyarchy: Participation and Opposition.* New Haven: Yale University Press, 1971.

Frydman, Roman, Andrzej Rapaczynski, and John Earle. *The Privatization Process in Central Europe.* Oxford, Eng.: Oxford University Press, 1993.

Hockenos, Paul. *Free to Hate: The Rise of the Right in Post-Communist Europe.* New York: Routledge, 1993.

Horak, Stephan M. *Eastern European National Minorities, 1919–1980: A Handbook.* Littleton, Colo.: Libraries Unlimited, 1995.

Huntington, Samuel P. *The Third Wave: Democratization in the Late Twentieth Century.* Norman: University of Oklahoma Press, 1991.

Kaiser, Robert J. *The Geography of Nationalism in Russia and the USSR.* Princeton: Princeton University Press, 1994.

Karp, Regina Cowen, ed. *Central and Eastern Europe: The Challenge of Transition.* London: Oxford University Press, 1993.

Kurski, Jaroslaw. *Lech Walesa: Democrat or Dictator?* Boulder: Westview Press, 1993.

Lapidus, Gail W., ed. *The New Russia: Troubled Transformation.* Boulder: Westview Press, 1994.

Latawski, Paul, ed. *Contemporary Nationalism in East Central Europe.* New York: St. Martin's, 1995.

Mestrovic, Stjepan. *The Road from Paradise: Prospects for Democracy in Eastern Europe.* Lexington: University of Kentucky Press, 1994.

Michta, Andrew A. *The Government and Politics of Postcommunist Europe.* Westport, Conn.: Praeger, 1994.

Millar, James R., and Sharon L. Wolchik, eds. *The Social Legacy of Communism.* New York: Cambridge University Press, 1994.

Milor, Vedat, ed. *Changing Political Economies: Privatization in Post-Communist and Reforming Communist States.* Boulder: Lynne Rienner, 1994.

O'Donnell, Guillermo, and Philippe C. Schmitter, eds. *Transitions from Authoritarian Rule: Tentative Conclusions About Uncertain Democracies.* Baltimore: Johns Hopkins University Press, 1986.

Pereira, Luiz Carlos Bresser, Jose Maria Maravall, and Adam Przeworski. *Economic Reforms in New Democracies: A Social-Democratic Approach.* Cambridge, Eng.: Cambridge University Press, 1993.

Pridham, Geoffrey, and Tatu Vanhanen, eds. *Democratization in Eastern Europe: Domestic and International Perspectives.* New York: Routledge, 1994.

Przeworski, Adam. *Democracy and the Market: Political and Economic Reforms in Eastern Europe and Latin America.* Cambridge, Eng.: Cambridge University Press, 1991.

Public Policy and Social Conditions. Regional Monitoring Report No. 1. Florence, Italy: UNICEF, November 1993.

Sachs, Jeffrey, and David Lipton. "Poland's Economic Reform." *Foreign Affairs* 69, no. 3 (Summer 1990):48–66.

Welsh, Helga. "Political Transition Processes in Central and Eastern Europe." *Comparative Politics* 26, no. 4 (July 1994):379–394.

Yergin, Daniel, and Thane Gustafson. *Russia 2010—and What It Means for the World.* New York: Vintage, 1995.

CHAPTER FIVE

Allison, Graham, and Gregory Treverton, eds. *Rethinking America's Security: Beyond Cold War to New World Order.* New York: Norton, 1992.

Baylis, Thomas. *The West and Eastern Europe: Economic Statecraft and Political Change.* Westport, Conn.: Praeger, 1993.

Campbell, Kurt G., and Thomas G. Weiss. "The Third World in the Wake of Eastern Europe." *Washington Quarterly* 14, no. 2 (Spring 1991):91–108.

Dienstbier, Jiri. "Central Europe's Security." *Foreign Policy,* no. 83 (1991):119–127.

Fukuyama, Francis. "The End of History?" *National Interest,* no. 16 (Summer 1989).

Gurr, T. R., and Barbara Harff. *Ethnic Conflict in World Politics.* 2d ed. Boulder: Westview Press, 1994.

Huntington, Samuel P. "The Clash of Civilizations?" *Foreign Affairs* 72 (Summer 1993):22–49.

Kennedy, Paul. *The Rise and Fall of the Great Powers: Economic Change and Military Conflict from 1500 to 2000.* New York: Random House, 1987.

Latawski, Paul. *The Security Route to Europe: The Visegrad Four.* London: Royal United Services Institute, 1994.

Moynihan, Daniel Patrick. *Pandaemonium: Ethnicity in International Politics.* Oxford: Oxford University Press, 1993.

Pinder, John. *The European Community and Eastern Europe.* New York: Council on Foreign Relations, 1991.

Shearman, Peter, ed. *Russian Foreign Policy Since 1990.* Boulder: Westview Press, 1995.

Shtromas, Alexander. *The End of Isms: Reflections on the Fate of Ideological Politics After Communism's Collapse*. London: Blackwell, 1994.

Slater, Robert O., Barry M. Schutz, and Steven R. Dorr, eds. *Global Transformation and the Third World*. Boulder: Lynne Rienner, 1993.

Weiss, Thomas G., ed. *The United Nations and Civil Wars*. Boulder: Lynne Rienner, 1995.

CURRENT EVENTS

The pace of change is so rapid in East-Central Europe that one has to follow newspapers and journals to keep up with events. The best U.S. newspaper for this purpose is the *New York Times*, which usually has daily stories from the Soviet successor states and from East-Central Europe. The *Christian Science Monitor*, the *Washington Post*, and the *Wall Street Journal* also have good coverage of the region. Other publications that have good coverage include the *Economist* (London) and the *New York Review of Books*, which has occasional essays and thought pieces by intellectuals in the United States and Western Europe (e.g., T. G. Ash and Martin Malia) and East-Central Europe (e.g., Vaclav Havel and Adam Michnik).

For translated materials *from* the media in these countries, there are a number of useful sources. The *Current Digest of the Post-Soviet Press* provides a weekly digest of translated articles from the former Soviet Union. *CDSP* is indexed quarterly and annually, which makes it a useful research tool. There are also several English-language publications emanating from Russia, including the weekly *Moscow News*. In East-Central Europe, there are also some English-language newspapers, such as The *Warsaw Voice* and The *Prague Post*, though they are not easily available in the United States.

The Open Media Research Institute (OMRI), the successor to the Radio Free Europe/Radio Liberty Research departments, publishes a useful bimonthly publication called *Transition: Events and Issues in the Former Soviet Union and East-Central and Southeastern Europe*. OMRI also publishes the *OMRI Daily Digest*, a six-page report focusing on news and developments in the region, which is available free of charge through electronic mail. Individuals may subscribe by sending an email message to: LISTSERV@UBVM.CC.BUFFALO.EDU. The subject window should be blank; in the body of the message, write: SUBSCRIBE OMRI-L FIRSTNAME LASTNAME (substituting your first and last names where shown).

There are also a burgeoning number of World Wide Web sites with information about the former communist states. An excellent starting place for these is REESweb of the University of Pittsburgh, which is a directory of internet resources from and about the countries of Eurasia and Eastern Europe. This site includes many links to other sites, including the official home pages of many of the countries in the region (http://www.library.pitt.edu/~cjp/rees.html).

For current information on Bosnia, the Department of Defense offers "BosniaLink," a resource for news and information on the U.S. military operation there, including maps, fact sheets, briefing transcripts, news releases, and speeches (http://www.dtic.dla.mil/bosnia/).

Some libraries also subscribe to two U.S. government publications that translate material from the postcommunist media: *Foreign Broadcast Information Service (FBIS), Daily Report: Central Eurasia* (for the former Soviet Union); and *Daily Report: East Europe.* Weekly news on Germany and summaries of the German press are provided in the German Information Office publication *The Week in Germany.*

□ □ □

Video Resources

There are several series of documentary videotapes that bring to life some of the key events of Eastern European and Soviet history. One of these, *The Eagle and the Bear*, is a series consisting of fifty-two videos, each twenty-three minutes in length, about the Cold War. They include some very good documentaries on East-Central Europe (available for purchase from MTI Film and Video, 108 Wilmot Road, Deerfield, IL 60015; telephone 1–800–621–2131).

Dateline: 1944—Yugoslavia. Tito's consolidation of power in wartime Yugoslavia, Allied jockeying over the country, and Tito's maneuvering for independence.

Dateline: 1945—Berlin. The occupation and division of Berlin at the end of World War II.

Dateline: 1948—Berlin. The blockade of Berlin and the legendary Berlin Airlift, a crisis point in the early Cold War.

Dateline: 1956—Budapest. The Hungarian Revolution and its crushing by Soviet tanks.

Dateline: 1961—Berlin. The Cold War face-off between Khrushchev and Kennedy over Berlin and the establishment of the Berlin Wall.

Dateline: 1968—Czechoslovakia. The background to the Prague Spring and Warsaw Pact intervention.

Dateline: 1980—Gdansk. The dockworkers' strikes in this coastal city and the emergence of Lech Walesa and Solidarity, the first independent trade union in the Soviet bloc.

Dateline: 1980—Poland. A follow-up to *1980—Gdansk* traces the sixteen-month life of Solidarity and its crushing with the implementation of martial law.

Dateline: 1989—Berlin, Hungary, Prague, and Romania (four tapes). The background to and events of the revolutions of 1989.

MTI Film and Video also distributes two good series on Gorbachev's Soviet Union. The first series, *Inside Gorbachev's USSR*, includes four sixty-minute videos (available for purchase or rental), narrated by Hedrick Smith for PBS, that look at democratization, perestroika, glasnost, and nationalism through the eyes of ordinary citizens (some of whom also appear in Smith's fine book *The New Russians*).

The Taste of Democracy. The process of democratization in the country and in the new Congress of Peoples' Deputies.

Looking for Perestroika. The plans and pitfalls of economic reform, including interviews at a coal mine, a state farm, and a private enterprise.

Comfortable Lies, Bitter Truths. The struggle over glasnost in the bureaucracy, the media, and the schools.

Coming Apart. Under the impact of glasnost, the resurgence of religious movements, ethnic rivalries, and movements for independence in five different republics.

Hedrick Smith produced a sequel to this series entitled "After Gorbachev's USSR," which aired on PBS in February 1992 (available from PBS Video; telephone 1-800-328-PBS1).

The second series available from MTI is called *The Second Russian Revolution,* a six-part series made for BBC Television and the Discovery Channel. These videos, each about fifty minutes long, use documentary footage and interviews with senior Soviet officials and chronicle the rise of Gorbachev and his efforts to change the Soviet Union. An additional video, *Anatomy of a Coup,* looks at the failed coup attempt of August 1991.

On the crisis in Bosnia, the following two videos are particularly good for gaining an understanding of the historical and cultural aspects of the conflicts. *Bosnia: We Are All Neighbors* portrays conversations by an anthropologist with several Muslim and Catholic families in a village near Sarajevo before and after the fighting. Fifty-three minutes long, it aired on PBS in May 1994 (see PBS telephone number above). *Breakup in the Balkans,* produced in 1993 by the Center for Defense Information, provides a good review of the history of the conflict and a discussion of current options, including the role of NATO and the UN (twenty-eight minutes). Available from the Center for Defense Information, 1500 Massachusetts Avenue, N.W., Washington, D.C. 20005 (telephone 202-862-0700).

Glossary

Anti-Semitism. Antipathy toward Jews; it took extreme form in Germany under Adolf Hitler, who pursued a deliberate policy of extermination of European Jews.

apartheid. The policy of "separate development" of the races implemented by the white minority government in South Africa from the 1940s until the election of the majority rule government in 1994.

Brezhnev Doctrine. This refers to the Soviet policy, enunciated by party leader Leonid Brezhnev, that justified Soviet intervention in the neighboring socialist states (e.g., Czechoslovakia in 1968) that strayed too far from the Soviet model.

Central Committee. One of the top policy-making bodies of the communist parties in Eastern Europe and the Soviet Union; formally elected by the party congress and formally approved by members of the politburo.

Charter 77. The document signed in 1977 by a group of Czechoslovak intellectuals (including Vaclav Havel) that called for greater respect for human rights and for the fundamental freedoms provided for in the Helsinki Accords; the term came to be used to refer to the human rights movement in Czechoslovakia, though Charter 77 was never a formal organization.

Civic Forum. The loose coalition formed in Czechoslovakia by Vaclav Havel and others in November 1989 to coordinate the protests against the communist government; together with Public Against Violence, the coalition won the first free parliamentary elections in June 1990.

civil society. A concept developed in the 1970s in Eastern Europe. Its underlying idea is that people can and should live as much as possible outside the official structures and patterns of life prescribed by the communist authorities.

Cold War. The term used to describe the war-like state of tension between the Soviet Union and the United States in the post–World War II era.

collective security. The original principle behind the League of Nations and the United Nations, which held that aggression against one state should be treated as aggression against all states and therefore it should be resisted by common action of all states.

collectivization. The policy pursued by communist regimes in the Soviet Union and Eastern Europe to replace private farms with collective farms (kolkhozy) and state-owned farms.

Comecon. The Council for Mutual Economic Assistance (also abbreviated CMEA), the organization created by Moscow in 1949 to coordinate trade and integrate the economies of the European communist states; dissolved in 1991.

Cominform. The Communist Information Bureau, formed in 1947 to coordinate policies among the European communist states; dissolved in 1956 as part of Moscow's efforts at reconciliation with Yugoslavia.

Comintern. The Communist International (or Third International), established in 1919 in Moscow to give communist leadership to the world socialist movement; dissolved by Soviets in 1943 to reassure World War II allies.

Commonwealth of Independent States (CIS). The successor to the Union of Soviet Socialist Republics, it was first constituted in December 1991 by Russia, Ukraine, and Byelorussia (now Belarus), and later joined by the former Soviet republics of Moldavia (now Moldova), Armenia, Azerbaijan, Turkmenistan, Uzbekistan, Kirghizia (now Kyrgyzstan), Kazakhstan, and Tadzhikistan (now Tajikstan).

Conference on Security and Cooperation in Europe (CSCE). This organization is composed of most states in Europe and North America, whose representatives signed the Helsinki Agreements in 1975 and the "Charter for a New Europe" in 1990, and who meet periodically to discuss peace and security issues. Renamed the Organization for Security and Cooperation in Europe (OSCE) in 1995.

consociational democracy. A form of democracy, but distinguished from competitive majority rule democracy, that might promote political stability in ethnically fragmented states. Such a system is characterized by power-sharing among elites representing the different subcultures; decision making by compromise or consensus; and proportional distribution of public goods among the subcultures.

containment. The guiding doctrine of U.S. foreign policy in the postwar period, first enunciated in 1947 by George Kennan (a U.S. State Department official), who called for "the firm and vigilant containment of Russian expansive tendencies."

Council of Ministers. The top executive body of the government structure in communist party states, including heads of most government ministries.

currency convertibility. This term refers to the goal of most postcommunist governments—to give their national currencies real values by making them freely exchangeable at market rates with other (especially Western) currencies.

democratization. One of the elements of Gorbachev's reform program in the Soviet Union that included a reduced role for the communist party, greater opportunity for independent interest groups, increasingly competitive elections to state and party bodies, and an enhanced role for the national legislature.

European Bank for Reconstruction and Development (EBRD). An international bank founded in 1990 to promote investment, privatization, and competitiveness in the postcommunist states. Acting in conjunction with the IMF and the World Bank, the bank was funded by 39 countries, including the EC countries, the United States, and Japan.

European Community (EC). A network of organizations whose aim is economic integration and political unity. It has a common membership of twelve Western European states and evolved from the European Economic Community (EEC), first formed in 1957.

European Union (EU). The new name for the European Community, adopted in 1992.

ethnic cleansing. The policy and practice pursued by some Serbs in Bosnia of removing Muslims from predominantly Serb areas, usually by forcible removal from their homes but sometimes accompanied by murder and rape.

G-7 (Group of Seven). The seven major industrial nations (Canada, France, Germany, Great Britain, Italy, Japan, and the United States), whose leaders meet periodically to discuss world economic issues.

GATT (General Agreement on Tariffs and Trade). An international organization, with a membership of over 100 states, that promotes the expansion of free trade; founded in 1947.

glasnost. The Russian word that means openness or publicity. The idea of openness was part of Gorbachev's reform program and was meant to reduce restriction on the media and open up previously forbidden topics for discussion.

gross national product (GNP). The total value of goods and services produced in a country and a standard measure of the size of a country's economy.

hegemony. This term means predominant influence or control; for example, when exercised by one state over another or, within a country, by one group over the rest of society.

Helsinki Agreements (also Helsinki Accords or Helsinki Final Act). A major diplomatic treaty signed by thirty-five nations in Helsinki in 1975 at the conclusion of the Conference on Security and Cooperation in Europe (CSCE). Besides numerous provisions promoting peace and security in Europe and East-West cooperation, the agreements also obliged all signatory states to promote human rights.

International Monetary Fund (IMF). A specialized agency of the United Nations, with over 150 member states, that promotes monetary stability by helping countries fund balance-of-payments deficits.

iron curtain. A phrase coined by Winston Churchill in a 1946 speech to describe the Soviet policy of isolating the communist states of Eastern Europe from the West.

irredentism. A policy advocating the acquisition of some region included in another country, usually based on ethnicity.

NATO (North Atlantic Treaty Organization). A regional mutual defense alliance formed in 1949, aimed at blocking the threat of Soviet military aggression in Europe. In 1995, its sixteen members included Belgium, Canada, Denmark, France, Germany, Greece, Iceland, Italy, Luxembourg, Netherlands, Norway, Portugal, Spain, Turkey, United Kingdom, and the United States.

New Economic Mechanism (NEM). The economic reform program introduced in Hungary in 1968 that was intended to reduce central planning and strengthen the role of the market. The reforms led to the elimination of most mandatory production targets for factories and enterprises, and enhanced enterprise autonomy in purchasing, production, and sales.

New Forum. The coalition of opposition forces that emerged in East Germany during the antigovernment demonstrations in the fall of 1989.

new thinking. The foreign policy component of Gorbachev's reform program in the late–1980s, which called for a reduced Soviet role in the Third World, improved East-West relations, and emphasis on global interdependence.

nomenklatura. A Russian word referring to the list of government positions whose appointees required party clearance. The term was used in all the European communist states to describe the political elite itself.

Organization for Security and Cooperation in Europe (OSCE). See Conference on Security and Cooperation in Europe.

Partnership for Peace (PFP). A program initiated by President Bill Clinton to bring the former communist countries into closer cooperation with NATO. By April 1995, twenty-six nations had joined the Partnership, including all of the former Warsaw Pact nations and their successor states, excepting only Tajikistan.

perestroika. The Russian word for economic restructuring, which was the cornerstone of Gorbachev's reform program in the late 1980s.

politburo. The top policy-making body in communist party states, consisting of ten to fifteen government and party leaders formally appointed by the party's central committee.

privatization. The postcommunist policy of selling or transferring state-owned industrial enterprises and agricultural land to the private sector.

Public Against Violence. The Civic Forum's political counterpart in the Slovak part of Czechoslovakia, which helped to lead the "velvet revolution" in 1989.

relative deprivation. A social science theory that explains the rise of social and revolutionary movements in a society. This theory holds that such movements develop after a period of some change and improvement in society, during which people come to expect further improvements that, however, are not forthcoming. This fosters frustration and grievances, which stimulate the formation of social and revolutionary movements.

resource mobilization. A social science theory that challenges the theory of relative deprivation. It contends that social and revolutionary movements develop because of long-term changes in group resources, organization, and opportunities for collective action. Grievances are a secondary factor.

samizdat. From the Russian words for "to publish on one's own," this refers to the illegal underground publications in the Soviet Union and Eastern Europe that proliferated during the 1970s.

second economy. This term refers to the black market or unofficial private sector in the communist countries, which operated outside of the official state sector.

socialist internationalism. A traditional principle of Soviet foreign policy that subordinated national interests to international socialist ones. This was used to justify both Soviet intervention in Eastern Europe (i.e., with the Brezhnev Doctrine) and Soviet support for Third World liberation movements.

Solidarity. The Polish trade union movement that was formed after the dockyard strikes in 1980, banned by martial law in December 1981, and legally reconstituted after the roundtable agreements in 1989. After winning partially free parliamentary elections in June 1989, Solidarity formed the first noncommunist government in Eastern Europe.

Titoism. The term, derived from the name of the Yugoslav party leader, Josip Broz Tito, was used by Soviet leadership in the 1950s to criticize Yugoslav-like nationalist deviation elsewhere in Eastern Europe.

totalitarianism. A term first developed to describe the highly-centralized and dictatorial one-party states in Europe during the 1930s: Nazi Germany (under Hitler); fascist Italy (under Mussolini); and communist Soviet Union (under Stalin). Later used by critics of communism to describe all communist party states, the concept holds that citizens in such states are totally controlled by the state.

Truman Doctrine. This refers to a speech made by President Harry Truman in March 1947 when the United States for the first time pledged support for "free people who are resisting attempted subjugation"; the doctrine became a basis for the U.S. policy of containment of communism.

Warsaw Pact. The Warsaw Treaty Organization (WTO) was the Soviet-dominated military alliance in Eastern Europe. It was formed in 1955 in response to German entry into NATO and dissolved in 1991. Members in 1990 were Bulgaria, Czechoslovakia, Hungary, Poland, Romania, and the USSR.

Western European Union (WEU). A mutual security organization of ten European states formed in 1948 but largely moribund until designated in 1991 as the defense component of the European Union.

xenophobia. Fear or hatred of foreigners or of other strangers (e.g., national minorities); related to the mass emotions of nationalism and ethnocentrism.

Yalta Agreements. The provisions concerning the postwar order in Europe signed by Franklin Roosevelt, Winston Churchill, and Joseph Stalin at a February 1945 summit meeting in the Soviet resort town of Yalta. Though they called for democratic governments in Eastern Europe, they also affirmed predominant Soviet influence in the region.

Chronology

1914–1917	World War I.
1917	The Bolshevik Revolution in Russia.
1919	The Communist International (Comintern) is established.
1939	The Soviet Union and Nazi Germany sign the Molotov-Ribbentrop nonaggression pact.
1941	Germany attacks the Soviet Union.
1945	The Yalta Agreements are signed by Stalin, Churchill, and Roosevelt.
1946	Churchill declares that an "iron curtain" has descended in Europe.
1947	The "Truman Doctrine" speech delivered to Congress. The Communist Information Bureau (Cominform) is established.
1948	Tito-Stalin split leads to expulsion of Yugoslavia from Cominform.
1949	The Council for Mutual Economic Assistance (CMEA) is established. The Soviet Union detonates its first atomic bomb. The North Atlantic Treaty Organization (NATO) is established.
1950–1953	The Korean War.
1953	Stalin dies and a power struggle ensues. Nikita Khrushchev defeats all rivals by 1958.
1955	The Warsaw Treaty Organization (WTO) is established in reaction to West Germany's entry into NATO. Khrushchev visits Yugoslavia, signs communiqué with Tito recognizing "national roads to socialism."
1956	Khrushchev makes his "Secret Speech" at the Twentieth Party Congress. The USSR begins a program of "destalinization." The Cominform is dissolved. Poland experiences civil unrest and the USSR suppresses rebellion in Hungary.
1961	The Berlin Wall is erected.
1962	Cuban missile crisis.
1964	Khrushchev is removed from power. Leonid Brezhnev becomes Communist Party of the Soviet Union (CPSU) General Secretary.
1968	Hungary begins its New Economic Mechanism, the most thoroughgoing reforms in Eastern Europe. The Prague Spring reforms in Czechoslovakia are ended by Soviet and

Warsaw Pact intervention in August. Legislative elections in Yugoslavia present two or more candidates for most seats for the first time.

1970 Riots and strikes in Poland protesting food price increases. Party leader Wladyslaw Gomulka is replaced by Edward Gierek.

1972 The first Strategic Arms Limitations Talks (SALT I) between the United States and the USSR.

1975 Leaders of thirty-five countries, including the United States and the Soviet Union, sign the Helsinki Accords.

1976 Another attempt to raise food prices in Poland meets with a response similar to that of 1970; the Workers' Defense Committee (KOR) is formed by intellectuals to defend arrested workers.

1977 Vaclav Havel and other dissident intellectuals in Czechoslovakia sign "Charter 77."

1978 Polish Cardinal Karol Wojtyla is elected Pope John Paul II.

1979 SALT II treaty is signed (but is never ratified by the U.S. Senate). The Soviet Union invades Afghanistan to support a communist faction.

1980 Polish shipyard workers in Gdansk and Szczecin strike to protest food price increases; strikes spread across country; government agrees to creation of independent trade union Solidarity. Yugoslav leader Tito dies; replaced by collective leadership.

1981 Martial law is declared in Poland on December 13; Solidarity is banned.

1982 Brezhnev dies and is succeeded by Yuri Andropov.

1983 Martial law formally lifted in Poland.

1985 March Mikhail Gorbachev assumes the position of CPSU General Secretary.

1986 The Soviet Union suffers a major nuclear disaster at Chernobyl in the Ukraine.

1987 U.S. President Ronald Reagan and USSR General Secretary Mikhail Gorbachev sign the Intermediate-Range Nuclear Forces (INF) Treaty in Washington, D.C.

November Boris Yeltsin, first secretary of the Moscow City Communist Party Committee and a nonvoting member of the politburo, is dismissed from both positions for criticizing what he called the slow pace of reform.

1988 August Ten thousand demonstrate in Prague on the twentieth anniversary of the WTO invasion.

December At the United Nations, Gorbachev announces plans for a major demobilization of Soviet troops.

1989 Early in the year, the Hungarian Communist party panel investigating the 1956 rebellion judges the events to have been "a popular uprising against an oligarchy which was humiliating the nation." The Communist party in Poland agrees to roundtable talks with Solidarity.

February   The Hungarian Socialist Worker's Party (HSWP) removes the clause from the country's constitution guaranteeing the leading role of the HSWP.

March   The Soviet Union holds the first contested elections since 1917 to elect the new 2,500-member Congress of People's Deputies. Boris Yeltsin and others opposed to the Communist party are elected. In the Kosovo region of Yugoslavia, thousands of ethnic Albanians clash with police.

May   Vaclav Havel is released from detention following an international condemnation of Czechoslovakia's poor human rights record. Hungary opens its border with Austria, opening the way for East Germans and others to flee to the West.

June   Solidarity practically sweeps the first free elections for the Polish Parliament.

July   Extensive strikes by Siberian and Ukrainian miners protesting poor working conditions and low wages and demanding accelerated reform.

August   A noncommunist government takes power in Poland under Tadeusz Mazowiecki.

September   The ruling communists and the opposition in Hungary agree on constitutional changes, a multiparty system, and free elections in 1990.

October   During Gorbachev's visit to East Germany during its fortieth anniversary celebrations, protests and demonstrations break out and grow to hundreds of thousands of people by mid-October. Honecker is replaced as party leader by Egon Krenz.

November   The fall of the Berlin Wall. Mass protests (350,000) in Prague in November result in the resignation of Communist party leaders. Karel Urbanek replaces Milos Jakes as the party leader, and Havel emerges as the opposition leader at the helm of the Civic Forum. After growing protests in Bulgaria, party leader Todor Zhivkov is replaced by Petar Mladenov, the foreign minister.

December   In Albania, antigovernment demonstrations are met with force by authorities. An alliance of opposition groups in Bulgaria forms the Union of Democratic Forces. In Romania, protestors and police clash in the mining town of Timisoara. After protests spread, party leader Nicolae Ceausescu and his wife Elena are arrested, tried, and executed on December 25. The National Salvation Front assumes power. Alexander Dubcek returns from "retirement" and is elected speaker of

	the Parliament in Czechoslovakia. Vaclav Havel is elected president.
1990 January	Poland begins its austere economic reform policy, the shock-therapy approach. In Yugoslavia, government initiates economic stabilization plan; League of Communists renounces communist monopoly of power.
February	The two-plus-four negotiations concerning the unification of Germany take place in Ottawa, Canada.
March	First free elections in Hungary and East Germany (GDR).
June	Free elections are held in Bulgaria and the communists (renamed Socialists) win a majority in Parliament. The Russian Parliament under the leadership of Boris Yeltsin proclaims the Russian Federation to be a sovereign country.
August	Iraq invades Kuwait.
September	The four Allies from World War II meet in Moscow and sign the "Treaty on the Final Settlement with Respect to Germany" officially relinquishing all occupational rights.
October 3	German unification.
November	Lech Walesa elected president of Poland. Delegates from NATO and the WTO meet and sign the treaty on Conventional Forces in Europe (CFE). Delegates from thirty-four European and North American states meet in Paris to sign the "Charter for a New Europe."
December	Eduard Shevardnadze resigns as Soviet foreign minister, warning of possibility of a hard-line coup attempt.
1991 January	The United States, allied with several other countries and with the backing of the United Nations, unleashes the air strike of the Persian Gulf War.
June	Parliaments of Slovenia and Croatia pass declarations of independence from Yugoslavia. Yugoslav government refuses recognition, and the country tumbles into civil war.
July	Signing of Strategic Arms Reduction Treaty (START I). The Warsaw Treaty Organization is officially dissolved at its last meeting in Prague.
August	A failed coup devised by hard-line communists against Gorbachev leads to the breakup of the Communist party and the Soviet Union.
September	The Baltic republics of Estonia, Latvia, and Lithuania declare their independence and are soon admitted to the United Nations. Miners' protests in Romania lead to the resignation of the prime minister and the formation of a new coalition government.
October	First totally free parliamentary elections in Poland; no party wins more than 12 percent of the vote. The second multiparty election in Bulgaria leads to the formation of a government under the opposition group, the Union of Democratic Forces.

December	The Soviet Union is dissolved after sixty-nine years of existence. Russia ratifies the Commonwealth of Independent States.
1992 January	Germany and other members of the EC recognize independence of Slovenia and Croatia. Yeltsin government frees most prices in Russia, leading to massive price increases.
March	Voters in a referendum in Bosnia-Herzegovina approve sovereignty and independence from Yugoslavia. Civil war erupts as Yugoslav-backed Serbs attempt to seize Bosnian territory for independent Serb state.
March	In second of free elections in Albania, Democratic party ousts communists from power.
March	Most of eighty-eight territorial units of the Russian Federation sign a Federal Treaty.
June	Presidents Georgy Bush and Boris Yeltsin sign START II accord.
October	In parliamentary elections in Lithuania, postcommunist party wins a majority of seats.
November	Bill Clinton defeats George Bush in U.S. presidential election.
1993 January	Czechoslovakia formally divided into the Czech Republic and Slovakia.
February	Former communist Algirdas Brazauskas elected president of Lithuania.
September	Polish parliamentary elections are won by the postcommunist parties, which then form a government.
September–October	In Russia, legislative gridlock leads President Yeltsin to disband the legislature. Group of deputies occupies the parliament building. Troops loyal to Yeltsin shell the parliament and arrest the insurgents.
December	Parliamentary elections in Russia result in strong showing for antireformist parties.
1994 January	President Clinton proposes NATO "Partnership for Peace" program.
April	First all-inclusive democratic elections in South Africa result in victory for Nelson Mandela and his African National Congress.
May	Hungarian parliamentary elections result in victory for the postcommunist Hungarian Socialist Party.
September	U.S. forces intervene in Haiti to restore President Jean-Bertrand Aristide to power.
October	In German parliamentary elections, Chancellor Helmut Kohl's center-right coalition maintains a slim parliamentary majority.
December	Bulgarian Socialist Party (postcommunist) returns to power after winning elections.

December	Russian military launches major assault on Chechnya to quash separatist movement there.
1995 January	Austria, Finland, and Sweden join the European Union.
July	Bosnian Serbs take control of town of Srebrenica, a UN-declared "safe area."
August	Croatian offensive in Krajina region defeats Serb forces there.
September	NATO, led by American fighter planes, launches major military operations against Serb positions in Bosnia.
November	Representatives of Serbia, Bosnia, and Croatia agree to Bosnian peace accord in Dayton, Ohio. Formally signed in Paris in December.
November	Postcommunist Aleksander Kwasniewski defeats Lech Walesa in Polish presidential elections.
December	In Russian parliamentary elections, communist party wins largest number of votes.
December	As agreed in the Dayton peace accord, the UN hands over Bosnian peacekeeping duties to NATO.
1996 February	Wlodzimierz Cimoszewicz is named prime minister of Poland, replacing Jozef Oleksy following allegations that he had earlier been a spy for Moscow.
February	The UN and Yugoslavia lift sanctions on the Bosnian Serbs after the Serb withdrawal from designated areas of Sarajevo.

□ □ □

About the Book and Author

Eastern and Western Europe continue to change in their relationship to one another and in their ongoing dynamic with the post-Soviet states. Economic development, electoral upheaval, and the Bosnian crisis all color the transition from communism to democracy and from a Cold War outlook to a new global order still taking shape.

In this fully revised and updated edition of his popular and critically acclaimed text, David Mason brings the revolutionary events of 1989 into context with the transitional yet turbulent 1990s. We see new parties, new politics, new constitutions, and new opportunities in light of economic shock therapies, "left turns" in recent elections, and dissolving sovereignties and alliances. Despite savage ethnic conflict, economic scarcity, and political insecurity, Mason shows us that East-Central Europe is consolidating and reemerging as a region to be reckoned with on the global stage.

David S. Mason is professor of political science at Butler University. His publications include *Public Opinion and Political Change in Poland* and *Social Justice and Political Change: Public Opinion in Capitalist and Post-Communist States*.

BOOKS IN THIS SERIES

Kenneth W. Grundy
**South Africa: Domestic Crisis
and Global Challenge**

□　□　□

Georg Sørensen
**Democracy and Democratization:
Process and Prospects in a Changing World**

□　□　□

Steve Chan
**East Asian Dynamism: Growth, Order, and
Security in the Pacific Region, second edition**

□　□　□

Jack Donnelly
International Human Rights

□　□　□

V. Spike Peterson and Anne Sisson Runyan
Global Gender Issues

□　□　□

Sarah J. Tisch and Michael B. Wallace
**Dilemmas of Development Assistance:
The What, Why, and Who of Foreign Aid**

□　□　□

Ted Robert Gurr and Barbara Harff
Ethnic Conflict in World Politics

□　□　□

Fredric S. Pearson
**The Global Spread of Arms: Political Economy of
International Security**

□　□　□

Deborah J. Gerner
One Land, Two Peoples:
The Conflict over Palestine, second edition

☐ ☐ ☐

Karen Mingst and Margaret P. Karns
The United Nations in the Post–Cold War Era

☐ ☐ ☐

Gareth Porter and Janet Welsh Brown
Global Environmental Politics, second edition

☐ ☐ ☐

Bruce E. Moon
Dilemmas of International Trade

☐ ☐ ☐

Barry B. Hughes
International Futures: Choices in the Creation
of a New World Order, second edition

Index

Abkhazia, separatists in, 86
Abuladze, Tengiz, 45
Activism, unofficial, 60–61
Adamec, Ladislav, 61, 70
Afghanistan
  invasion of, 28
  withdrawal from, 48, 171, 180
Agriculture
  collectivization of, 15–16, 20, 22
  percentage labor force in, 18(table)
  privatization of, 44
  See also Farms
Albania
  democratization in, 152
  elections/new government in, 112
  former communists in, 114
  irredentism in, 188
  liberation of, 39
  loans/investments for, 176
  PRC and, 24
  revolutions of 1989 and, 72
Alexander, King, assassination of, 87
Alia, Ramiz, 49, 50(table), 112
Alliance of Free Democrats, 107, 135
Alliances, revising, 156–158
Alternative society, creating, 37
Anatomy of Revolution (Brinton), 68
Andropov, Yuri, 41
Angola, Soviet collapse and, 180
Antipolitics (Konrad), 37
Anti-Semitism, 38, 113, 143
  return of, 107, 144, 150–151, 153
Antonescu, Ion, 151
April Action Program, 24
Aristide, Jean-Bertrand, 175
Armenia
  former communists in, 114
  Nagorno-Karabakh and, 146
  secession of, 82
  warfare in, 86

Arms race, 155, 171
  slowing, 42, 177–179
Assembly of National Fronts, 82
Authoritarian rule, 113, 114
  demise of, 117, 118
  movement from, 117, 122, 153
  persistence of, 117
  regime change from, 117(figure)
  restraint in, 70
Azerbaijan
  Nagorno-Karabakh and, 146
  warfare in, 86

Baker, James
  on Gulf Crisis/Soviets, 173
  "two-plus-four" and, 77
Balcerowicz, Leszek, 104
  plan by, 131, 132
Baltic republics, 7
  nationalistic forces in, 81
  secession of, 82
  UN mission to, 159
  See also Estonia; Latvia; Lithuania
Banking system, creation of, 123, 126, 127
BBC. *See* British Broadcasting Corporation
Belarus, 7
  nuclear weapons in, 178
Benda, Vaclav, essay by, 37
Berisha, Sali, 112
Berlin Wall, 57(photo), 59(photo), 76
  fall of, 56–58, 75
Bielecki, Jan Krzysztof, 104–105
Bierut, Boleslaw, 22
Black market, 37, 124
Bosnia, 7
  crisis in, xi, 167, 175, 184
  embargo on, 91, 92

nationalism in, 142
peacekeeping forces in, 95, 161, 189
referendum on, 88
Serb control of, 90
Bosnian Serbs, 88, 92
aggressiveness of, 6, 91, 93
Botez, Mihai, on NATO/Hungary, 161
Brandt, Willy, 76, 77
Brcko, dispute over, 94
Brezhnev, Leonid, 4, 26, 34, 41
Brezhnev Doctrine, 26, 28, 41, 67, 143
end of, 48–49, 54, 171
Brinton, Crane, 69
on revolutionary movements, 68
British Broadcasting Corporation
(BBC), 44, 72
BSP. *See* Bulgarian Socialist party
Bujak, Zbigniew, 70
Bulgaria
elections/new government in, 111,
113
EU association agreement with, 168
foreign debt of, 128
loans/investments for, 176
nationalism in, 147, 149–150
postwar influence in, 9
transformation for, 58–60, 123
Tripartite Pact and, 10
Turkish minority in, 147, 149
Bulgarian Agrarian National Union,
111
Bulgarian Communist party, 60, 111
Bulgarian Socialist party (BSP), 111
Bundestag, all-German elections to, 78
Bundeswehr, WTO and, 157–158
Bush, George, 184
conceptual vacuum and, 172
Gulf Crisis and, 174
new world order and, 173, 179, 183
START and, 178
United Europe and, 164

Calfa, Marian, 62
Campaign posters, 107–108
Capitalism
social justice and, 136–138
traditional, 131
Castro, Fidel, 180
CDU. *See* Christian Democratic Union
Ceausescu, Elena, 62
Ceausescu, Nicolae, 48–49, 50(table),
62
fall of, 70, 71, 109–110
Censorship, 15, 25, 44, 64
Center Alliance, 104

Central Committee, defined, 16
Central Europe
civil society and, 36–39
concept of, 38–39
development of, 164
Central planning, 29, 33, 114, 129
dismantling, 5, 139, 141, 152
"Centseimus Annus" (John Paul II),
138
CFE. *See* Treaty on Conventional
Forces in Europe
Charter 77, 36, 61, 110
"Charter for a New Europe" (CSCE),
158
Chauvinism, 142, 143
Chechnya, civil war in, 86, 147
Chernenko, Konstantin, 41
Chernomyrdin, Viktor, economic
reform and, 136
Children of the Arbat (Rybakov), 45
Christian Democratic party, coalition
with, 108
Christian Democratic Union (CDU),
77, 78, 79
Churchill, Winston
iron curtain speech by, 13, 17
postwar order and, 12
at Yalta, 9
CIS. *See* Commonwealth of
Independent States
Civic Forum, 36, 61, 68, 71, 118
Public Against Violence and, 95
Civil liberties, 115, 116, 151
Civil society, 40
concept of, 36–39
development of, 37, 165
"Clash of Civilizations?, The"
(Huntington), 185
Clinton, Bill
foreign policy of, 174–175
PFP and, 160
worldview of, 184
CMEA. *See* Council for Mutual
Economic Assistance
Coalition governments, 11, 99
Cold War, 75
end of, 3, 6, 39, 96, 154, 155, 171, 172,
179, 180, 182, 185, 188, 189
interpretations for, 12–14
NATO and, 160
stability of, 5
Collectivization, 15–16, 165
abandonment of, 22
Comecon. *See* Council for Mutual
Economic Assistance

Cominform. *See* Communist
Information Bureau
Comintern. *See* Communist
International
Committee for Social Self-Defense
(KOR-KSS), 35
Committee of Free Trade Unions for
the Baltic Coast, 27
Common European Home, 164, 168
Common Foreign and Security Policy,
165
Commonwealth of Independent States
(CIS), 82, 168
as confederal arrangement, 151
ethnic composition of, 145(figure)
loans/investments for, 177
market economy for, 136
nationalism in, 144, 146–147
Communism
challenges to, 19–29
collapse of, 1, 2–5, 29, 31–39, 71, 73,
80, 87, 96, 98, 99, 112–113, 155, 156,
171–172, 179, 183–186, 188, 189
consolidation of, 26
containment of, 2, 6, 13, 14, 172, 179,
182, 183
institutions of, 14–17
nationalism and, 186–187, 188
performance of, 29, 31–39
roll back of, 23
socioeconomic changes by, 17–19
threat of, 186
Communist Information Bureau
(Cominform), 17, 20, 21, 22
Communist International (Comintern),
2, 12
Communist parties, 11
membership drop in, 100
renaming of, 100, 101(table)
Communist Party of the Russian
Federation, 83
Communist Party of the Soviet Union,
nationalism and, 75
Competition
domestic/international, 125
increasing, 126, 172
political, 115, 119
Confederation of Independent Poland
(KPN), samizdat by, 36
Conference on Security and
Cooperation in Europe (CSCE),
158, 196(n22)
Conflict Prevention Center, 158
Conformity, 23
diversity and, 4–5

Congress of Peoples' Deputies
disbandment of, 82
elections for, 45
political monopoly issue and, 80
Consumer goods, 124, 138, 139
shortage of, 18, 123, 131
Contact group, plan by, 92
Control, 23
diversity and, 21
Convertibility, 123, 124, 127, 196(n18)
Cooperation, 47, 154
Council for Mutual Economic
Assistance (Comecon, CMEA), 14,
17, 24, 62, 133, 176
changes for, 156–157
collapse of, 157, 169, 189
trade within, 48, 156
Council of Ministers, 16
growth targets by, 15
Creditworthiness, problems with, 128,
176
Croatia, 7
nationalism in, 87, 142
recognition for, 88
violence in, 87–88
CSCE. *See* Conference on Security and
Cooperation in Europe
Cultures, 38
nationalism and, 142
Velvet Curtain of, 185
Currency reform, 124, 182
Czechoslovakia, xi
challenge from, 24–26
EC and, 167
economic problems for, 96, 123, 169
IMF and, 164
invasion of, 25
transition for, 60–62
velvet divorce in, 95–96
Czech Republic, 7, 96
EU association agreement with, 168
foreign aid for, 141
former communists in, 114
loans/investments for, 176
NATO and, 160
shock therapy and, 141
Czechs, Slovaks and, 95–96

Dahl, Robert
on democracy, 115, 121
on nationalism, 151
on tolerance/mutual security,
118–119
on transitions, 120

Dayton Agreement, 94(map), 94, 161, 175
DCR. *See* Democratic Convention of Romania
Decentralization, 21, 48, 80, 82
"Declaration on Liberated Europe," 10
Defense spending
  cutting, 46, 47–48
  increase in, 182
  strain of, 155
De Gaulle, Charles, United Europe and, 164
Democracy, 2, 5, 6, 168
  consociational, 120
  consolidation of, xi, 117, 118
  economic reform and, 151–152
  liberal, 116, 185
  persistence of, 117, 120
  prior experience with, 121
  procedural minimum for, 115
  promotion of, 172
  regime change to, 117(figure)
  theories of, 115, 121
  transition to, 117
Democratic Action, 104
Democratic Convention of Romania (DCR), 111
Democratic Forum
  campaign poster by, 108, 109(reproduction)
  coalition with, 108
Democratic Left Alliance (SLD), 106
Democratic party (Albania), 112
Democratic Russia Movement, 81
Democratization, 5, 42, 43, 45–46, 72, 183
  assessment of, 153
  models of, 121
  political, 122
  problems/prospects of, 115, 119
  speed/timing of, 71, 129–130
  theories of, 115–121
Deprivation, relative, 65, 67, 68
Desert Storm, 173, 174, 188
Destalinization, 21, 22, 23, 45
Dienstbier, Jiri, on EC membership, 167
Dissent, 64, 72
  spread of, 35–36
Diversity
  conformity and, 4–5
  control and, 21
  political consciousness and, 66
Djilas, Milovan, on communist party, 33–34

Dubcek, Alexander, 24, 25, 26, 61
  election of, 62
  Prague Spring and, 60
Dudayev, Dzhokhar, 147
Dulles, John Foster, roll back and, 23

East Central Europe (ECE), 6–7
  changes in, 189
  map of, 8
  postcommunist government in, 103(table)
  security concerns of, 170
Eastern Europe, 6–7
  Cold War and, 39
  economic growth in, 19(table), 20(table)
  foreign debt of, 32(figure)
  party leaders in, 50(table)
Eastern Germany, public transfers to, 79, 177
East Germany. *See* German Democratic Republic
East-West relations, 3, 155
  changes in, 179–180
EBRD. *See* European Bank for Reconstruction and Development
EC. *See* European Community
ECE. *See* East Central Europe
Eco-Glasnost, 59, 60
Economic decline, 41, 43, 112, 169
  foreign aid and, 182
  impact of, 67–68
Economic growth, 18–19, 32
  decline of, 29, 30(figure)
  in Eastern/Western Europe, 19(table)
  estimating, 29
  generating, 132–133
Economic reform, 5, 43, 48, 73
  components of, 123–129
  democracy and, 151–152
  foreign debt and, 128–129
  nationalism and, 151–152
  phasing of, 130(figure)
  programs for, 122
  resistance to, 31
ECSC. *See* European Coal and Steel Community
Ecu (European currency), concerns about, 167
EEC. *See* European Economic Community
Eisenhower, Dwight, 184
Elections, 100, 104–112
  monitoring, 102

Energy, price changes for, 31, 32, 42
Estonia, 7
  citizenship laws in, 147
  economic problems for, 136
  elections in, 81
  EU association agreement with, 168
  former communists in, 114
  Russian minority in, 86, 170, 187
  See also Baltic republics
Ethiopia, Soviet collapse and, 180
Ethnic cleansing, 89–90, 150
Ethnic tensions, 144, 153, 165, 188, 189
EU. *See* European Union
Europe, restructuring of, 158–161,
    164–165, 167–168
European Bank for Reconstruction and
    Development (EBRD), 129
  aid from, 177
  aid program by, 129
  EC and, 165, 167
  ECE and, 164
  privatization and, 132
European Coal and Steel Community
    (ECSC), 143
European Community (EC), 143, 179
  ceasefires and, 88
  ECE and, 164, 165
  membership in, 165, 167–168
  See also European Union
European Economic Community
    (EEC), 143
European organizations, membership
    in (by country), 162–163(table)
European Union (EU), 143, 165, 189
  Association agreements, 118, 168
  ECE and, 3, 169
  growth of, 185, 188
  membership in, 168
  NATO and, 167
  See also European Community

Farms
  collective, 15
  state-owned, 126
  See also Agriculture
Federal Treaty (1992), 86
  Chechnya and, 147
Five-Year Plans, 15
Foreign aid, 122
  economic decline and, 182
  problems with, 127–129
  transition and, 128
Foreign debt, 32, 99, 113, 135
  Eastern European, 32(figure),
    129(table)

economic reform and, 128–129
  problems with, 127–129, 131, 176
Foreign policy
  control of, 17
  domestic policy and, 47
  new thinking in, 3, 46–48, 99,
    174–175
  problems in, 4
Fragmentation, 70–71, 80, 144, 169
  economic/political, 113, 135
Free Trade Union movement, samizdat
    by, 36
French Revolution (1789), 68, 99
  impact of, 1–2

Galbraith, John Kenneth
  on economic recovery, 130
  on free-enterprise models, 130
  on traditional capitalism, 131
GATT. *See* General Agreement on
    Tariffs and Trade
GDR. *See* German Democratic
    Republic
General Agreement on Tariffs and
    Trade (GATT), ECE and, 49
Georgia
  secession of, 82
  UN mission to, 159
  warfare in, 86, 146
German Democratic Republic (GDR)
  end of, xi, 56–58
  exodus from, 55–56, 57
  perestroika and, 56
  WTO and, 76, 77
  See also Eastern Germany
Germany (Federal Republic of
    Germany)
  aid from, 177
  economic problems for, 80
  NATO and, 76–77
  unification of, 1, 75–80, 97, 164, 165
Gierek, Edward, 26
Glasnost, 43, 44–45, 46, 60, 80, 143, 144,
    150
  defined, 42
  reform and, 49
  spread of, 72
GNP. *See* Gross national product
Gomulka, Wladyslaw, 22, 26
Gorazde, 90
  safe haven in, 91
Gorbachev, Mikhail, 3, 61, 164,
    197(n33)
  Brezhnev Doctrine and, 49
  communist collapse and, 4–5

coup against, 82, 135, 174
criticism by, 45, 51
democracy and, 45, 46, 122
Eastern Europe and, 48–49, 72, 80
GDR and, 56, 57, 58
German reunification and, 76
on Germany/NATO, 77
INF Treaty and, 177–178
interdependence and, 155, 173
new thinking of, 171, 183, 188
reform by, 34–35, 42–49, 51, 70, 72, 81, 135
rise of, 40, 41–42
at UN, 47–48
union treaty and, 81–82
Gosplan, planning by, 15
Governments
collapse of, 75
political structure of, 16
Gradualist approach, 129, 135, 136
Gromyko, Andrei, on Gorbachev, 42
Gross national product (GNP), growth of, 18, 32
Grosz, Karoly, 51, 100
"G–24" group, aid from, 129
Gysi, Gregor, 58

Hard currency, 128, 169
Havel, Vaclav, 38, 198(n37)
Charter 77 and, 36
election of, 62
essay by, 37, 61
velvet divorce and, 95, 96
on WTO, 158
Helsinki Agreements (Helsinki Accords) (1975)
dissident movement and, 35
human rights and, 159
Hitler, Adolf, 13, 143, 150, 184
Honecker, Erich, 50(table), 56, 197(n33)
fall of, 58
refugees and, 57
Human rights, 5, 36, 45, 158, 159
Hungarian Democratic Forum, 107
transition and, 135
Hungarian National Bank, economic reform and, 134
Hungarian revolution (1956), 22–24, 54
Hungarian Socialist party, 55, 100, 107, 109
Hungarian Socialist Workers' party, 55, 107
dissolution of, 55
new name for, 100, 101(table)

Hungarian Workers' party, domination by, 11
Hungary
democratic politics in, 114
EC and, 167
economic transition in, 54–56, 123, 133–134
elections/new governmnet in, 10–11, 107–109, 113
EU association agreement with, 168
goulash communism in, 51
industrial production in, 139
liberalization in, 22–23
loans/investments for, 176
multiparty system for, 55
NATO and, 160
postwar influence in, 9
privatization in, 127
subsidies in, 126
Tripartite Pact and, 10
Huntington, Samuel
on modernization/development, 66
on Velvet Curtain of culture, 185
Husak, Gustav, 25, 50(table), 51, 59, 60, 62
Hussein, Saddam, 173, 174

Ideology, decline of, 184–185, 189
IGOs. See Intergovernmental organizations
Iliescu, Ion, 63, 111
on political pluralism, 110
IMF. See International Monetary Fund
Independent Smallholders' party, 10–11, 107
coalition with, 108
privatization and, 127
Industrialization, 17, 20
forced, 43
state control of, 15
INF. See Intermediate-Range Nuclear Forces Treaty
Inflation, 113, 123, 135, 136, 141
measures against, 131–132, 139
problems with, 133
Integration
economic, 78–79, 165
political, 78
separatism and, 151–152
Interdependence, 47, 48, 155, 173
growth of, 3–4
Interfactory Strike Committee (MKS), demands of, 27–28
Intergovernmental organizations (IGOs), 143

Interior ministries, communist
    domination of, 11
Intermediate-Range Nuclear Forces
    Treaty (INF), 177–178
Internationalism, 153
    nationalism and, 186
    socialist, 17, 23, 34, 47, 143
International Monetary Fund (IMF),
    49, 164
    aid from, 129, 177, 182, 189
International politics
    problems of, 98
    revolution in, 154
Intolerance, 120, 144
Iron curtain, 56, 164, 189
Irredentism, 142, 143, 188
Izetbegovic, Alija, 90, 91, 93
Izvestia, 54

Jakes, Milos, 51, 60, 61
Jaruzelski, Wojciech, 28, 49, 50(table)
    economic reform by, 52
    elections and, 104
    Solidarity and, 5, 34, 52, 53, 69
John Paul II (Karol Wojtyla), 27, 138

Kadar, Janos, 23, 50(table), 51, 54, 59
Kafka, Franz, 60
Kania, Stanislaw, 28
Karadzic, Radovan, 91, 92, 93, 94
Katyn, massacre at, 55
Kazakhstan
    nuclear weapons in, 178
    Russian minority in, 187
Kennan, George, article by, 13
Kennedy, John, 184
Kennedy, Paul, on major powers, 186
Khadafy, Muammar, 172
Khasbulatov, Ruslan, 82
Khrushchev, Nikita, 4
    destalinization and, 21, 22, 23, 45
    dissidents and, 35
Kirghizia, Russian minority in, 187
Kirkpatrick, Jeane, 64
Kiszczak, Czeslaw, 52
Klaus, Vaclav, velvet divorce and, 96
Kohl, Helmut, 78, 80
    border issue and, 76
    reunification and, 77
    tax increases by, 79
Konrad, Gyorgy, 37, 38
KOR. See Workers' Defense Committee
KOR-KSS. See Committee for Social
    Self-Defense

Kosovo region, Albanian claims to, 188
Kozyrev, Andrei, on Russian minority,
    86
KPN. See Confederation of
    Independent Poland
Krajina, 88, 93
Krenz, Egon, 58
    Leipzig demonstrations and, 69
Kundera, Milan, 38, 165
Kwasniewski, Aleksander, 106–107
Kyrgyzstan, Russian minority in, 187

Latvia, 7
    elections in, 81
    EU association agreement with, 168
    former communists in, 114
    Russian minority in, 187
    See also Baltic republics
LDP. See Liberal Democratic party
League of Communists, 75, 86
Left turn, xi, 114, 114(figure), 120, 141
Leipzig, demonstrations in, 58, 77
Lenin, Vladimir, 2, 14, 33, 35, 44
Lenin Shipyards (Gdansk), strike at,
    27–28
Liberal democracy
    deficiencies in, 116
    universalization of, 185
Liberal Democratic party (LDP), 83,
    136
Liberalization
    economic, 5, 156
    political, 24
Liberal party, 110
"Liberman" reforms, 31
Lijphart, Arend, 120
Limited sovereignty, 26, 49
Lithuania, 7
    elections in, 81, 113
    EU association agreement with, 168
    See also Baltic republics
Logic of Collective Action, The (Olson),
    66

Maastricht Treaty, 167
McCarthy, John, on social movements,
    66
Macedonia, 7, 87
    Albanian claims to, 188
    UN mission to, 159
Malia, Martin, on boomerang effect, 80
Mandela, Nelson, 181
Mao Zedong, 23
Marcos, Ferdinand, overthrow of, 70

Marer, Paul, 29
Market economy
    building, 81, 99, 114, 121–139, 141,
        152, 176
    leap to, 131, 132, 135
Marshall Plan, 13, 14, 154
Martial law, 41, 52, 121
Marx, Karl, 33
    on substructure, 122
    on superstructure, 36
Mazowiecki, Tadeusz, 53, 54, 105, 131,
        171
    Democratic Action and, 104
Meciar, Vladimir, velvet divorce and,
        96
Media
    impact of, 68, 69
    openness for, 45, 72
Medvedev, Roy, on Stalinism, 45
Michnik, Adam, 29
    on nationalism, 144, 152
    strategy of, 37
Milosevic, Slobodan, 87, 92, 93, 98
    nationalism and, 142
Minorities, problems with, 120, 143, 151
MKS. See Interfactory Strike
        Committee
Mladenov, Petar, 60, 111
Mladic, Ratko, 94
Modernization, theories of, 66, 67
Moldova, 7, 146
    Russian minority in, 86
    Russian relations with, 170
    secession of, 82
    UN mission to, 159
Mostar, destruction of, 92
Movement for Rights and Freedom,
        111
Movement for the Defense of Human
        and Civil Rights (ROPCiO),
        samizdat by, 35–36
Multiparty systems, 100, 102, 112
Munich Agreement (1938), 13
Muslims, 88, 92, 175
    aggression against, 6, 93
    ethnic cleansing of, 89–90
    nationalism and, 147
    Serbs and, 95
Mutual security, developing, 118–119

Nagorno-Karabakh, 86, 146, 159
Nagy, Ferenc, 11

Nagy, Imre, 23, 24, 54
Napoleon, 2, 10
National fronts, 46, 116
Nationalism, 2, 38, 97, 112
    chauvinism and, 142
    communism and, 186–187, 188
    economic, 181
    economic reform and, 151–152
    globalization and, 151–152
    matryoshka, 146–147
    negative aspects of, 5, 21, 75, 120,
        142, 143, 144, 150, 152, 153, 155,
        188
    positive aspects of, 143, 151
    reemergence of, 86, 141–144,
        146–147, 150–152, 186–189
    regional, 147, 150–151
    violence and, 141
Nationalities, in ECE, 149(table)
Nationalities problem, 86, 146–147
National Salvation Front (NSF), 63,
        109–110
NATO. See North Atlantic Treaty
        Organization
Nazism, revival of, 80, 153
NEM. See New Economic Mechanism
New Economic Mechanism (NEM), 51,
        133, 134
New Forum, 58, 60, 68, 71
New thinking, 42, 46–48, 49, 171, 181,
        183, 188
New world order, 155, 173, 179,
        183–189
Nomenklatura, 16, 46, 68, 118
Non-Proliferation Treaty (NPT), 178
Noriega, Manuel, arrest of, 172
North Atlantic Treaty Organization
        (NATO), 13, 17, 185, 189
    Bosnia crisis and, 3, 93
    Cold War and, 160
    CSCE and, 159
    EC and, 165
    ECE and, 3, 164, 169, 170
    EU and, 167
    OSCE and, 159, 161
    peacekeeping by, 94, 95, 161, 175
    reorganization of, 159–161, 178, 179
    WEU and, 167
    WTO and, 14, 157, 160
Novotny, Antonin, 24
NPT. See Non-Proliferation Treaty

NSF. *See* National Salvation Front
Nuclear weapons, 155, 171
   reducing, 177, 178, 179
Nyers, Rezso, 100

Ochab, Edward, 22
Oder-Neisse line, recognizing, 76
OECD. *See* Organization for Economic
   Cooperation and Development
Oil
   price fluctuations for, 32, 42
   subsidized prices for, 169
Olson, Mancur, on social movements,
   66–67
One-party rule, end of, 102, 116, 152
Opposition movements, 40, 114, 152
Organization for Economic
   Cooperation and Development
   (OECD), ECE and, 176
Organization for Security and
   Cooperation in Europe (OSCE),
   175
   CSCE and, 158
   NATO and, 159, 161
OSCE. *See* Organization for Security
   and Cooperation in Europe
Ostpolitik, 76

Palestine Liberation Organization, 188
"Pamyat" (Memory), 150
"Parallel Polis, The" (Benda), 37
Paris summit, 159
Participation oriented movements,
   65–66
Parties
   antireformist, 83
   formation of, 100, 102, 107
   political structure of, 16
   state and, 16–17
Partisans, 19–20
Partnership for Peace (PFP), 160
Party leaders, listed, 50(table)
Party of Democratic Socialism, 79
Party of Social Democracy, 110
Peace dividend, 155, 171–172, 174
Peasant party, 110
Peloponnesian War, The (Thucydides), 4
People power, 70, 71
Peoples' democracies, 10, 115–116
People's Republic of Congo, Soviet
   collapse and, 181

Perestroika, 42, 43–44, 68, 72, 80, 122,
   134, 144
   national fronts and, 46
   reform and, 49
   South African version of, 181
PFP. *See* Partnership for Peace
Pluralism, 2, 115, 152, 183
   movement to, 122, 153
   political, 53
   socialist, 45–46
Poland
   aid to, 177
   anti-Semitism in, 150
   challenge from, 22–24, 26–29
   democratic politics in, 114
   EC and, 167
   elections/new government in,
     104–107, 113
   EU association agreement with, 168
   foreign debt of, 52, 128
   IMF and, 164
   loans/investments for, 176
   martial law in, 41, 52
   NATO and, 160
   new borders for, 9
   postwar influence in, 10
   privatization in, 127
   shock therapy in, 123, 129, 131–133
   subsidies in, 126
   transition for, 52–54, 107
Polish Beer Lovers party, 105
Polish Peasant party (PSL), 106
Polish United Workers' party
   (PUWP/PZPR), 16, 67, 106
   decline of, 28, 54
   new name for, 101(table)
   reserved seats for, 53
Politburo. *See* Political Bureau
Political Bureau (politburo), 16
Political legitimacy
   decline of, 33–35, 41, 70
   socioeconomic accomplishments
     and, 34
Political order, rebuilding, 73, 100, 102,
   104–112
Political process, 122
   postrevolutionary, 112–114
Political succession, lack of, 64
Politics
   changes in, 5
   international, 98, 154
   tuning out, 39

Polyarchy (Dahl), 115, 118, 120
Postcommunist governments,
    formation of, 102, 103(table), 104-
    112
"Power of the Powerless, The"
    (Havel), 37, 61
Power oriented movements,
    emergence of, 65
Poznan, unrest in, 22
Pozsgay, Imre, 100
Prague Spring (1968), 4, 24–26, 68
    political legitimacy and, 34
Pravda, 26, 47
    on Czech invasion, 25–26
    on glasnost, 44
Prices, 130
    equilibrium, 124
    lifting controls on, 131, 136, 141
    subsidized, 124
Primakov, Yevgeniy, 173
    on domestic policy/foreign policy,
    47
Privatization, 44, 78, 108, 123, 126–127,
    134
    attitudes toward, 138
    from below, 133
    large-scale/small-scale, 139
    laws on, 135
    problems with, 127
    rapid, 132
PSL. *See* Polish Peasant party
Public Against Violence, Civic Forum
    and, 95
Purges, 17, 21
PUWP. *See* Polish United Workers'
    party
PZPR. *See* Polish United Workers'
    party

Radio Free Europe, 60, 72
Radio Liberty, 44
Rakosi, Matyas, 22
Rásputin, Valentin, anti-Semitism of,
    150
Reagan, Ronald
    conceptual vacuum and, 172
    dissidents and, 64
    military spending by, 42
Reform, 69
    from above, 46, 112
    acceleration of, 48
    market-oriented, 48
    models for, 49

    speed/timing of, 129–130
    See also Economic reform
Refugees, 57
    aid for, 91
Repentance (film), 45
Republic of South Africa, changes in,
    181
Resource mobilization, 66, 68
Reunification, 1, 75–80, 97, 164, 165
Revolutionary movements
    fragmentation of, 70–71
    natural history of, 68
    political elite and, 69
Revolutions
    bottom-up, 72
    lessons from, 70
    nonviolent, 69
    self-limiting, 67
    social movements and, 63–71
    theories of, 65, 69
Revolutions of 1989, 19, 51–63, 99
    EC and, 165
    impact of, 2, 71, 152–153
    revolutionary patterns and, 69
    Soviet collapse and, 80
    suddenness/thoroughness of, 63
Rights of contestation, concession of,
    118
Rights of individuals, interests of the
    people and, 116
Rise and Fall of the Great Powers, The
    (Kennedy), 186
Romania
    anti-Semitism in, 150–151
    elections/new government in,
    109–111
    EU association agreement with, 168
    loans/investments for, 176
    nationalism in, 149
    postwar influence in, 9
    transition for, 62–63, 123
    Tripartite Pact and, 10
    WTO and, 24
Romania Mare, anti-Semitism and, 150
Romanian Communist party, 62
    new name for, 101(table)
Roosevelt, Franklin D.,
    postwar order and, 12
    at Yalta, 9
ROPCiO. *See* Movement for the
    Defense of Human and Civil
    Rights
Roundtable agreements, 53, 54, 55, 60

"Rush to Capitalism, The" (Galbraith), 130
Russia, xi
  economic problems for, 141
  IMF and, 164
  NATO and, 160, 161
  nuclear weapons in, 178
  PFP and, 160
  shock therapy in, 136
  See also Commonwealth of Independent States; Successor states
Russian Federation, 168
  heterogeneity of, 187–188
  unraveling of, 147
Russian mafia, threat of, 141
Russian minorities, concern for, 86, 170, 187
Russian Orthodox church, 46
Russian Revolution (1917), 1, 68, 99, 184
Rutskoi, Aleksandr, White House occupation and, 82
Rybakov, Anatoly, 45
Ryzhkov, Nikolai, on defense spending, 48

Sachs, Jeffrey, 131, 136
Safe havens, 91, 93
Sakharov, Andrei, 35, 46
SALT. See Strategic Arms Limitation Treaty
Samizdat, 36, 44
Sandel, Michael, on nationalism/separatism, 151–152
Sarajevo, 6, 90
  assassination in, 86
  mortar attack on, 93
  population of, 82
  safe haven in, 91
Schmitter, Philippe, democratization and, 117, 118
SEA. See Single Europe Act
Second economy/society, 37
Secretariat, 16
Secret police, 15, 64
Self-determination, 6
  democracy and, 120
  national, 142–143
Self-management, 21, 43
Separatism, 142, 188
  integration and, 151–152
  problems with, 144

Serbia, 93–94
  domination by, 89
  nationalism in, 149
Serbs, 82, 175
  chauvinism of, 142
  ethnic cleansing by, 149
  loyalty oaths for, 88
  Muslims and, 95
  violence by, 88–89
  See also Bosnian Serbs
Sharlet, Robert, 36
Shatalin, Stanislav, plan by, 81
Shevardnadze, Eduard
  on interdependence, 47
  resignation of, 174
Shock therapy, 81, 82, 123, 127, 164
  abandoning, 136
  using, 129, 131–133, 141
Single Europe Act (SEA), implementation of, 168
Sino-Soviet conflict, 24, 62
Skocpol, Theda
  on government breakdown, 69
  on social revolutions, 68
Slansky, Rudolph, 21
SLD. See Democratic Left Alliance
Slovakia, 7, 96
  EU association agreement with, 168
  nationalism in, 149
  NATO and, 160
  Tripartite Pact and, 10
Slovaks
  Czechs and, 95–96
  struggles of, 188
Slovenia, 7, 87
  national tensions in, 87
  recognition for, 88
Smith, Anthony, on nationalism, 142
Social compact/contract, 34
Social Democrats (SPD), 77, 78
Socialism, 137–138
  depression for, 122
  with human face, 24, 29
  national roads to, 17, 21, 22, 26
  pursuit of, 14–15
Socialist Unity party, new name for, 101(table)
Social justice, capitalism and, 136–138
Social movements
  creation of, 66–67, 68
  governments founded on, 113
  integrative, 118
  lessons from, 70
  literature on, 66

media and, 68
revolutions and, 63–71
theories of, 64, 65
Society for People Living Below the
    Minimum Standard, The, 109
Solidarity, 4, 26–29, 39–40, 70, 95, 71,
    104, 107, 110, 138
  crackdown on, 5, 29, 34, 51–52
  demands of, 67
  democratization and, 121
  demonstration by, 106(photo)
  emergence of, 41, 65, 67
  factions within, 105
  members of, 28
  recognition of, 52–53, 69
  as social movement, 67
Somalia, peacekeeping forces in, 188,
    189
Sorensen, Theodore, on national
    security, 172
South Ossetian Autonomous Region
  civil war in, 146
  separatists in, 86
Sovetskaia Rossiia, on Iraq, 174
Soviet Constitution, 116
  amendment of, 46
Soviet Union
  alliances with, 12
  challenges to, 41
  collapse of, xi, 1, 80–83, 86–87, 146,
    158, 168–170, 179, 181, 186
  democratization of, 45–46
  Eastern European impact on, 80–83,
    86–87
  economic problems for, 31, 42, 81,
    169
  Law on Cooperatives (1988), 43–44
  Law on Press Freedoms (1990), 44
  Law on State Enterprises, 43
  reform in, 4, 48
  successor states of, 84–85(map), 98
  United Europe and, 164
  U.S. relations with, 155
  See also Commonwealth of
    Independent States; Russia;
    Successor states
SPD. See Social Democrats
Srebrenica, 90, 91, 93
Stalin, Joseph, 4, 10, 14, 15, 41
  on Communism/Poland, 39
  criticism of, 21, 22, 23, 45
  dissidents and, 35

postwar order and, 12
Yalta Agreements and, 9, 13
Yugoslav challenge and, 20, 21, 39
See also Destalinization
Stalinism, 35, 45
Standard of living
  decline of, 113, 135
  economic problems and, 42
  improvement in, 33
START. See Strategic Arms Reduction
    Treaty
State enterprises, privatization of, 123,
    127, 132, 133, 134
State farms, 15
  privatization of, 123
State Property Agency, privatization
    and, 108
States
  collapse of, 73, 75
  parties and, 16–17
Stock markets, 127, 134
Strategic Arms Limitation Treaty
    (SALT), 177, 178
Strategic Arms Reduction Treaty
    (START), 178
Subsidies, 169
  cuts in, 126, 182
  elimination of, 123, 125–126, 131
Successor states, 98
  economic problems for, 141
  ethnic composition of, 145(figure)
  loans/investments for, 176, 177
  map of, 84–85
  market economy for, 135–136
  nationalism in, 144, 146–147
Superpowers, 173–174
  decline of, 185–186
Supply and demand, 123, 124, 125, 139
Supreme Soviet, 46
  disbandment of, 82
  Stalin condemnation by, 45

Tajikistan
  civil war in, 86, 147
  UN mission to, 159
Tatar Autonomous Republic, 146
  separatism in, 187–188
Tatarstan, 147
  independence for, 86
Theories of Nationalism (Smith), 142
Third World
  changes in, 179–183

international politics and, 185
  relations with, 155, 183
Thucydides, 4
Timisoara, protest in, 63
Tito, Josip Broz, 75, 86, 98
  independence of, 20, 39
  liberation by, 10
  regional initiatives of, 20, 21
  separate roads principle and, 22
Tokes, Laszlo, 63
Tolerance
  decline in, 152
  developing, 118–119
Tomasek, Frantisek, 61
Trade, obstacles to, 123, 169–170, 176
"Tragedy of Central Europe, The"
  (Kundera), 38
Transformation
  economic, 5, 122
  fast track, 131
Transition, 115, 117, 120
  economics of, 78, 122, 139,
    140(table), 141, 153
  first phase of, 138–139, 141
  problems with, 2, 98, 153
Transnational corporations, influence
  of, 188
Treaty on Conventional Forces in
  Europe (CFE), 158
Treaty on the Final Settlement with
  Respect to Germany (1990), 77
Treuhandanstalt, East German
  economy and, 78
Tripartite Pact, 10
Truman, Harry S, 13, 176
Truman Doctrine, 13, 14
Tudjman, Franjo, 92, 93
"Two-plus-four negotiations," 76
Tyminski, Stanislaw, 104

UDF. See Union of Democratic Forces
Ukraine, 7
  economic problems for, 141
  independence for, 82
  nuclear weapons in, 178
  Russian minority in, 86, 187
  Russian relations with, 170
  UN mission to, 159
UN. See United Nations
Unemployment, 79, 113, 135, 136, 170
  problems with, 133, 141

UNICEF, report on economic changes
  in ECE, 139
Unification. See Reunification
Union of Democratic Forces (UDF), 60,
  68, 111
Union treaty, 81–82, 135
United Nations (UN)
  Bosnia crisis and, 3, 91
  ceasefires and, 88
  ECE and, 169
  Gorbachev at, 47–48
  Hungarian uprising and, 23
  new role of, 188
  peacekeeping forces from, 188–189
  sanctions by, 159, 173
United States
  aid from, 177, 181–182
  communism collapse and, 171–172
  debt problems of, 186
  foreign policy changes for, 6, 185,
    189
  relations with, 47, 155
United States of Europe, hope for, 143,
  164–165
Universalism, 143
Urbanek, Karel, 61
Urbanization, 17
Velvet Revolution, 60–62, 70, 99
Videnov, Zhan, 111
Voice of America, 44
Voting
  majority system, 102
  monitoring, 102
  plurality, 102

Walesa, Lech, 27, 52, 53
  Center Alliance and, 104
  elections and, 104–105, 106
Warsaw Treaty Organization (WTO),
  14, 17, 62
  East Germany and, 76, 77
  end of, 3, 157–158, 159, 170, 178, 189
  Hungary and, 23
  NATO and, 160
  Prague Spring and, 24–25
Western Europe
  economic growth in, 19(table),
    20(table)
  rebuilding of, 39
Western European Union (WEU)
  EC and, 165
  NATO and, 167

WEU. *See* Western European Union
White House (Russia),
   occupation/shelling of, 82–83
Wilson, Woodrow, 97, 143, 175
Wojtyla, Karol. *See* John Paul II
Workers' Defense Committee (KOR),
   26, 35, 67
World Bank
   aid from, 129, 177, 182, 189
   ECE and, 164
   on economic transformation, 153
   on Polish economy, 133
   privatization and, 132
   on Third World, 181
World Economic Development Report, on
   Third World, 181
WTO. *See* Warsaw Treaty Organization

Xenophobia, 120, 143, 144, 170

Yalta Agreements, 9, 10, 13
Yavlinsky, Grigory, plan by, 81
Yeltsin, Boris, 81
   Chechnya and, 147
   elections and, 83, 86
   Gorbachev coup and, 82
   IMF and, 164
   on NATO, 161
   price controls and, 136
   Serbia and, 92

shock therapy and, 82
START and, 178
Yugoslavia
   autonomy of, 20–21
   challenge from, 19, 21–22
   civil war in, 87–95, 97, 153, 188
   collapse of, xi, 1
   former republics of, 89(map), 98
   liberation of, 39
   loans/investments for, 176
   postwar influence in, 9, 10
   privatization in, 127
   rapprochement with, 23
   revolutions of 1989 and, 72
   sanctions against, 159

Zald, Meyer, on social movements, 66
Zantovsky, Michael, on NATO
   membership, 161
Zaslavskaya, Tatyana, on glasnost, 44
Zepa, overrunning of, 93
Zhdanov, Andrei, on Truman
   Doctrine/Marshall Plan, 14
Zhirinovski, Vladimir, 86, 98, 136, 170
   antics of, 83
   anti-Semitism of, 150
Zhivkov, Todor, 50(table), 58–59, 111
   challenge to, 59
   resignation of, 60
Zyuganov, Gennadi, 86